ON THE NARROW ROAD

Journey into a Lost Japan

LESLEY DOWNER

Summit Books
New York London
Toronto Sydney Tokyo

for
my mother and father

SUMMIT BOOKS
SIMON & SCHUSTER BUILDING
ROCKEFELLER CENTER
1230 AVENUE OF THE AMERICAS
NEW YORK, NEW YORK 10020

ORIGINALLY PUBLISHED IN GREAT BRITAIN BY JONATHAN CAPE LTD.

COPYRIGHT © 1989 BY LESLEY DOWNER

LIBRARY OF CONGRESS CATALOGING IN PUBLICATION DATA

DOWNER, LESLIE.
ON THE NARROW ROAD : JOURNEY INTO A LOST JAPAN / LESLEY
DOWNER.
P. CM.
BIBLIOGRAPHY: P.
INCLUDES INDEX.
ISBN 0-671-64047-X
1. MATSUO, BASHŌ, 1644–1694. OKU NO HOSOMICHI. 2. MATSUO,
BASHŌ, 1644–1694—JOURNEYS—JAPAN. 3. JAPAN—DESCRIPTION
AND TRAVEL—TO 1800. 4. AUTHORS, JAPANESE—EDO PERIOD,
1600–1868—JOURNEYS—JAPAN. 5. DOWNER, LESLEY—JOURNEYS—
JAPAN. 6. JAPAN—DESCRIPTION AND TRAVEL—1945—   I. TITLE.
PL794.4.Z5A36325 1989
895.6'13—DC19   89-31356
                                                               CIP

BOMC offers recordings and compact discs, cassettes
and records. For information and catalog write to
BOMR, Camp Hill, PA 17012.

Contents

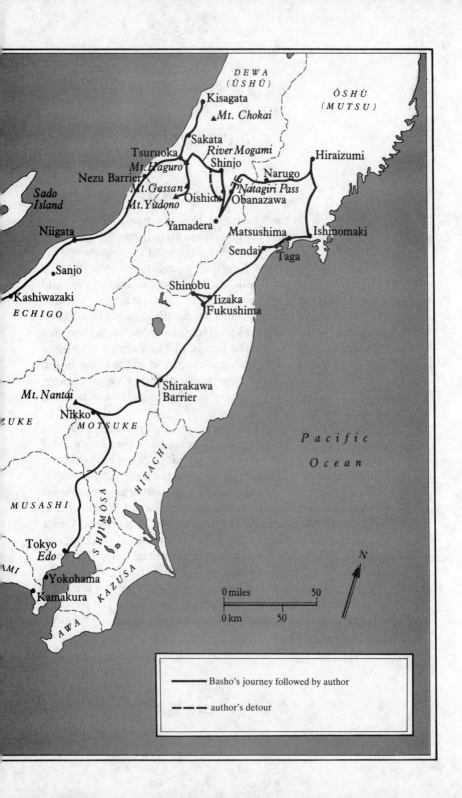

DEWA
(ŪSHŪ)

Kisagata

▲ Mt. Chokai

Sakata

River Mogami

ŌSHŪ
(MUTSU)

Tsuruoka

Shinjo

Hiraizumi

Mt. Haguro

Nezu Barrier

Narugo

Mt. Gassan

Natagiri Pass

Mt. Yudono

Oishida

Obanazawa

Sado
Island

Yamadera

Matsushima

Ishinomaki

Niigata

Sendai

Taga

Sanjo

Kashiwazaki

Shinobu

ECHIGO

Iizaka

Fukushima

Shirakawa
Barrier

Mt. Nantai

ZUKE

Nikko

MOTSUKE

Pacific

Ocean

MUSASHI

HITACHI

SHIMŌSA

Tokyo
Edo

Yokohama

N

Kamakura

KAZUSA

AMI

AWA

0 miles   50

0 km   50

——— Basho's journey followed by author

- - - author's detour

Acknowledgments

Many people helped to make this journey and this book possible, and I am deeply grateful to all of them.

Of all the friends in Japan who have, in the Japanese way, unstintingly given me hospitality and kindness, I would particularly like to thank the people of Shimokoya and Matsuhashi; the Hasegawa family in Yamagata, who provided a home for me in the north; and Shohachiro and Sachiko Ojima who gave me a home in Tokyo. Thanks are due too to Professor Umetsu and the Nishizuka family of Obanazawa; Professor Ogawa of the Dewa Sanzan museum; and all the other Basho enthusiasts who gave so generously of their time and knowledge. In the text I have changed some personal names to avoid embarrassment.

Without the help and encouragement of my agent, Xandra Hardie, the book would probably never have been begun; and without the support and wise suggestions of my editor, Anne Chisholm, would certainly never have been finished.

Finally, I am deeply indebted to the Great Britain–Sasakawa Foundation and its Administrator, Mr Donald Warren-Knott OBE; to Mr Narisada and the staff of the Toyko Head Office and the London office of the Japan National Tourist Organisation; and to Japan Air Lines. Without their help, this book would not have been possible.

The illustrations at the beginning of each section are from Buson's picture scroll of 'The Narrow Road to the Deep North' and are included by kind permission of the Itsuo Museum, Ikeda City, Osaka.

Introduction

This year, the second year of Genroku, I have decided to make a long walking trip to the distant provinces of the far north. Though the hardships of the journey will pile up snowy hairs on my head, I will see with my own eyes remote places of which I have only heard – I cannot even be certain that I will return alive.

It was a fine spring morning when the poet Matsuo Basho set out on this last long journey of his, to the wild north of Japan. The sky was hazy and the moon still faintly visible. From Fukagawa, on the outskirts of Edo (old Tokyo), he could see Mount Fuji in the far distance, its perfect cone etched against the morning sky and, closer at hand, the hills of Ueno and Yanaka, covered in pink cherry blossom. 'Heavy of heart, I wondered when I would see them again,' he wrote.

He had so little expectation of ever returning that he had sold his house in Fukagawa. He made few preparations for the journey – patched his trousers, put new cords on his hat, had moxa treatment on his legs to make them stronger – and took little more than the clothes on his back ('plus a paper coat to protect me in the evening, *yukata*, rainwear, ink, brushes'.)

His closest friends and disciples were there to see him off. They boarded the boat together and went with him the few miles up the Sumida river through the suburbs of Edo to Senju, where they disembarked. Here they said their farewells and Basho set off along the great highway to the north, accompanied only by one friend and companion, Kawai Sora. His disciples stood watching and waving until the small black-clad figures disappeared from sight.

'My heart was overwhelmed at the thought of the three

1

thousand ri that lay ahead, and as we separated, perhaps for ever, in this illusory world, I wept,' he wrote, and added a haiku

yuku haru ya	Spring passes!
tori naki uo no	Birds cry,
me wa namida	Fish have tears in their eyes

It was the twenty-seventh day of the third month by the old lunar calendar, May 16th 1689. The Stuarts had just lost their throne to William of Orange; Milton had died a few years before; Louis XIV was ruling from Versailles; and Newton had discovered gravity. In Japan, there was peace for the first time in centuries, which meant that the roads were safe for travellers, and poetry and the arts were flourishing. Thanks to the strong rule of the Tokugawa shoguns, the country was enjoying a renaissance; and Matsuo Basho was one of its leaders.

Basho was on the road for five months, a hard journey for a man who, at forty-five, already felt old and frail. There are many drawings and paintings of him from that time. He has a crumpled, kindly face, rather gaunt, a little greying stubble around his chin and tired eyes that gaze into the far distance. He dresses like a priest in black robes and flat cap, and carries a bamboo staff and wide-brimmed sedge hat.

Like a priest, he owned nothing. (He was never ordained, but, in the tradition of the wandering philosopher-poet, was, as he put it, 'not a priest nor a layman but more like a bat, wavering between bird and rat'.) Wherever he went his disciples and admirers welcomed him, offered him hospitality, showed him their poems for correction and organised gatherings where they all sat down together to write poetry.

In this fashion Basho travelled, visiting local poets and places which had inspired poets in the past. For six weeks he walked the Oshukaido, the great north road through the eastern coastal plain, up into the remote province of Oshu.

Then he turned inland, into steep and rugged mountain country where often 'the forests were so thick that we couldn't hear one bird cry, and under the trees it was so dark that it was like walking at midnight'. Sometimes he found nowhere better to stay than a stable; and at times he was afraid for his life. But it was also in these backward regions, as far as it was possible to be from the cultured world of Edo, that he had some of his strangest and most moving encounters. Finally – the climax of the journey – he met the near-legendary yamabushi, the hermit priests of the northern mountains; and spent a week with them at their sanctuary.

The final part of the journey was also the hardest: a walk of two and a half months, through the heat of the summer, along the Hokurikudo, the highway which led back down the western Japan Sea coast, ending at the town of Ogaki on October 18th.

For the next four years Basho mulled over his experiences. Then he produced a book which he called *Oku no hoso-michi*; *oku* means the interior, the back country, the northern provinces (the title for someone else's wife is *Oku-san*, 'Honourable Interior', 'Honourable Person-at-the-back'); *hoso* is narrow, *michi* road or roads. In English its most famous and evocative title is *The Narrow Road to the Deep North*.

Nearly three hundred years have passed – 1989 will be the 300th anniversary of Basho's journey. Basho is now admired as Japan's greatest poet, as familiar a name in Japan as Shakespeare is in the West. *The Narrow Road to the Deep North* is on the curriculum of every school; and every Japanese (and many non-Japanese too) knows and loves his haiku.

Before I reached Japan I had come across the haiku and pondered over the syllables of the most famous

furu-ike ya
kawazu tobi-komu
mizu no oto

There are many translations; the one which I first read was in the Penguin edition of Basho

Breaking the silence
Of an ancient pond
A frog jumped into water –
A deep resonance

The original is much more compact (and does not include the words 'a deep resonance' – hardly an appropriate expression for the sound of a frog jumping into water). Translated as near as possible word for word, it runs

Old pond –
Frog jumps in
Sound of water

A picture, a happening, a sound – and many profound philosophical ripples.

When I was a child I loved to look at Hokusai's woodblock prints, the *Thirty-six Views of Mount Fuji*, at the lines of tiny figures with their straw hats and staffs, endlessly struggling across a stylised landscape of wild crags and thread-like bridges, with Fuji ever present in the background.

It was not until years later that I decided to go to Japan, attracted first by its pottery and later by its food and Buddhist culture, and began to learn the language. Somehow it never occurred to me to doubt my first images of the place. *The Narrow Road* and the other books I read only confirmed them. As a result, when I finally went there, I was as ill-prepared for a country of neon and high-rise blocks as anyone could ever be.

It was 1978. I had taken a job as a teacher in a girls' university in the provincial city of Gifu. There, far removed from Tokyo and its foreign enclaves, I hoped to find 'real Japan', the Japan of my imaginings. Instead I found myself the only foreigner (I discovered five others a few months later) in a city of 400,000 Japanese, crammed into concrete houses stretching endlessly along streets lined with hoardings, shadowed with wires and cables.

Shortly after I settled in Gifu I was invited to Iga Ueno. Hisae Tsuji had read about me in the paper (the novelty of my arrival had been greeted by newspaper articles and TV interviews). There were no foreigners in Iga Ueno; and, as she told me later, she thought it would be good for her two small sons to meet one. In this way she hoped they might absorb a little English – perhaps by some process of osmosis.

Her husband was less enthusiastic. They met me at the station after a train journey that took half a day, trundling around mountains and across gorges to a picturesque part of the country, not far from the old city of Nara. He was a surly unsmiling fellow. Unlike Basho, who was neither a priest nor a layman, he was both – by profession a maths teacher, by heritage a priest. (This was not at all rare; I knew many people who had inherited a temple but also carried on a normal job.) Irrespective of his natural inclinations, it was his duty to maintain the temple where his mother still lived, and conduct the occasional funeral.

After supper he had a cup of saké, then another. He had been silent and sullen all day. Suddenly his face swelled and turned as red as the pickled plums we had been eating. For a few minutes he was voluble. 'Imagine – a foreigner in my house! We are the only ones in the whole neighbourhood. No one else has ever had a foreigner in their house! I'll tell them all – I want to tell them . . .' As he reached for the telephone he toppled gently over (we were sitting on the floor, so he did not have far to fall). He was snoring even before he hit the tatami. 'More tea?' said Hisae, raising her voice a fraction as the snores increased in volume.

The following day he drove the car, a brown Nissan, proudly to the front of the house and we lumbered off around the narrow streets. He handled it with care, as if it were seldom used; I suspected he had brought it out for my benefit.

Like all Japanese towns, Iga Ueno had its share of concrete and electric wires. But between the houses there were inlets, paddy fields, brown and sunken at this time of year; the shops crammed side by side along the main street were not concrete but dark wood; and all around were hills. It was bitterly cold. The wind was whipping across the barren brown ground of the park. I was still not used to these bleak winter landscapes and yearned for some grass.

'First we see the Ninja Castle,' said Hisae, striding briskly up the hill, a complaining child hanging on to each hand. Iga Ueno, for all its present drabness, had been the headquarters – the city, in effect – of the infamous ninja mercenaries, masters of the poisoned barb, the spiked chain that coiled around your neck just as you thought you had escaped and, it was said, the art of invisibility. They were also adept at scaling impossibly steep walls and could travel vast distances at superhuman speed.

A girl swathed all in black like a *ninja* (except for bright lipstick and painted eyes) showed us the special features of their stronghold – swivel doors, false floors, trap-doors which slid away pitching the enemy into pits lined with spikes. 'Now everybody,' she trilled, 'watch very carefully.' She crouched prettily next to a panel in the wall, then in a split second pushed it round and disappeared.

'It's a revolving panel,' explained Hisae kindly. 'She didn't really disappear.' The two little boys, who had been watching wide-eyed, now began wailing again and pinching each other. Their father yawned loudly. 'That's enough,' he grunted. 'Let's go.'

'Now Basho's hut.' Shivering, we trailed after Hisae back down the hill. She didn't bother to explain who Basho was. Foreigner though I was, I must at least know that.

There was a gate to push open, then a cobbled path leading to a small house, with walls of clay embedded with rice straw, a wooden door, a latticed window. In front was a tree – 'A basho tree,' said Hisae importantly. (Father and children had not come this time; they were waiting in the car.) It looked tropical to me – and rather sad in this chilly climate – with a thick furry trunk like a palm tree and enormous frayed leaves that creaked and flapped forlornly in the wind.

basho nowaki shite	Banana tree in autumn
tarai ni ame o	gale –
kiku yo kana	All night hearing
	Rain in a basin . . .

Basho took his name from the basho tree, the banana tree. He liked to compare himself to it: 'Broken in the wind, the leaves flutter like a phoenix's tail and torn by the rain they are like a tattered green fan. Although there are flowers, they are not bright; and as the wood is completely useless for

6

building, it never feels the axe. But I love the tree for its very uselessness.'

It was the smallest house I had ever seen: one little room, a few dusty straw mats, a tiny table in the middle of the floor with a box on it and a sign – 'Basho's writing equipment' – and, hanging on the wall, a round hat and a strange matted tattered garment like an ancient pelt or the discarded feathers of some enormous bird. 'Basho's rain-cape,' said Hisae. She was enjoying her new role as guide.

She left but I lingered, poked cautiously at the 'rain-cape' – surprisingly dense and heavy – and sat on the edge of the matting, trying to imagine the poet who had, from time to time, stayed here.

Iga Ueno was Basho's home. He was born here in 1644, the second son of a low-ranking samurai. When he was a boy, he was sent to Ueno Castle, the seat of the Todo family, to serve as a page. He and Todo Yoshitada, the daimyo's son, became firm friends and took up the study of haiku together.

As a young man, Basho left and moved to the great new city of Edo, 300 miles away to the east. Gradually he became established as one of the city's leading poets and gathered a coterie of students and admirers around him.

He had been settled there for several years when news came that his mother had died. The following year, 1684, he set out on the long walk back. It took him a month. He wrote about it in the first of his travel diaries, *Nozarashi Kiko – The Records of a Weather Exposed Skeleton*: 'At the beginning of the ninth month I returned to my native place; the miscanthus in the north chamber (his mother's room) had withered away with the frost and there was nothing left of it. Everything was changed from old times. My brother's hair was white, his brows wrinkled. He said only "We are alive." Without a word, he opened his relic bag: "Do reverence to mother's white hairs! This is Urashima's magic box – like Pandora's box – but when Urashima opened his, he aged like Rip van Winkle. You too have turned into an old man!" For a while I wept.'

Looking at the skein of his mother's hair, white as frost, Basho wrote:

te ni toraba kien	If I took it in my hand it
namida zo atsuki	would melt
aki no shimo	My tears are so hot!
	Autumn frost

In the end I spent five years in Japan. Basho and his haiku seemed to colour my experience of the country and through him I came closer to the Japan I had been looking for. Sometimes I daydreamed about following the 'narrow road to the deep north'. But I left without ever doing so.

Back in London, I took a job with a Japanese company; but still I yearned to return to Japan. Gradually the desire to follow the narrow road grew stronger and stronger. One day I mentioned to my Japanese boss that I was thinking of going to Tohoku, the north-east.

'To Tohoku?' he said incredulously – he was a forthright man: 'You don't want to go there – there's nothing there. They're all yokels. You won't understand their dialect. Anyway, it's dangerous. You can't go up there on your own.'

I knew that Tohoku was the most backward, underdeveloped part of Japan, that guide books to the country gave it little more than a page or two – that was part of the attraction. But above all I wanted to walk along with Basho, see Japan through his eyes. And I was curious about the hermit priests that he had stayed with in the northern mountains. 'They don't exist,' snapped my boss. 'Haven't existed for five hundred years.' But as he assured me he had never been there, I thought I would like to see for myself.

So it was that I found myself back in Tokyo. The first part of the journey I planned to cover by train – the smokestacks of Tokyo, the traffic-filled highways, hardly invited walking. But once I was well out of the city, like Basho, I would walk.

Across the Plain

1

The Barrier at Shirakawa

'The old barrier, is it? But . . .'

The grizzled old fellow at the information desk at Shirakawa station tilted his head to one side and drew his breath through his teeth with a long hiss.

'Nothing there now, you know,' he said firmly. 'Really no reason to go there. Nothing at all to see.'

'Nothing at all,' echoed the large untidy woman at the desk opposite.

Still pondering, he ground his cigarette into a large ashtray and slowly lit another. He had enormous hands, dark and work-stained, and a weather-beaten face creased and wrinkled like old leather – as if he had spent most of his life out in the fields, not bent behind a desk in this bleak sunless station. Tokyo, with its skyscrapers and crowds of pale plump faces, was less than two hours away; but this old fellow could almost have been from another race.

'Anyway' – he paused – 'you can't get there.' The woman nodded vigorously.

'No bus, you see.'

My guide book disagreed. A thirty-minute bus ride from the station to the barrier, it said. But looking around the deserted concrete corridors, I was inclined to believe the old man. There couldn't be much call for public transport from here.

Perhaps I would have to walk – an unattractive prospect. Thirty minutes on the bus was a good number of miles; and I had not been planning to begin my walk around the north country at Shirakawa, which could, after all, hardly be called the north country at all, really just a distant suburb of Tokyo.

The pair looked at me apologetically.

I thought a little. Was there perhaps a train?

The old man's face brightened and he waved a stubby finger at me. Yes, of course! How could he have failed to think of that? From under the heap of papers on his desk he extracted a volume the size of a telephone directory and began to thumb methodically through, muttering as he ran his finger slowly down the lines of tiny figures. I waited patiently. Finally he looked up, beaming triumphantly and stabbing the page with his finger.

'Here, here – here's a train for you. 15.37 next one.'

'But that's nearly four hours from now!'

So I really had managed to escape from Tokyo. Despite the inconvenience, I felt a sort of wry satisfaction. It was good to know I was back in the countryside, back in *inaka* – identifiable not so much by its appearance (there was still plenty of concrete around) as by its endearing inefficiency.

I had only had a few days in Tokyo this time. But that was long enough to get used to its ways again – stations where you never have to wait, trains that are never late, telephones that never break down, shop girls who bow to you and smile. It all went together with the high tech façade of the place, the insistent newness of it, the looming skyscrapers and streets crowded with people in chic black or sewer-rat grey, all inexplicably in a hurry.

In the countryside, on the other hand, no-one was in a hurry. 'Countryside', actually, is rather a mistranslation. *Inaka* really means anywhere that is not Tokyo – the provinces, in other words, the boondocks, the sticks. It is difficult to say in Japanese – in my limited Japanese, at any rate – 'the country-side is wonderful', 'I wish I lived in the country'. For the word *inaka* carries overtones of contempt and dismissiveness. When people say they come from the country, they say it abjectly, apologetically. Unlike Londoners, Tokyoites do not drive out to the country at the weekend or yearn for a country cottage. Everyone, if they had the chance, would live in Tokyo.

Four hours to the next train, while inconceivable in Tokyo, was only to be expected of *inaka*. Had I been Japanese, I would

12

have sat down quietly to wait. But I had no intention of doing that.

'In that case I shall walk,' I announced.

The two looked at me not so much with concern as plain astonishment. People do not normally step out of line in Japan, and particularly not in the countryside.

'But – but – it's twelve miles,' they spluttered in chorus. 'You can't walk. It's impossible! It's too far!'

Strolling along the empty road in the sunshine, between the paddy fields spreading flat to humpy hills, I didn't care even if they were right. Perhaps it was too far and there would be nothing to see when I got there. But there was a breath of air on my face and I could hear birds singing and crickets chirping. For the first time I realised that it was nearly summer. Somewhere in those hills over there, I thought, must be the old barrier which marked the beginning of the north country.

The barrier was not always so difficult to find. For a thousand years it barred the main highway up through the coastal plains from the civilised south to the wild north. It was a checkpoint where every traveller had to stop – it was a serious offence to skirt round it through the fields – and present their papers to the guards, a rough bunch, who would interrogate them as to the purpose of their journey and, from time to time, search them.

There were more than seventy of these barriers throughout Japan. At one time, when the country was divided into small warring kingdoms, they had been border posts. Later, in 1603, after the warlord Tokugawa Ieyasu had brought the whole country under his control (when, in England, another small island country, the Stuarts had just succeeded the Tudors and William Shakespeare was writing *Hamlet* and *Lear*), he maintained the barriers as a system of road blocks, one way of controlling his unruly subjects.

But from earliest times the barrier at Shirakawa was somehow special. There was a magic, a glamour about it. For it was here that travellers crossed over into the untamed northern territories, the remote land of Oshu. When poets came this way, it was customary for them to mark their crossing with a

poem; and even poets who did not make the long journey were
expected to produce a poem on the subject.

Nöin Hoshi, an eleventh-century priest, wrote the most
famous poem of all

> *miyako o ba*
> *kasumi to tomoni*
> *tachishikado*
> *aki-kaze zo fuku*
> *Shirakawa no seki*

> Though I left the capital
> With the spring mist –
> The autumn wind blows
> At Shirakawa Barrier

For six months, from spring to autumn, so the story goes, he
vanished from the streets of Kyoto, the capital. Late that
autumn he reappeared and presented his wonderful poem to
the public. He had walked, he said, five hundred miles, all the
way from Kyoto to the barrier. But there were a few doubters
who must have scrutinised the soles of his soft aristocratic feet;
for, says the story, there was not one callus on them.

In 1689, when Basho decided to set out on his final long
journey, it was the magic of the barrier at Shirakawa that drew
him to the far north. He had been travelling for the last two
years with very little rest – to Kashima to see the harvest moon
(in the event he had to write a haiku on the heavy rain instead),
home to Iga, to Mount Yoshino to see the cherry blossoms . . .

Only a few months earlier, he had trekked up into the
mountains of central Japan (at first he went on horseback; but
he felt so nervous jogging along the narrow mountain paths
that he decided he would rather walk) to Sarashina in the
province of Kiso, determined that this year, at least, he would
see the harvest moon, rising over Mount Obasute. He was not
back in Edo until the ninth month of 1688, tired and thin from
his travels.

Kiso no yase mo	Kiso thinness too
mada naoranu ni	Still not mended
nochi no tsuki	Late moon-viewing

Instead of resting in Edo, he stayed just long enough to 'brush the cobwebs from my dilapidated house on the river-bank'. It was as if the gods of the road had bewitched him. Echoing Nöin's words, he wrote: 'The spring mist filled the sky and, in spite of myself, the gods filled my heart with a yearning to cross the Shirakawa barrier.'

There were no surly border guards and no crowds of travellers when I finally reached the barrier – no merchants in sedan chairs, no *daimyo* on horseback with retinues of foot soldiers and servants and porters; no pilgrims, no priests; no ladies in palanquins or travellers in capes and straw hats, like the colourful figures in Hokusai's woodblock prints. In fact, I nearly walked straight past it along the rough country road.

Probably the road had changed less than anything. Until the rule of the Tokugawas came to an end, in 1867, wheeled vehicles were the prerogative of the emperors, who rode around Kyoto in carts drawn by oxen. Everyone else, no matter how far they had to go, walked or went on horseback or in a palanquin. The roads had to carry men and horses, nothing else – no heavy stage-coaches, no carriages – and even the great highways were fairly rough and narrow.

Perhaps, I thought, stepping over a puddle, the old man had been right. Perhaps there really was nothing here. Certainly, no one else was coming this way – no cars to hitch a ride from, no people to check if I was on the right road. It was the middle of June. In Tokyo, the rainy season was overdue. Water rationing had begun and in the middle of the day the taps produced nothing more than a thin trickle (though there was still no restriction on the nightly bath).

Up here, by the looks of it, there was no problem. The paddy fields were brimming with water and crammed with young rice plants, dazzlingly green. Occasionally, from somewhere out in the middle of them, an invisible frog sounded off like a miniature fog-horn. A grey heron dipped and soared overhead.

I sat down at the side of the road, wondering if I should turn back. I was glad that I had left my bags at the station. Beside me stood a tall stone figure sprouting green moss on its head like a thatch of hair. It must have been eight foot tall, with big stone earrings, a solemn round baby's face and a faded cloth bib around its neck. Evidently the place was not always deserted, for someone had laid offerings in front of it – coins, an empty cup, packets of biscuits, a few fresh rhododendrons in a vase.

Facing me was a stone pillar, half hidden in the grass, some worn hieroglyphs carved down its side. The hillside rose right behind in a tangle of trees. Laboriously I read the characters one by one: 'Old – Barrier – of – Shirakawa'.

It had taken me five and a half hours. Basho and his travelling companion, Kawai Sora, took three and a half weeks.

'After many unsettled days of travel, we finally reached Shirakawa barrier and felt we were on our way at last.' It was the twenty-first day of the fourth month, June 10th 1689.

Looking at the famous barrier, it was as if he were seeing it through the eyes of all the poets who had passed through before him: 'I understood the feeling of Taira Kanemori (a tenth-century warrior poet), who wished he could send a message back "somehow, to the capital" . . . Nöin's "autumn wind" lingered in my ears and Minamoto Yorimasa's "maple leaves in autumn" before my eyes, even as I was moved by the green leaves of summer. Seeing Fujiwara Toshimichi's "white unohana blossom", added to the white blossoms of the briar rose, made me feel as if I were crossing in the snow, like Oe no Sadashige. And one man of old (Taketa Kuniyuki) straightened his helmet and put on new clothes before crossing, according to Kiyosuke's records.'

Basho himself did not write a poem then. The two travellers had another twenty miles to walk that day, to the post town of Sukagawa, well into the land of Oshu. They spent four or five days there, staying with Tokyu, a local poet. 'The first thing he asked was, "What did you write when you crossed the Shirakawa barrier?"

'"What with the hardships of the long journey," I replied, "I was tired in body and spirit; and besides, my soul caught up by the beauty of the landscape and my heart pierced by the thought of the ancient poets who had passed this way, I could hardly bring myself to compose a poem.'''

But he could not pass the barrier in silence. He wrote

furyu-no	Culture's beginning:
hajime ya oku no	Rice-planting song
ta-ue uta	Of the far north

Shirakawa was the crossing point between the world of *furyu*, which Basho was leaving behind him – elegance, refinement, the cultured life of Edo – and *oku*, the back country, the rustic land of Oshu. But all that fine culture, he saw, was rooted in the humble rice-planting songs of the north – the world which he was about to rediscover.

No rice-planting songs came floating up to me on the silent hillside, though in the distance I could hear the splutter of a rice-planter being driven up and down a field. It was a wild, unkempt sort of place; hard to imagine that anyone had ever lived here. I headed straight for the top of the hill, up a long flight of broken stone steps, then on, clambering between enormous old pines and cedars and over gnarled vines, as thick as good-sized saplings, which humped and twisted across the ground and coiled around the trunks.

I reached a clearing at the top and peered through the trees over the surrounding country. Far below, the old highway, the road which I had been walking along, wound away into the distance. Surely, I thought, the hills of the north should have a different cast to them. There should be some dramatic change in the landscape to mark the beginning of the land of Oshu. But in each direction there were only the same bland round hills.

There seemed to be nothing left of the barrier at all. In the middle of the clearing was a neglected old temple, with copper glinting from beneath the grime on its roof and a large padlock on its wooden doors. Hanging in front was a thick straw rope with a tasselled end and, tucked up under the eaves, two rusting round bells. I tugged the rope to make the bells jangle, then clapped my hands and made a wish.

This was the spot, apparently, where the main fortress of the old border garrison stood. Sixty soldiers had lived here, with a stockade and ditch all around to protect them and a guardhouse at each of the four gates.

Pushing aside branches and brambles, I scrambled down the slope behind the temple. After a few yards I found the ditch, as deep as a moat, stretching around the hill with a wall of earth covered in grass mounded up on each side of it. Further round it broadened to a deep hollow with a signboard in front reading 'South Gate'.

So that was all that was left – no ruins, not even a rock, just a dent in the hillside. Only three hundred years before, when Basho came, the border had been full of life. There must have been inns for travellers who arrived late and geisha to entertain them, somewhere for porters and palanquin bearers to rest, stables with fresh horses. Now there was not a trace.

Things disappear quickly in Japan. There are villages in the countryside where the whole population has left, moved to the city – and within months the roofs have caved in, the walls toppled and a mat of vines and weeds hangs over the skeletal remains of the houses. What with earthquakes, volcanoes, typhoons, fires and the hot steamy days of summer when everything rots, no one builds for posterity. And the old is not valued as it is in England. Usually 'old' simply means worn-out, useless, in need of replacement . . .

'Got any change?'

'Hundred yen do?'

'Fifty's enough.'

The silence was broken by voices and the clatter of money falling into the wooden collection box. Standing in front of the temple were three men, old soldiers perhaps or farmers on holiday, in white shirts, baggy grey trousers and boot-lace ties. Each had a large old-fashioned camera in a leather case slung over his shoulder. They clapped their hands twice and bowed, short stiff military bows, then, as I passed, turned and bowed again. I bowed back.

I caught up with them at the bottom of the stone steps. One, an old fellow with a sagging bloodhound face, stopped in his tracks and jabbed a finger at me.

'Doko? Where . . . ?' he asked.

I must have been the first foreigner he had ever seen.

'England,' I grinned.

'America?'

'England.'

The others gathered round. One, as I had guessed, was a farmer. My inquisitor was, he said, 'something in architecture', which I took to mean a carpenter, while the third was 'a local government officer', a labourer, in other words. They had known each other since primary school and were having one of those little jaunts that Japanese men do, leaving their wives at home.

'We stayed at a hotspring last night,' announced the architect.

'Was it fun?' I asked.

They all chuckled. 'Yes – because we played,' said the government officer. I did not know precisely what they meant – and, as a woman, I was unlikely ever to find out. But I did know that taking the waters is only one of the pleasures that hotsprings have to offer. Admittedly most encounters are not as romantic and tragic as that of Shimamura and Komako the geisha in Kawabata's famous novel *Snow Country* – most of the women, indeed, hardly qualify for the epithet geisha (*gei* – arts; *sha* – person) – but there are still plenty of opportunities for old farmers to 'play'.

Now it was time for photographs. First I posed with the farmer at the bottom of the stone steps to be photographed with his camera. Then the performance had to be repeated twice for the other two. Finally the architect carefully placed his large and heavy camera in my hands and explained with great care exactly which button I should press, and the three lined up with military precision in front of the stone *torii*, the gateway marking the entry to the temple. They all stopped smiling and stood as stony-faced as the eight-foot image over the road, like three Victorian patriarchs, while I pressed the button.

'Come and look at the museum,' said the architect. It was hardly a museum really, just some dusty glass cases along the back wall of a neighbouring house, with a couple of birds in cages hanging overhead. There were the usual things – some rocks (perhaps fossils), broken roof tiles, a lance, a rusty helmet, some books open to show maps and a long document covered in tiny hieroglyphs. Frowning with concentration and mouthing each syllable, he read the document through, then turned to me.

'When this barrier was built, there were Ainu here, see. That was why they built it – to keep the Ainu back. Then they pushed them up north, all the way to Hokkaido. That's where they are now, the Ainu – in Hokkaido.'

A simple enough theory and one that has been popular for years. The barrier was built somewhere around the eighth century, by soldiers who marched up from central Japan, from the land of Yamato, based around the Kyoto-Nara region. It was one of the first in a chain of fortresses slung across the northern neck of the country, a sort of Hadrian's Wall built partly to restrain the ferocious northern tribes – the Picts and Scots of Japanese history – but mainly to establish the control of the Yamato armies over the area.

All this is beyond dispute. Less certain is the identity of the northerners. The men from Yamato eventually conquered the whole of Japan, and as a result, the only histories we have are theirs, written by them, seen through their eyes.

Predictably the northern tribes, the hairy Emishi ('enemies of the Emperor') or Ezo, come out rather badly. 'Among the (north-) eastern savages the Emishi are the most powerful', notes the *Nihongi*, the Record of Japan (completed around 720); 'their men and women live together promiscuously, there is no distinction of father and child. In winter they dwell in holes, in summer they live in nests. Their clothing consists of furs and they drink blood . . . Both men and women tie up their hair in the form of a mallet and tattoo their bodies . . . They are of a violent disposition and are much given to oppression'.

For many years scholars believed that the Emishi were the same as the hairy Ainu, the gentle non-Japanese tribes who live in the northern island of Hokkaido – an attractive theory, evoking a picture of the superior Japanese, the embodiment of civilisation and culture, driving the barbarous non-Japanese tribes into the sea.

In fact there is no evidence that the Ainu were ever in Honshu, the main island. It seems that the Ezo or Emishi and the Ainu were completely different peoples. (Although old textbooks and dusty museums like to preserve the story.) So who were the Ezo? I suspected that they were simply the ancestors of the people who still live in Tohoku, in Oshu. I hoped, in other words, that they still existed and that I would find them when I crossed the barrier.

By 1150, the Ezo presented so little threat that they were even the subject of courtly poetry. A gentleman called Fujiwara no Chikataka wrote

Ezo ga sumu
Tsugaro no nobe no
hagizakari
koya nishikigi no
tateru naruran

In the fields of Tsugaru
Where the Ezo live
Bush clover blossoms
Like brocaded courting wands
At a maiden's house

The three old fellows gave me a lift back to the station. Before we parted company, we had to repeat the ritual of photographs, posing in twos, then threes, then all together with the self-timer, in front of the vast concrete building which rose anachronistically out of the paddy fields.

Finally they drove off. I watched them vanishing into the distance, still bowing through the back window of the car. I bowed even deeper myself, grateful for the company and the lift.

It was still early, time enough to get the Bullet Train on to Fukushima.

'We were worried,' said the old man in the information office. 'Didn't know what would happen to you. Anyway, you're just in time for the train.'

2
Sword and Satchel

The landscape north of the border looked depressingly similar to the landscape south of the border, and I quickly settled down to pore over Basho and sip Japanese Railways' green tea – a tiny plastic container of hot water, a tea bag to dunk in it and a cup big enough for two mouthfuls. There was one stop (which I timed – fifty seconds precisely) at Koriyama, a town memorable only for its lack of any attractive features. It was a hotch-potch of concrete, a clutter of squat grey faceless buildings without a hint of green, stretching as far as the distant mountains on the horizon. Factories with plumes of smoke hanging from the chimneys, rows of identical apartment blocks, more factories . . . It didn't look a place for human beings.

'Only five ri (twelve miles) from Tokyu's house, beyond the town of Hiwada, are the Asaka hills, just off the highway. This is a marshy area,' wrote Basho. Was that, I wondered, now Koriyama?

The two travellers – Basho and Sora – had come to see the Asaka *katsumi*, the beautiful blue irises which were said to bloom in the marshes and which had inspired poets in the past. 'The season for gathering irises was drawing near, so we asked people which plant was the one called katsumi, but there was no one who knew. As we searched around the marshes, asking people, walking around enquiring "Katsumi, katsumi?" the sun went down behind the mountains. At Nihonmatsu, "Two Pines", we turned to the right, took a quick look at the cave of Kurozuka, and stopped at Fukushima for the night.'

At first reading, it seemed a rather ludicrous story. Who had they asked, I wondered, and what had the locals made of these two middle-aged men in black picking their way across the marshes, saying 'Katsumi, katsumi?' But then I remembered all the flower-viewing excursions I had been taken on – two hours by car to see an ancient cherry tree, a visit to a temple in Kamakura to see the hydrangeas, a day-trip by coach to a park famous for its lilies . . . In Japan there was nothing bizarre about going a long way to see a particular flower at the height of its season.

'Katsumi, katsumi'. Not long after I arrived in Japan, a kind neighbour phoned one morning. Today, she said, the plum blossoms were at their height. Of course, I would not want to miss them. As I was new to town, perhaps I didn't know Bairin Park, 'Plum Forest Park'. That was the place, she said, to see plum blossoms. Those were the best plum blossoms in town. She told me where it was and I jumped on my bicycle immediately and set off.

The road I had to cycle down was full of traffic, with rickety old trams (some of the last remaining in Japan) rattling down the middle. Bairin Park, she had said, was on this road. Surely not, I thought. Plum Forest Park could not be on a noisy road like this. I must have misunderstood.

I stopped in a shop to ask and was directed to a small open square right beside the road.

It was difficult to see the plum trees for all the people – people walking from tree to tree, stopping to peer long and hard at a particular blossom; people photographing other people lined up beneath the branches; and several men crouched over complicated cameras, inches from a particularly photogenic cluster, taking close-ups.

No one but me could see the concrete – or so it seemed. What I saw was a small, dingy square, paved with concrete, walled with concrete, with a few sad dusty plum trees in the middle.

Later, I became a connoisseur of plum blossom – delicate, more delicate than the celebrated cherry, and with a certain sadness, appearing as it does in February when the snow is still on the ground. I had learned the Japanese way of seeing. When I went to Bairin Park, I saw lovely plum blossom, nothing else. I no longer noticed the concrete that propped up the hills, the concrete breakwaters in the sea, the dense network of wires crisscrossing above the streets.

Then I went back to England and my training deserted me. Looking down now on Koriyama's concrete and, later, on Fukushima's neon, I rather wished that I could still see with Japanese eyes.

At first sight there was nothing in Fukushima to suggest that I had crossed into another land, that this had once been the country of the Ezo. It seemed identical to every other Japanese city I had ever seen – the same concrete, the same neon, the same covered arcades with Bach throbbing out of loud-speakers and plastic leaves sprouting from the lampposts, a touching reminder that, out there beyond the concrete, it was early summer, the season of green leaves.

ara toto	Ah – magnificent!
aoba wakaba no	Green leaves, young leaves,
hi no hikari	The sun shining

But at least Fukushima was small, and all around, in the distance, at the end of each long flat street, were mountains.

Feet on desk, the information man at the station was watching baseball on television. I expected him to snap to attention with the efficiency of a Tokyo official. But instead he turned reluctantly after I had rung the bell several times, with an expression of utter amazement that anyone could want information – particularly at this most important moment in the match.

'Inns? These are all right. Near the station. Cheap,' he snapped, thrust a couple of leaflets into my hand, slammed the window of his little glass capsule shut and returned to the baseball.

The innkeeper at Yamamoto Ryokan, the nearest inn, was also preoccupied. He had a round face and hair cut flat across the top as if it had been sheared off with a hedgetrimmer.

'No empty rooms,' he said, casting an anxious glance towards an open door from which came an endless stream of words – baseball commentary, I guessed. It was all rather

24

discouraging. I hoped it was not an inauspicious beginning to my journey.

'Do you have a *zashiki* – Japanese-style room?' I had put my bags down heavily on the floor and had no intention of picking them up again and dragging them a step further. Besides, the place looked half empty; it had a shabby, unused look to it.

'You won't want one of those,' he said. 'They don't have showers.'

That was fine, I said. I could use the communal bath, like everybody else.

He looked deeply perturbed. Foreigners, as everyone knows, have showers, and only Japanese bath together. Foreigners, in fact, are shocked by communal bathing.

Finally he hit on a solution. 'You can take your bath after dinner,' he said. 'Everyone will have finished by then. You won't be disturbed. You can lock the door. Of course, you won't be wanting breakfast,' he added.

'I know it's Japanese-style, but it'll be fine,' I sighed.

He would, of course, suggest that I should have the last bath. I was, after all, both a woman and a foreigner. I had been here long enough to know the pecking order for the bath: all the men of the family, from oldest to youngest; then, once the bath water (which is never changed, simply topped-up) was getting a little chilly – once there was a slight scum on the surface (despite the fact that everyone washes outside) – came the women, with the mother of the house last of all, of course.

Next morning I parcelled up some of my books and clothes and posted them back to a friend in Tokyo. With my load thus lightened, I was anxious to begin walking. As yet, I had not discovered the narrow road itself; I had not yet had a glimpse of Basho's actual path.

Basho was in Fukushima on the first day of the fifth month, June 18th 1689. 'The next day, enquiring for the stone of Shinobu Mojizuri, we went to the village of Shinobu. In a little hamlet in the shadow of a distant hill we found the stone, half buried in the earth.'

It was easy enough to find Mochizuri; even the bad-tempered man in the station information office could tell me how to get there. But to find the path that Basho took from Fukushima was more difficult.

Kawai Sora kept his own diary, full of practical details – the weather, the distance from one place to another, what they ate, how much their lodgings cost, the names of everyone at each poetry gathering. Perhaps, I thought, it might provide a clue.

I studied the old-fashioned writing, showed it to the innkeeper who shook his head dismissively and said, 'Can't understand that!' and finally, with the help of a dictionary and a bit of guesswork, worked out a few sentences: '5th month, 2nd day. Fine weather. Leave Fukushima. Having covered a distance of 10 cho (1190 yards) from the town, there are two rivers. At the first river we do not cross, but go to the right 7 or 8 cho (800 yards), then cross the Abukuma river by boat. From there we go 17 or 18 cho (1½ miles) in the direction of the mountains, and in a valley is the stone of Mojizuri. There is a fence around it. There is a temple to Kannon. There are six or seven cedars and cypresses. There is a small shallow spring called Tiger Spring.'

Sora had been Basho's friend and devoted pupil for many years. He was five years younger, forty when they set out together for the north, and had also accompanied Basho on the journey to Kashima to see the harvest moon. 'My companion', Basho wrote at that time, 'is a wanderer, like a samurai without a lord.' Before leaving for the north, he took religious vows, shaved his head, and put on priest's robes.

He was a close neighbour of Basho's in Fukagawa. 'He lives almost under the very leaves of my banana tree and helps me with carrying wood and fetching water', wrote Basho. For Sora he wrote some of his most relaxed and affectionate haiku. One winter evening, for example, when Sora had dropped in and was building a fire and heating water for tea, Basho wrote

kimi hi o take	You light a fire,
yoki mono misen	I'll show you something good:
yukimaroge	A huge snowball

In the end I took the bus to Mochizuri, then walked the last hundred yards to Mochizuri Kannon Temple. It sits right on the edge of the Fukushima plain, at the exact point where the rice fields run up against the mountains.

The temple itself was invisible among the trees at the foot of the mountain. All I could see was a huge bell in a sort of wooden scaffold with a signpost in front of it. I went to look at it. The signpost read *shizen hodo* – *oku no hosomichi*: FOOTPATH – NARROW ROAD TO THE DEEP NORTH.

So there really was a 'narrow road to the deep north' – and I was standing on it. It disappeared enticingly around the edge of the hill. I felt inclined to set off along it straightaway; I was longing to walk along Basho's path. But first I had to see the famous stone of Shinobu.

It was big, bigger than I had expected, and more impressive. In fact, it was the size of a small house, with a rough blotchy surface covered in different varieties of moss, dull shades of blue, green and pink. It lay face down on the ground surrounded by a stone fence and a locked gate and right behind it was the cliff from which, apparently, it had tumbled.

There was a winding path to the top of the cliff, flanked by ancient cedars and cypresses, dotted with stone images and small faded wooden shrines. I climbed along it, fanning myself vigorously to beat off the mosquitoes, and peeped into one small shrine, hoping that the contents were not secret. Inside I glimpsed an altar, surprisingly lavish, with tiers of candles, gold images, heavy drapes, ornate gold lilies.

At the top of the path was a plateau and a small two-storeyed pagoda, also unusually lavish in its decoration, with curving copper roofs and protruding beams ending in grotesque lion and elephant heads, brightly painted. Nearby a *semi*, a particularly noisy species of cicada, was whirring like an electric drill while a mechanical voice droned from loudspeakers fixed in the trees. 'This pagoda is one hundred and seventy-six years old. It is a reproduction of the famous Toshogu shrine at Nikko . . .'

The commentary continued as I walked around the tiny

museum in the grounds. The woman who had sold me a ticket came bustling in after me, pausing in front of each dusty cabinet to give me the history of the contents. In spite of her official role, she looked a homely sort, broad of base, with thick splayed legs ending in white ankle socks, curly hair and a fine set of gold teeth.

The first exhibit was a yellowing scroll with a faded painting of Basho. 'The great poet Matsuo Basho,' she intoned. It was the same voice, the same intonation, as the voice which still droned from the trees. 'It was three hundred and five years ago to the day that he honoured our temple with his presence, together with his disciple, Kawai Sora. He came to see the famous dyeing stone of Shinobu Mochizuri, which, since olden times, had been used for making designs on silk.'

She gave me a kindly smile. 'On your own, are you?' While the first voice had been high-pitched and used a Japanese laden with formal phrases, this one was several tones lower. 'That's very good. I'm impressed.' She turned to the next exhibit and reverted to the tour guide again.

So we continued around the museum, admiring tattered scrolls with faded characters brushed on them and wooden carvings darkened with age. There seemed to have been an endless number of emperors and great men who had wondered whether they still dyed using the stone, and had come to visit, and had written a poem. Before reciting each one, she would pause, fold her hands, close her eyes, and half speak and half sing it, like some blind bard. I wished my Japanese was better so that I could understand more of what she was saying.

Finally we came to the pride of the collection. In a glass case in the middle of the room was a ragged piece of silk, neatly folded, blotched with pink and yellow. 'And if you would care to examine this piece of material' – her enthusiasm overcame her and she switched in mid-sentence to everyday Japanese – 'just last year it was, imagine – they hadn't used the stone for centuries and centuries. Let's try it, they thought, let's see if it works. Professor Shimizu from the high school it was, he organised it. They came down here, put a piece of silk on the stone, and that was how it came out. Even in Basho's time it was centuries since they had used the stone.' I was a bit baffled by the dyeing process but said it was beautiful anyway.

'On your own, are you?' she said again as we walked back to her ticket office in the gateway of the temple. She lowered her voice a little, took a step closer and said, 'I didn't want to get married either, you know. Wanted to be a carpenter; or an architect. Parents were against it, though. Had to have *o-miai*. They said I had to. I was twenty-two. Didn't like him at first – not at all. But I married him anyway. I have four children now, and ten grandchildren. Ten.'

'Tell me that story again,' I said, 'the one about the minister. I didn't understand it properly. Tell me it in ordinary Japanese.'

She beamed. We settled down on each side of the open window of the ticket office, she inside on her stool, me outside, elbows propped on the ledge.

'Around 859, in the Heian period, a minister of state from the capital was passing this way. He was going to Matsushima. It got late and he lost his way and asked to stay at a farmer's house. The farmer lived near here, near the Shinobu dyeing stone. The minister fell in love with the farmer's daughter. He stayed and stayed. He didn't tell her he was a minister of state.

'Finally a command came down from the capital: he had to go back. He told her he was a minister. "But I will return," he said. "I will return in a hundred days." She waited day after day for a message and every day she prayed to the goddess Mochizuri Kannon for his return. After ninety-nine days still no message came and she became ill. At last a poem came; but she died of sadness anyway. They say that on the hundredth day, she was looking at the dyeing stone and saw his face; and after that she polished it every day to see his face.

'He was Minamoto Toru. He was Minister of the Left of the Kawara District. Do you know his poem? It's in *Hyaku nin Isshu*, "A hundred poems by a hundred poets".'

She closed her eyes and recited:

29

'*Michinoku no
Shinobu moji-zuri
tare yue-ni
midare some nishi
ware narunaku ni*'

'Who has caused this confusion, this secret love
That paints my heart
Like the Shinobu dyeing stone
In the land of Michinoku?
Would that it were not I who suffers so.'

She carried on. She was well into the swing of it now. 'The stone used to be up at the top of the hill. Until the Sengoku period, the sixteenth century, they made designs on silk with it. They put pieces of silk over it, laid ferns on top – shinobu ferns, hare's foot ferns – then rubbed with another stone. But the village girls kept wasting barley, polishing it to see their lovers' faces, and the farmers got angry and toppled it down into the valley. It landed with the mirror face downwards and was covered in moss and earth. You know Basho's haiku, don't you?

'*sanae toru
temoto ya mukashi
shinobu zuri*

'Hands planting rice –
Recall the old days,
Rubbing ferns

'It was rice-planting time when Basho came – they planted rice later in the year in those days. The women he saw planting rice, in the old days would have been rubbing ferns on the stone.

'Go by train,' she said firmly when I asked her which way I should go along the Narrow Road footpath. It was simple. To get to Ioji, Basho's next stop, all I had to do was take the bus back to Fukushima, wait a bit at the station ('only a few hours,' she said, 'perhaps three or four'), then take the train out again.

'But I want to walk,' I insisted. 'I want to walk along the narrow road to the deep north.'

'You want to walk . . . Well . . . Well, what an idea! I'm impressed. But Ioji is very far,' she clucked, 'and the footpath doesn't go there. And it's a road, not a footpath.'

I kept my doubts to myself; I was sure that I would be able to follow Basho's path through the mountains. The directions she gave were like a secret code: 'Wherever the road forks, go left. Keep to the edge of the mountains; never go right, or you'll be in mountain country. Watch out for a carpenter's workshop. It's big. Maruyoshi, that's the name to watch for. Ask there for Kamada Bridge and look for a big bare mountain.'

Before I left, I asked if I could take her photograph. 'If I was young I wouldn't mind,' she said, giving me a beautiful gold-toothed smile. 'Now I'm too old and ugly.'

As soon as I was outside the temple, I saw that she was right. There was no footpath. The road ran along the edge of the hill for a few yards, then branched into three and all the branches disappeared into the maze of roads crisscrossing the fields.

I set off, keeping the mountains to my right, following the map she had drawn for me, but soon found I had stepped off the edge of it and was walking blindly.

It was ordered, orderly country, as geometric, as precision-tooled as the skyline of Fukushima on the far horizon and as unlike the rolling fields of England as I could imagine. The landscape in Japan never rolls. Either it is flat, or it is mountains, shooting abruptly out of the plain, covered in trees and useless for farming. You can mark the point where the plain stops and the mountain begins. It is a young, sharp-edged landscape, to English eyes – to my eyes, at any rate – more foreign, more other, than any I have seen.

The paddy fields looked not man-made but machine-made, they were so perfect – perfectly square, perfectly flat. Here and there, becalmed in the middle of them like stranded ships, were small neat houses with shiny red roofs, surrounded by greenhouses, rows of cabbages and onions and dark red perilla plants, or orchards full of green peaches.

I walked along for half an hour or so, fairly confident that I was going in the right direction, following along the edge of the mountains as I had been told. Then I came to a second road, at right angles to mine, branching off to the left and disappearing across the paddy fields. Which instruction was I to follow, I wondered, 'stick to the mountains' or 'keep to the left'?

There was one small shop where the roads met. Standing outside it, talking in the sunshine, were two people, a man and a curly-haired woman in a voluminous white garment which looked like a smock but seemed to function as a pinafore or pinny. All the women around here wore them – long-sleeved, tied at the back at neck and waist, decorated with lace, and efficiently covering their clothes nearly down to the knee.

These were the first people I had seen for miles. I glanced at them as I passed, wondering whether to disturb their conversation and ask the way to Maruyoshi's.

Suddenly the woman noticed me and darted forward, thrusting a sheet of paper into my hand.

'There's your road,' she said urgently, pointing to the road through the fields. 'That one there. That's the way to Kamada Bridge.' On the paper was a neatly drawn map, a grid of thin pencil lines, showing the next stage of my journey.

It was uncanny. I stared at her in amazement. Did she have second sight? It seemed a miraculous example of the Japanese ability to communicate without words. She was already shunting me off along the road and the man was offering me a lift in his car.

'Kokuho-san from the temple called,' she smiled. How disappointing, I thought. What a mundane solution to the mystery. Walking through these fields, I had forgotten that telephones existed. 'It's a long way, you know. Better take a lift as far as Kamada Bridge.'

I never found Maruyoshi or the big bare mountain, but after stopping many times to ask directions, eventually came to Kamada Bridge. Ioji, I was beginning to realise, was a lot further than I had thought. My pleasant country stroll had turned into a marathon hike through the industrial suburbs of

Fukushima, and on the far side of the bridge – a massive concrete affair, shaking under the weight of lorries rumbling ponderously across – were endless rows of factory chimneys and banks of neon signs lighting up an enormous drive-in complex of pinball parlours.

I stopped for a bowl of noodles and to find out how Basho had fared. He too apparently had a difficult time finding his way that day.

'Crossing the river on the Tsuki-no-Wa ferry, we came to a post town called Se-no-Ue,' he began. It was hard to imagine that a ferry with the romantic name of Tsuki-no-Wa, 'Ring of the Moon', had ever plied back and forth across that sluggish grey river with its concrete banks. It must have been one of those flat-bottomed, punt-like boats that Hokusai and Hiroshige drew (a hundred years or so after Basho's time), poled along by a bow-legged ferryman with a shaven head and skimpy loincloth, packed with passengers and parcels and covered with a straw canopy to keep the sun off them. In those days, I thought, the river must have been silent – just the splash of the pole dropping into the water, birds singing, semis whirring . . . And from there they went on to Se-no-Ue, 'Above the Rapids', another romantic name.

'The ruins of the castle of the Sato lords were said to be one and a half ri (3½ miles) to our left, in the foothills of the mountains. Having been told to go via Saba Moor, near the village of Iizaka, we were walking along, *tazune tazune*, asking and asking – asking directions again and again – when we came to a place called Maruyama (Round Hill). It was here that the hall once stood . . . In an old temple nearby, the family tombs remain.'

The temple was easier to find than the castle ruins. The woman in the noodle shop drew a complicated map which took me off the main road into some sort of industrial estate. Right in the middle of it, on the other side of a factory, I came across Se-no-Ue station. By now I was hot and tired and bad-tempered, cross at the lorries which roared along the narrow roads, pushing me aside, and cross at the woman who had directed me into this miserable labyrinth of grey streets.

But I felt more cheerful when I discovered the station. Despite losing my way so many times, I was still on Basho's path. I asked directions again and had another map carefully drawn for me.

Finally I hitched a lift with a surly lorry driver and sat perched in his cab listening to baseball on the radio as we rolled along Route 13, one of those enormous, endless, dusty Japanese highways loaded with traffic. He dropped me off near Ioji. A swarthy man selling strawberries outside a supermarket had never heard of Maruyama, the site of the castle, but directed me to Ioji Temple. 'Just up the road,' he said, and, as I thanked him, put a box of strawberries into my hand.

It was a relief to leave the main road. I followed quiet backstreets down to the large and beautiful old temple, in its tranquil garden. As I came through the gates, a very old man raking the ground looked up and grinned widely, revealing a mouthful of gold teeth.

'America?' he quavered.

'*Igirisu* – England.'

'Oh, oh – Japanese very good' – this was in English. He took a few hobbling steps towards me. 'This way, this way', beckoning for me to come closer. His cheeks were sunk so deep his face was like a skull and his trousers, rolled at the ankles, flapped around his thin legs as he limped along, but his face beamed with welcome.

Against the wall was a large stone, carved with characters. 'Here, here.' He still insisted on speaking fractured English. 'Matsuo Basho – you know?' Inscribed on the stone was the haiku which Basho had written here

oi mo tachi mo	The satchel too, the long
satsuki ni kazare	sword too –
kami nobori	Celebrate May
	With flying carp!

He lapsed into Japanese. 'Matsuo Basho visited on June 18th, but by the old calendar that was the first day of the fifth month – you understand?' I thought a little, then I understood. Basho was here four days before the Boys' Festival, the fifth day of the month (Girls' Festival is on the third of the third month and Tanabata, the Star Festival, on the seventh of the seventh). And at that time, as now, enormous multicoloured paper carp were hung out like flags above every house where there were sons, one for each. Nowadays the fifth day of the fifth month is May 5th, and when I was at Ioji the paper carp had long since been taken down for the year.

'When we went into the temple and asked for tea, we learned that Yoshitsune's long sword and Benkei's satchel were among the treasures here,' wrote Basho. Sora tells the story differently: 'Went from Se-no-Ue to Saba Moor. There is the Sato lords' temple. Did not enter temple gates. Went to the west . . . Cloudy from midday, rain fell from early evening.'

It is hard to imagine that Sora got it wrong. His diary is quite matter of fact, quite down to earth. Probably the two travellers were tired; as I had discovered, it was a long walk from Shinobu to Ioji. Their feet must have been sore (as mine were); they had been walking all day in rough straw sandals. They wanted to get to an inn and rest. For the old poet it was enough, perhaps, simply to stand by the gate of the temple. He knew that the sword and the satchel were there; he didn't need to see them in order to write about them.

'This way, this way.' The old man was hobbling across the temple grounds, beckoning me to follow. He slid open the wooden doors closing off a side section of the main temple and, shuffling off his shoes, stepped inside, shouting 'Oi, oi! Okakusan da yo! Visitor!'

There was no response. We waited. Then he shouted again, giving me a reassuring grin. 'You've come all this way . . . We'll make sure you see them.' I wondered what it was I was going to see.

Another few minutes passed. A woman appeared, finishing off a mouthful of food, a pale thin woman in a grey blouse and skirt. 'Two hundred yen,' she said, without bothering to look at me.

I stepped in, blinking, dazzled from the glaring sunshine outside. I was in another museum, a very small one this time, just a row of old dusty objects in a glass case; hopefully it would not take long. I was looking forward to a hot bath.

The woman finished chewing and positioned herself at the end of the row. Clasping her hands in front of her, she closed her eyes and began to speak, her voice rising and falling in a rhythmical expressionless monotone.

I listened hard. It was a mishmash of archaic Japanese and formal expressions, peppered with the honorific *de gozaimasu* – difficult to understand much at all, except for the names 'Yoshitsune' and 'Benkei', repeated again and again. Looking at her blank expression, I wondered if she had any more idea than I did of the meaning of what she was saying.

She finished speaking and stood waiting for me to leave. There were voices at the door, shoes were removed, and a group of elderly men crowded in, all in brown suits, all with weathered farmers' faces. The woman took their two hundred yens and began speaking again, exactly the same words, exactly the same voice, like a tape-recorder. This time I understood a little more.

'Honoured guests: the antique relic which you see before you may truly be considered to be Benkei's *oi* – Benkei's satchel . . .'

For '*oi*', my dictionary had 'satchel, chest, pannier, portable bookcase carried on the back, portable shrine'; but none of these did justice to the enormous object in the case. It was a huge wooden box covered in gold and copper leaf, ornately worked with images of temples and pagodas, welded with strips and studs of copper, a beautiful piece of work. Twenty kilos at least, I thought. The men crowded around the case. 'Must have weighed a ton,' one was saying. 'Still, when I was young I could carry heavy things – they must have been stronger than us in the old days.'

They hurried on. But I stayed and looked. Suddenly the dusty old objects were much more interesting. If this was really Benkei's satchel – if that was really Yoshitsune's sword – then I was seeing the Japanese Excalibur with my own eyes, I was looking, as it were, at Lancelot's armour, Robin Hood's bow, Richard the Lionheart's sword.

Benkei and Yoshitsune first met on Gojo Bridge in Kyoto. Musashibo Benkei was a giant, a Little John, a Goliath – eight foot tall according to some stories, ten according to others, a quarrelsome, brawling, battling warrior monk and a member of the order of *yamabushi*, the fierce hermit monks of the mountains. This enormous hairy fellow, with a fearsome grimace, bloodshot eyes, pitchblack armour and a twelve-foot halberd, had been terrorising Kyoto nightly, blocking Gojo Bridge and forcing anyone who dared to cross to give up their sword. For some reason he had taken an oath to collect a thousand swords – and the thousandth person to cross was a young boy, twelve or thirteen years old.

The incident is celebrated in countless paintings and woodblock prints, in chronicles, epic poems and the Noh play '*Hashi Benkei*', 'Benkei on the Bridge'. The boy strolled nonchalantly on to the bridge, playing his flute, dressed like a courtier in rich brocades – 'a white blouse, white bloomers and a silver-plated corselet', says the *Gikeiki*, the fifteenth-century chronicle of his exploits, 'with at his waist a magnificent sword decorated with gold'. On his feet were high wooden *geta* and he had a woman's cloak slung over his head.

Benkei challenged him. Such an effeminate character was bound to be easy prey. He slashed with his halberd again and again; but the boy parried his blows and each time the blade swept by, sprang high into the air out of its way – nine feet into the air, says the *Gikeiki*, sometimes without even landing on the ground. Finally Benkei was exhausted. The boy drew his sword and forced him to concede defeat. His name, he said, was Minamoto Yoshitsune. Benkei swore eternal loyalty to him. 'Once Benkei had become Yoshitsune's retainer, he followed him as faithfully as a shadow, performing innumerable gallant deeds'.

To Basho, Yoshitsune must have been a more real figure than he was to me. He had lived five hundred years earlier, in the second half of the twelfth century – an equally mythic time in the West; the time of the Crusades and Richard the Lionheart (a figure akin to Yoshitsune, and nearly an exact contemporary), of knights in armour, jousts, tournaments, courtly love and strolling troubadours.

Basho's purpose, I was beginning to realise, was a poetic one. While I wanted to see Ezo country, the farmers and peasants of the far north, Basho was visiting places which had inspired poets in the past. Many poets had written about these places, but few actually visited them; and Basho's aim was to revive his poetic spirit by seeing the places themselves. 'Do not seek to follow in the footsteps of the men of old; seek what they sought', he wrote. And the stories and legends surrounding Yoshitsune had always been a particular inspiration.

The year before his journey to the north, in 1688, Basho travelled down through Yoshino (to see the cherry blossoms) and on to Nara and the Inland Sea. His companion for much of the journey was one of his favourite students, a man called Tsuboi Tokoku, who had been exiled to Irako Point, a long lonely peninsula south of the city of Nagoya. When he was sent into exile, Basho had written sadly

shirageshi ni	For the white poppy:
hane mogu cho no	Torn off wings – the
katami kana	butterfly's
	Keepsake . . .

Tokoku met Basho at Ise and they set off together; they had been separated for four years. 'Merrily as we left, we scribbled on our bamboo hats: "No home in the universe – we two pilgrims".'

It was April when they reached the Inland Sea. They were just a little south of Kyoto, near the area which is now Kobe, in the very centre of the ancient kingdom of Yamato, where many of the most dramatic scenes of Japanese history had taken place. Here, right behind a strip of beach, the mountains towered 'so high and straight that they looked like a standing screen', according to the old epics.

The guide refused to enter this wild country and Basho had to promise him dinner to make him go. Finally he agreed and led them, 'slipping time and time again', along rocky paths deep into the hills, then scrambling across a narrow ridge with precipices to either side, until they found themselves above Ichi-no-tani, the site of Yoshitsune's most spectacular victory.

'Looking down over Gong Hanging Pine (the pine on which Yoshitsune hung his war gong) I saw the site of the camp at Ichi-no-tani right below my eyes.' The enemy – the Taira clan and their armies, twenty thousand of them – had set up camp on the beach, protected by the near vertical mountains behind them, stockades to each side and the sea in front. It was 1184. As they sat around their camp fires, playing their flutes, singing, dancing, making poems, they thought themselves perfectly safe.

Years before, they had defeated Yoshitsune's family, the Minamoto clan, and set themselves up in Kyoto as the virtual rulers of Japan. Yoshitsune was a baby then, and they bundled him off to a monastery to be brought up as a monk. But as soon as he became a young man, he escaped to join Yoritomo, his older brother, who was preparing for battle.

At Ichi-no-tani, the odds seemed hopeless. The Minamoto had only two thousand men and the Taira were in an impregnable position. The cliffs behind them were so steep, it was said, that even monkeys dared not descend. But Yoshitsune led a handful of warriors on horseback to the top of the cliffs – the very point from which Basho looked down – and they plunged, slipping and sliding, 'the stirrups of the men behind almost striking the helmets and armour of those before', straight down and into the enemy camp. 'Their actions seemed more those of demons than of men and their war cries echoed among the cliffs like those of a hundred thousand.'

Like the bards of the time, Basho, five hundred years later, was moved more by the sufferings of the defeated Taira than the exploits of the victors. Looking down on the windswept shore, he thought of their final defeat, at Dan-no-ura, when the despairing Taira lords leapt into the sea rather than be captured, taking with them the two-year-old Emperor Antoku. Red Taira banners floated on the waves as thickly as maple leaves in autumn, and the waves lapping the beach, it was said, were red with blood.

'The chaos of that age, the turmoil of that time, rose in my mind and images gathered – the second lady-who-had-become-a-nun (the Emperor's grandmother) reverently gathering the child Emperor in her arms, his little legs tangled in the robes of the Queen (his mother), and all tumbling in confusion into the boats, imploring the gods; the ladies of the court – maids-of-honour, ladies-in-waiting – and the page-boys, gathering up precious musical instruments, *kotos*, *biwas*, wrapping them in cushions and *futons* (quilts), and throwing them into the boats; imperial food scattered, become bait for fishes; combs thrown away in disorder on the grass, flotsam for fishermen. Here on this shore there is the sadness of a thousand years and even the sound of the waves is like a lament.'

Thinking of the young Taira courtiers and their flutes, he wrote

Suma dera ya	Suma temple:
fukanu fue kiku	Hearing the unblown flute
ko shita yami	In shade beneath the trees

It was many years later that Yoshitsune, with his gigantic companion Benkei, visited the Sato temple at Ioji. By then he was no longer a brilliant and celebrated young general but a fugitive, on the run from Yoritomo, his elder brother. Thanks to Yoshitsune's victories, Yoritomo had become the most powerful man in Japan. He took the title of Shogun and set up his capital in Kamakura, in the Minamoto lands to the east, not far, in fact, from the tiny fishing village of Edo.

But he was a harsh, ambitious man and Yoshitsune was too popular. He turned against him and in spite of his declarations of loyalty, ordered his execution. Yoshitsune went into hiding and then, accompanied by a small band of loyal followers, fled north to the independent Ezo kingdom of Hiraizumi in the land of Oshu, the only part of Japan which was not under his brother's control.

Once he was safely in Hiraizumi, he made a special journey down to the Sato lands, to pay tribute to the memory of the two Sato lords and to comfort their wives and their old mother. The brothers, Tsuginobu and Tadanobu, had been two of his most devoted followers and both died in battle, defending him. Tsuginobu was struck by an arrow intended for Yoshitsune and Tadanobu single-handedly defended a mountain pass against several hundred enemy until he had escaped.

As a token of his esteem, he left the widows his long sword, his staff, some of the dishes he used and a piece of material from his robe.

Sadly, his sword was not in the museum – I did not, in the end, see Excalibur. But his staff was still there, a double piece of bamboo, two branches growing side by side, and so was the faded scrap of brocade which he cut from his robe. Beside them in the case was the Lotus Sutra, in neat gold characters on dark blue paper – 'This, honoured guests,' recited the woman in grey, 'is understood to have been inscribed by Lord Benkei' – and two hefty wooden grave markers which Benkei carved, one for each of the two brothers.

Outside the temple gates was a signpost pointing the way along the 'narrow road to the deep north footpath' to the remains of the Sato brothers' castle, Otori. A path led invitingly down the hill and disappeared into a wood. I looked at it suspiciously; I doubted if it went much further than the 'narrow road to the deep north footpath' I had set off along that morning. Halfway down the hill, the trees parted. Ahead of me was a wide shallow valley with a river running across it and, on the other side, low hills already in shade. One rose above the rest, picked out by the long rays of the evening sun, perfectly spherical. Surely this, I thought, was Maruyama, the Round Hill on which the castle stood.

'Looking upon the ruins of the Great Gate at the foot of the hill, I wept', wrote Basho. It was getting dark when I finally reached the hill. There was nothing left of the Great Gate, only a sign showing where it had stood. Panting up the narrow footpath which zigzagged to the top, I stood looking out over the plain which I had walked across that day. Below me was the river, winding across it like a silver ribbon, and the ridge on which the temple stood. It was civilised country, well tamed, every inch neatly marked into small squares of paddy, dotted with little houses. As I watched, lights were flickering on across the plain. Fukushima was a pin-cushion of light and beyond it mountain ranges receded, iron grey, vanishing into the darkening sky.

A tiny shrine at the top of the hill was all that marked the castle, at the edge of an expanse of grass ringed with trees. In the empty circle of sky above, a kite swooped and from one of the trees came a semi's rattling whirr.

Basho spent the night in the town of Iizuka, at the foot of the hill. Iizaka, as it is now called, is one of the hot-spring resorts for which the area is famous. Streams of hot water, full of healing minerals, gush out of the ground up here in the mountains and people come simply to take the waters.

I didn't like the place and decided straightaway to take the train back to Fukushima. There was something seedy about the battered old wooden houses and cheap new tin ones straggling down the hillside, the shoe shops full of plastic slippers and grubby little stalls selling souvenir cakes. Nearer the river were hotels, great blocks of concrete, one of which sported an elephantine woman of pink plaster, quite naked, reclining outside, with a large red mouth curled into an inviting smile and long flowing hair of a particularly intense shade of yellow. Not, I thought, an appropriate place for me to stay, and noted with distaste that this unsavoury creature was of course not Japanese, but foreign.

The river itself was invisible, gliding like black oil between the concrete backs of the hotels which towered on each side, ten storeys high. Songs and shrieks of laughter drifted from the open windows.

Basho had a miserable time of it here. 'That night we stayed at Iizuka', he wrote. 'As there are hot-springs, we took a room in a place with a bath, but it had nothing but an earth floor covered with straw mats. It was a dreadful, miserable hovel. There wasn't even a lamp, so we made our beds in the dim light from the fire in the hearth and lay down. As night came on, there was thunder and endless torrents of rain, which leaked through right above where I lay, and I was so tormented by fleas and mosquitoes, I couldn't sleep at all.'

42

3
The Tsubo Stone

Safely back in Fukushima, bathed, fed, and wrapped in the inn's standard issue cotton dressing-gown, I settled down at the low table in my room with a cup of tea and thought smugly of Basho and Sora curled up on the hard floor at Iizaka, contending with the fleas and mosquitoes. Not that fleas, or lice either, were a rarity in the inns in those days. When Basho came back from his journey of 1684, his last haiku, rather a cheerful one, was

natsugoromo	Summer clothes –
imada shirami o	Not yet finished
toritsukusazu	Picking out the lice

To add to his troubles at Iizaka, his 'old illness' came back, 'and I thought my end had come'. It was rather an unpoetic ailment, some sort of bowel complaint – a combination of colic and abdominal pains, perhaps caused by gall-stones, complicated by haemorrhoids – which had plagued him for years and which seemed to flare up whenever things were going badly. Perhaps it was the damp which brought on the attack; or perhaps he was just disgruntled at having to stay in such a hovel. (Though despite his frailty, he had still managed to walk all the way from Fukushima to Iizaka, whereas I had had to take a lift.)

In any case, the two travellers left as soon as they could, as soon as there was a glimmer of light, and took horses as far as the post town of Kori. Basho was still in poor spirits after the misery of the night and, as he jogged along, worried about the long journey ahead of them and about whether his health would hold out. Somehow he managed to worry himself into a

43

good mood. 'On this long pilgrimage to remote places, I am resigned to the impermanence of my human body; if I die on the road it will be the decree of heaven. So thinking, I recovered my vigour a little and stepping out more cheerily passed through the Great Gate of Daté'.

There were no fleas or lice in the inn at Fukushima, though the tatami mats were old and worn and the bedding had a well-used feel to it. There were however plenty of mosquitoes. I went in search of the innkeeper to borrow a mosquito coil. It was one of those dreadful nights that you get at the beginning of the rainy season, unbearably close and sultry, the air heavy with rain. My face was sticky with sweat and there were cold droplets trickling like syrup slowly down my chest and from each armpit.

The innkeeper's wife, a round-faced curly-haired woman who, like the inn, had a faded look about her, followed me back to my room and exclaimed with horror when she saw the open window, 'You'll catch cold!' She slid it shut with a bang, locked it, fanned herself for a moment groaning *'Atsui atsui* – so hot!' patted her face with a handkerchief and bustled out.

She was ready for me next morning. Down in the breakfast-room, she served me shredded cabbage, rice, sautéed bean-sprouts, a raw egg – standard fare – on a plastic tray, turned the television so that I could watch the baseball, then, when I was well settled, took a deep breath and said slowly and carefully in English, 'London – it is rainy and dark, I hear. I am learning English,' she added quickly, before I could answer, as if to justify her boldness. 'May I speak to you in English?'

I was used to being an *iki jibiki*, a 'walking dictionary'. When I lived out in the provinces, people used to come up to me on the street and say 'Excuse me, may I practise my English?' And once I had a phone call from someone who announced himself as a teacher at the local high school, then, without further ado, said, 'In the following sentence: "Some difficulty was experienced in rearing the algae", is the word "rearing" the gerund or the gerundive?'

The conversation went along the usual lines. 'How old are you? How many brothers and sisters do you have? What is

44

your hobby? Are you married? Why not? When will you return to your country?'

Finally, with a small sigh of relief on both sides, we switched back to Japanese. There were a few foreigners in Fukushima, she said. She occasionally saw one on the street. But she never dared speak to one. And she had never had one staying at her inn before.

'You should go abroad, mama. They're all foreigners there.'

The old boy perched next to me at the counter had downed his rice and egg with impressive speed, crunched his pickles and was now on his third cigarette, filling the little room with smoke. He must have been in his sixties, twenty-odd years older than the mama-san, with a face like crumpled parchment and no more than a couple of white hairs left on the dome of his freckled head. He was dressed in shorts and plimsolls, with a little pack which remained firmly in place on his back even while he was eating.

'I'm cycling,' he announced cheerfully. 'I cycled from Osaka.' From Osaka . . . Something like cycling from Land's End to John o' Groat's or Paris to Marseilles. 'I am cycling because my body is weak.'

He looked pretty strong to me, I said.

'I'm strong because I cycle' – patting the hard muscles of his spindly brown legs – 'but basically weak.'

'Please take good care of yourself,' said the innkeeper's wife. 'Today there is a fifty per cent chance of rain.'

I took the Bullet Train to Sendai. From here on I would be on local trains and very soon I would walk. I reclined in the seat, looking at the paddy fields flying by, savouring the luxury. The train was packed but silent. The man next to me, in *nezumi iro* – 'sewer-rat grey' – suit, like everyone else, took a document out of his briefcase and began to annotate it, sighing and making sucking sounds through his teeth.

That evening I met Horiguchi-san. We were squeezed elbow-to-elbow along the counter of a bar which held exactly six customers, down a backstreet in a rather seedy part of town, picking at the only bad meal I have ever had in Japan.

The large red-faced chef, overflowing out of his skimpy white jacket, was pressing raw fish on to stale rice with the air of a master while a pinched, tired-looking woman kept our saké cups full. She looked as if she had not seen daylight for years – hard to imagine anyone less like the plump, healthy Japanese women I was used to.

Horiguchi-san too had a dissipated air about him. He had thinning hair combed smoothly back with plenty of oil and the open-necked shirt and brusque manner of the Japanese journalist. He was gazing at me quizzically as I talked about finding unspoilt rural Japan; the Japan that Basho had known.

'Let's face it,' he yawned, disdainfully poking at a piece of raw fish. 'Wherever you go, Japan is the same.'

I hoped he was wrong. But so far, as so often in Japan, the present seemed pitiful, tawdry, compared to the magnificent past. Was there nothing left of Basho's Japan except faded paintings and rocks carved with haiku, everything carefully preserved, labelled, pickled in aspic for the benefit of coachloads of tourists? Was there nothing left to be discovered?

'What you don't seem to understand', said Horiguchi-san, 'is that there's a Basho boom.' He sat hunched on his stool, shoulders rounded, an equally tired-looking pink prawn hanging limply from his chopsticks. 'Ever since they opened the Tohoku Bullet Train, a few years back, there've been scores of them,' he explained, examining the prawn without enthusiasm. 'You get groups, you get couples, you get taxis, you get coaches – they go round each place where he wrote a haiku. There are books, there are television programmes . . . So you're bound to get statues of him and souvenir shops and things.'

'Heard of Basho, has she, that foreigner?' butted in a red-faced old fellow squashed in next to him. 'Well, that's something, isn't it. 'Course, they can't understand Basho, can they, these foreigners.'

'Where's she from?' asked the fat chef. 'America?'

'No,' I said patiently, 'England.'

'England, is it?' he said, ignoring me and addressing his remarks to Horiguchi-san. 'Good-looking, aren't they, these foreigners – trouble is, you can't tell them apart.' He chortled loudly.

'Mama,' he bellowed. The pale mama-san, endlessly smiling, refilled his saké cup.

'I realise', I persisted, ignoring him in my turn, 'that around here it's bound to be built up. But what I want to know is, once I turn inland, into the mountains, will I find wild, remote country, like Basho walked through?'

'Wild country? In Japan?'

Horiguchi-san raised an eyebrow in disbelief at such naïvety. I felt rather foolish. How could I have imagined that in this most advanced, industrialised of countries there could be anywhere unaffected by progress? No one, after all, would want to live as they had done in Basho's time. It was all rather dispiriting. The answer to my question was probably no.

'What about yamabushi?' I ventured. I still cherished the hope of finding hermit priests striding, Benkei-like, across the northern mountains, or pursuing esoteric practices, hidden away in caves.

'We Japanese', said Horiguchi-san wearily, 'never think of yamabushi. There haven't been yamabushi for five hundred years.'

Walking Sendai's neon-lit concrete boulevards, I tried to picture it as it must have been in Basho's time – dark winding lanes of wooden houses, jammed together higgledy-piggledy around the great white castle on the hill, from where the descendants of the 'one-eyed dragon', the pock-marked half-blind Daté Masamuné, ruled the city.

Basho and Sora arrived on the fourth day of the fifth month, June 21st 1689. It was 'iris thatching day', and there were blue irises everywhere, (not *katsumi* but *ayame*), spread over the roofs and under the eaves, brightening the dark streets and filling the city with their sweet smell. 'We took a room at an inn and stayed four or five days.'

They sought out a man called Kaemon, an artist and sculptor. 'We had heard he was a man of great sensitivity ("a man of heart"), so we made his acquaintance', wrote Basho.

As Japanese do, Kaemon dropped everything to take care of his distinguished guests. He knew many local places mentioned in old poems and one day took Basho and Sora to see them.

They climbed up on to Miyagi Moor to see the white bush clover ('it brought to mind the scenery in autumn', much celebrated in poetry) and admired the lilies-of-the-valley at Tsutsujigaoka, 'azalea hill', then entered the pine forest of Ki-no-shita, 'beneath the trees', where the trees were so close packed that 'not even a ray of sunlight could filter through'. 'In the old days too the dew that fell here must have been heavy', wrote Basho, and quoted the old poem

> *misaburai*
> *mi-kasa to mose*
> *Miyagi no no*
> *Ki-no-shita tsuyu wa*
> *ame ni masareri*

> In Ki-no-shita on Miyagi Moor,
> Where the dew falls heavier than rain –
> Servant, tell your lord
> To wear his bamboo hat

When they left the city, Kaemon gave them each 'a pair of *waraji*, straw sandals, with thongs dyed dark blue', the exact colour of irises. 'In this gift he truly revealed the soul of a poet', Basho wrote, adding a haiku

> *ayame gusa*   Irises
> *ashi ni musuban*   To bind our feet –
> *waraji no o*   Dark blue sandal thongs

In their new sandals, they tramped along a road which led out of Sendai and along the edge of the hills – called *oku no hoso-michi*, the narrow road to the deep north.

'The Tsubo stone monument: at Taga Castle in the village of Ichikawa.' A few miles outside the city was the site of the ancient castle of Taga, where the Tsubo stone stood, 'over six shaku (six feet) in height and three shaku wide'. The stone was overgrown with moss and they could just make out the characters engraved on it:

'This castle was built in the first year of Jinki (724) by Lord Azuma-bito of Ono, governor of the eastern provinces and representative of the Emperor. It was repaired in the sixth year of Tempyo-hoji (762) by Lord Asakari of Emi, member of the court and, similarly, governor of the eastern sea and the eastern mountains. Dated twelfth month, first day'.

Beside this inscription were distances to the different parts of the country in each direction – to Nara, the capital of the time, 1,500 ri, about 630 miles, a long way; and just up the road, a mere 120 ri, 50 miles, away, the land of the hostile Emishi, the Ezo.

> Though folk say
> That one Emishi
> Is a match for one hundred men,
> They do not so much as resist

gloats a little war-song, recorded in the *Nihongi*.

The last line, surely – 'They do not so much as resist' – is a case of wishful thinking. In similar vein, in 789, a general called Ki no Kosami sent a despatch to the Emperor, boasting that this barbaric enemy, 'who live in holes in the mountains and caves by the sea', would melt away like morning dew when he attacked. He had not, of course, yet done so – and spent many more months sending despatches explaining why the time was not yet ripe. 'Too cold', he wrote in the spring; 'too hot', in the summer. More likely, he was simply afraid to attack the fierce, reckless Ezo, every one of whom was reputedly worth a hundred of his own men, the men of the south.

Finally the Emperor sent a furious decree ordering him to attack immediately. He went into battle with 52,000 men and was thoroughly trounced: '25 killed, 245 wounded by arrows and 1,316 thrown into the river and drowned'. 'Over 1,200 reached the bank' – but naked; the Ezo had stripped them of their armour and thrown them naked into the water. On his side, Ki no Kosami notched up less than a hundred Ezo heads.

By the eighth century, the men of Yamato had managed to

set up their Hadrian's Wall of fortresses along the northern border, and Taga was one of the first and most important to be built. By now they had advanced deep into Ezo territory, well to the north of Shirakawa barrier. But the Ezo were still far from subdued. They roamed the country, 'gathering together like ants but dispersing like birds', and made frequent attacks.

Taga Castle did not last long. Built in 724, by 762 it was in need of repair, no doubt after a particularly successful Ezo attack, and in 776 it was burnt to the ground. Lord Asakari of Emi's Tsubo stone was not so much a distance marker as a defiant assertion: 'This far we have come in hostile territory; up to this point, the land is ours'.

The hero of the times, at least in the eyes of the Yamato historians, was Sakanoue-no-Tamuramaro. He marched north in 795, accompanied by '30,000 in leather armour and 3,000 in iron'. When he returned, bringing with him several captured Ezo princes, there were great festivities and he was given the title of Sei-i-Tai-Shogun, Barbarian-subduing-Generalissimo. Over the next few years he fought his way further and further north, until the whole of the island of Honshu, right to the distant tip, far beyond Taga, was controlled by the men from Yamato, and the land of Oshu was absorbed into the empire of Japan.

Thinking of all this, Basho looked at the ancient stone on which these men who had lived nearly a thousand years before had recorded their words and deeds. He was greatly moved.

'Mountains crumble, rivers change their course, new roads replace old, stones are buried and vanish into the earth and old trees yield to saplings. Time passes, one era replaces the next, and we cannot be certain that anything of them will remain. But here before my eyes was a monument which without a doubt had stood for a thousand years, through which I could see into the hearts of the men of old. This, I thought, makes travel worthwhile and is one of the joys of being alive, and forgetting the pains of the journey, I wept for joy.'

That was one of the things I was looking for too, some feeling of 'seeing into the hearts of the men of old'. Basho himself had become one of the 'men of old'. Three hundred years before, he had been following in their footsteps – and now here was I, following in his. And what for him had been reality, the prosaic present, had now slipped as inexorably into the past and disappeared as completely as the age of chivalry, the romantic era of Yoshitsune and Sakanoue-no-Tamuramaro.

I had trouble finding the Tsubo stone. First I took the wrong train and ended up at the wrong station. Then I had a long bus ride and finally a long walk along the edge of a busy highway, watching out for cars and stepping off the road on to the narrow verge whenever one roared past. And when I did find the stone, I was not sure whether it had been worth the journey.

The fact that it exists at all is remarkable, I suppose. There is little of the past left in Japan . . . And what there is is often so carefully preserved that there is no life left in it.

It was a large black rock, a cousin of Stonehenge, one side smooth, covered in tiny characters, the other rough. It stood just off the road, on a grassy hillside, encased in a wooden shelter. A little further up was a dusty plateau and a playground – swings, a slide, no children. I peered at the characters in the half-light but it was impossible to read them.

It was evening again and I wanted to see the castle, which has recently been excavated, before darkness fell.

Unsurprisingly, there is nothing much left – it had, after all, been built and burnt down again long before the Norman Conquest. The moon was rising as I climbed through a wood to the top of the hill, where, in the middle of a grassy plain, the foundation stones lay greyly, evenly spaced like draughts on a giant draughtboard.

This would have been the living quarters of the castle – a two-storeyed wooden edifice with a colonnaded verandah running around the outside, painted an unlikely shade of orange like the great Heian Shrine in Kyoto and roofed with local slate. Around this central building was a vast courtyard – nothing but grass now – and at the perimeter great earthen ramparts, which still stand, and beyond that a ditch.

In the distance a dog barked. There was an unearthly whistling in the air, reminding me unpleasantly of Japanese

films in which ghosts of long-dead warriors appear, and for
once I was glad to get back to the road and the traffic.

I spent the evening poring over the railway timetable.
Planning a train journey by anything other than the Bullet
Train is a highly demanding intellectual exercise, for the
Japanese as much as anyone. Bringing out a timetable on the
train or, even more effective, reading it, was guaranteed to
produce gasps of awe and amazement and exclamations of
'Can't understand that, can you? It's beyond me.' After a
couple of hours of flicking back and forth over the pages and
studying the mass of figures, symbols, little drawings and
Japanese characters, I finally hit on a train which stopped at my
destination – the ancient Ezo capital, Hiraizumi – without
taking hours about it, but which was not absurdly expensive.

The train was packed, and very noisy. Squashed in my
corner, a clammy body pressed up against me, I thought
wistfully of the sleek air-conditioned carriages of the Bullet
Train and its silent grey-suited occupants.

The four men opposite, all in short-sleeved shirts and boot-
lace ties, were playing cards on a briefcase balanced between
them, drinking can after can of beer and yelling with laughter.
In the next compartment was a family, all slumbering. Father
was spread across two seats, his feet, in transparent nylon
socks, propped on the one opposite, two children sprawled on
top of him. Mother, I noticed disapprovingly, had the least
space of all. She was balanced on the very edge of the seat, her
head resting uncomfortably on the back – though she still
succeeded in sleeping in this position. All around was a litter of
Cellophane bags, empty bamboo food boxes and beer cans
rolling noisily back and forth across the floor.

Facing me were two women, one older, one younger –
mother and daughter, perhaps. Ours was the sunny side of the
train and they had pulled the blind down to keep out the
frazzling heat. The older one might have come from the age
of Sakanoue-no-Tamuramaro. She was tiny, immaculately
dressed in a pale mauve kimono tied with a striped *obi*, her hair
coiled round and round into the largest, heaviest knot I had
ever seen. Surely when she let it down, I thought, sneaking an

admiring glance, it must reach the ground, like the *kurokami*, the long black locks of the court ladies in Heian times. She looked rather uncomfortable on her seat, her legs dangling not quite to the floor. After shuffling around a few times, she inched first one foot, then the other, delicately out of her sandals, pulled them up and folded them under her, so that she was kneeling as primly as a guest at the tea ceremony, then smoothed her kimono and sat gently swaying from side to side with the train, fanning herself.

When we changed direction so that the sun was no longer blazing in through the edges of the blind, I leaned forward and asked very politely if they would mind terribly if I opened it so that I could look at the scenery.

'Of course,' they shouted back (we had just rattled into a tunnel), looking rather startled, then asked the usual question – '*Hitori des ka* – on your own, are you?' followed, as always, by '*Sabishi ku-nai*? Aren't you lonely?'

I was launching brightly into my usual reply – it's more interesting, not lonely in the slightest, best way to meet people, etc., etc. (though the question always made me feel uncomfortably alone), when the older woman interrupted.

'I'm on my own too. It's the best way,' she said firmly. Time had not been kind to her. Her small round face, poking out from the layers of kimono, was puffy and glistening with sweat and her cheeks laced with broken veins.

'*Sensei*' – 'Teacher' – explained the younger one in respectful tones (so they were not mother and daughter after all) taught tea ceremony, Urasenke school, and flower arrangement.

'I was married, you know,' said the *sensei*. 'He died in the war, when I was twenty-six. I've been alone ever since. He was a bad man, anyway. I was twenty-two when I had *o-miai*. I really didn't like him, didn't want to marry him. He had a mistress all the time we were married . . .'

The younger woman was nodding sympathetically. Gradually her nods became deeper and deeper until eventually her eyes closed and her head rested on her chest.

Shiogama, Matsushima . . . The poetic places which Basho

had visited rolled slowly past like a never-ending extension of Sendai, a succession of concrete shops and houses lining concrete streets, interspersed with enormous hoardings – for Coca-Cola, and drinks with wonderful names like Poccari Sweat and Calpis – all enmeshed in cables and wires. Even Matsushima's 'pine-clad isles' were shored up with concrete, and across the bay I made out the chimneys of a power station dominating the famous view.

We stopped at a station and the doors slid open. Heat swirled into the carriage in a great gust.

Basho had been dreaming about 'the moon at Matsushima' even as he swept the cobwebs from his house in Edo and when he finally reached this celebrated place, he was not disappointed. 'It has been said many times before – yet truly Matsushima is the most beautiful place in the land of Japan.'

The white craggy islets, battered into fantastic shapes by the sea, with a thatch of gnarled pine trees, had been an inspiration to poets for centuries. 'Some stretch upwards, pointing a finger to heaven or, low-lying, seem to crawl across the waves. There are some piled-up in twos or threes, spreading away to the left or joining up to the right. Some, like loving mothers or grandmothers, carry babes on their backs or hold them close . . . What brush could show or words describe this wondrous creation of nature?'

The old poet was so moved that he could not write a haiku. 'I wrote nothing and lay down but did not sleep' and spent the night gazing at the view and reading poetry.

There is one haiku on Matsushima which has been attributed to Basho, though it is unlikely that he really wrote it. It is very famous and easy to remember and Japanese tend to quote it whenever Matsushima is mentioned. There are many theories about it – that it is, for example, an invocation to the god of the place or that the poet felt that any words would be inadequate to express his wonder at the beauty of the scene. *Ya* is like 'Lo!' or an exclamation mark.

Matsushima ya
aah Matsushima ya
Matsushima ya

54

4
City of Gold

The further we got from Sendai the greener the place became, until we were chugging gently along between fields bursting with rice shoots, dazzlingly emerald green, with tidy round hills on each side. By this time everyone but me was asleep, sprawled as innocently as children in an assortment of undignified Hogarthian postures, mouths gaping, legs splayed. Every now and then we rolled past a farmer working out in the fields, up to his knees in water, plucking out weeds and throwing them into the plastic basket on his back, or drew up at a little station in the middle of nowhere, grass and vines spilling across the platforms.

Matsushima was not the only place where Basho did not write a haiku – perhaps he felt that the most magnificent sights were beyond words. When he visited Mount Yoshino, famous for its cherry blossoms, he did not write about it. And the only haiku he wrote about Mount Fuji was on not seeing it

kiri shigure	Misty drizzle –
Fuji wo minu hi zo	A day you can't see Fuji!
omoshiroki	Interesting

– almost a comment on the way in which the Japanese flock to 'famous' sights and are blind to, for example, the beauty of a day when you *can't* see Fuji.

The process of writing itself was often very difficult for him. Once when he was travelling through the mountains of Kiso he met up with an old priest. That night they found lodgings ('a grass pillow') together. Probably, in the usual Japanese way, they were sharing a room. Basho took out his brush and ink to try and record his impressions of the day and to work on some haiku. It was hard that night. 'I lay down on the tatami . . . closed my eyes under the lamp, beat my head and groaned.'

The kind old priest, hearing his groans, thought he must be worn out from travelling or that he had something on his mind. To cheer him up, he started chatting. He talked and talked. He told him all about the pilgrimages he had been on when he was young. Then he went on to endless stories about the marvels of Amida Buddha, then this, then that, everything 'which he thought was wonderful'. His chatter was so disturbing, grumbled Basho, 'that I couldn't compose a single verse'.

Basho and Sora spent a couple of days in Matsushima, then, on the twelfth of the fifth month (June 29th) set off for Hiraizumi. The journey, as Basho tells it, was particularly tough. They wanted to see the Pine of Aneha and the Bridge of Odae, two of the most famous literary sights of the north country (in Yoshitsune's time they were already famous, and on his journey down from Hiraizumi to the Sato brothers' castle he stopped to see them). But by the time Basho came this way, the road was 'little used, fit only for hunters or woodcutters' and badly overgrown. Eventually the travellers completely lost their way and, as evening fell, found themselves at the coast, at a port called Ishi-no-maki.

It was a grim little place. Had there been concrete in Basho's day, it would have been full of it. 'Hundreds of cargo ships were gathered in the harbour, the houses of the land were struggling for space and smoke rose incessantly from all the furnaces. "Fancy coming to such a place, purely by chance," I thought and looked around for lodgings, but there was no one who would rent us a room. Finally we spent the night in a miserable little hut and as soon as it was light set off again on our confused wandering along unknown roads.'

That day too the walking was hard. They passed other places famous in poetry – the Ford of Sode ('Sleeve Ford'), Obuchi meadows, the reed moor of Mano – then trudged along a dyke that stretched 'far into the distance' and skirted Long Marsh, 'a depressing place'. By nightfall they still had miles to go. They had to lodge in a town called Toima and didn't reach Hiraizumi until the following day. 'We must have covered about twenty ri' – almost 50 miles.

Everyone seemed to know by some sixth sense that we were approaching Hiraizumi. By the time we had trundled past a few small grey sheds and were pulling into the station they were all wide awake, on their feet and standing in line at the door, ready to shuffle off as soon as the train stopped; even these little country trains didn't stop for long.

Hiraizumi looked sleepy enough, a nondescript little country town of faded wooden houses strung along dusty streets, with sunlight sparkling on the paddy fields just behind – hard to imagine that it had once been the Ezo capital, the centre of Ezo civilisation. On three sides were hills, covered in thick forest, while the fourth, bounded by a wide river, opened out into a shimmering plain of rice fields which stretched away to the hills, hazy on the horizon. It was a spectacular setting for such a dozy little town.

The air seemed cleaner, the hills, with their untamed forest, closer, the paddy fields somehow less tidy – as if I had managed at last to shake off the deadening influence of Tokyo and the concrete which smothers the surrounding countryside for hundreds of miles around it.

I watched my fellow passengers disappearing purposefully along the dusty street which led up the hill from the station. A few lingered, settling down on a bench at the bus stop. They looked like locals; whereas those others striding up the hill were visitors, come to sightsee the ancient capital. I sat down too. The rush and urgency of Tokyo were beginning to ebb out of me at last.

The people sharing my bench were all old. The man next to me had a watering-can in a plastic bag between his feet and a tie like a shoe lace around his neck. Beside him was a woman stooped under an enormous load of bowls stacked one inside the other, all wrapped in a huge purple scarf and tied to her back, and beyond her was another in a straw sunhat with a plastic bag full of onions. A couple more joined us, bobbing over on legs curved into two halves of a circle.

I couldn't help admiring their striped *mompei*, beautiful

baggy trousers carefully stitched by hand, quite unlike the cheap cotton ones with elasticated waists you find in country shops. One woman, as wizened as an old monkey, let me feel the fabric and pulled up her smock to show me how they were made, open from the knee upwards, front and back tied separately at the waist.

'But what's happened to your hat?' she said. 'You have no hat!'

By now more and more people were gathering at the bus stop – and they all had hats: straw hats with huge brims, gingham bonnets, baseball caps, knotted handkerchiefs and white towels.

'You must have a hat,' she said.

There was no arguing with her. She produced a white towel and knotted it around my head, then stepped back to admire her handiwork and made a comment. I didn't catch what it was – but they all laughed, great open-mouthed cackles, slapping each other on the back and roaring with appreciation. I grinned too. All those rules I had carefully learnt so as not to offend – that, for example, ladies do no more than simper politely and always cover their mouths with their hands, even when they smile or talk – clearly did not apply here. (In the past, in fact, teeth were considered so aesthetically unappealing that well brought-up ladies carefully blackened them every morning.)

But I got my revenge. '*Ikutsu?*' she asked, 'How old are you?' (using a particularly basic form of address, with no honorifics: not '*O-ikutsu-de-gozaimasho-ka?*', 'I wonder if you would mind terribly telling me your honourable age?' or even '*O-ikutsu-desu-ka?*' 'How old might you be?' but simply "Ow old?'). I returned the question and she answered, 'Sixty-six.' She looked so old and bent I had thought she must be eighty. She waited for me to respond with my age and when I didn't, looked sulky, and the crowd laughed again.

As soon as they had all disappeared on to the bus, I took the towel off straightaway.

It was still early so I left my bag at the station and ambled off down the road which ran between the river and the railway line. It turned out to be the main shopping area of town, lined with open-fronted shops and trestles loaded with vegetables, fruit and fish.

I stopped to watch the tatami-maker, in white vest and longjohns, cross-legged on the earthen floor of his shop, hand-stitching the straw mats. Then the fishmonger, an old fellow in vest, wellington boots and a long black apron right to the ground, beckoned me over, his enormous grin revealing a mouthful of teeth all bound at the roots with gold.

'Fresh in this morning!' he said, holding up a huge gleaming fish on a hook.

Next stop was the tofu shop to buy a block of freshly made beancurd for the next day's breakfast. It was dark and blissfully cool inside.

'What is your country, dear?' enquired the fat tofu lady as she scooped a slab of it out of the water. 'All the way from England?' She sighed with amazement. 'Such a long way, just to see our little town', and took fifteen yen off the price.

What intrigued me most was their faces. The backwardness, the feeling of having stepped back in time – that was not so unusual. But the faces here . . . There was almost a Mongolian cast to them – broad, flat, angular, deeply lined . . . So different from the round, fleshy, unfocused faces of Tokyo that they could have been another race.

Did the Ezo, I wondered – one of whom had been worth a hundred of the men of Yamato – did they look like this? These faces couldn't have changed much since Basho was here three hundred years ago.

'The glory of three generations of Fujiwaras is passed like an empty dream'. Long before Basho came, Hiraizumi was a great city, the City of Gold, capital of the north, home to a magnificent culture. But it was to last no more than a hundred years. For a hundred years, they say, its marvels outshone Kyoto – then vanished, as completely as the cherry blossoms.

Marco Polo knew about it – though by his time Hiraizumi and its wonders were no more than a memory. In the land of Zipangu, Japan, he wrote, 'they have gold . . . in measureless quantities. The ruler of the island has a very large palace entirely roofed with fine gold. Just as we roof our houses or churches with lead, so this palace is roofed with fine gold. And the value of it is almost beyond calculation. Moreover all the chambers, of which there are many, are likewise paved with fine gold to a depth of more than two fingers' breadth. And the halls and the windows and every other part of the palace are likewise adorned with gold. All in all I can tell you that the palace is of such incalculable richness that any attempt to estimate its value would pass the bounds of the marvellous.'

Admittedly Marco Polo is not the most reliable of reporters. He added for good measure that the people of Zipangu not only had idols with the heads of cattle, pigs, dogs and sheep, too horrible to speak of and 'no fit hearing for Christians', but were also cannibals.

In the matter of Japan's gold, however, he was not far off the mark. But it was not the Emperor in Kyoto who had palaces roofed with gold, but the Fujiwara lords in Hiraizumi.

A few centuries later, Christopher Columbus, inspired by tales of Hiraizumi's gold, set off to sail to the west, thinking that if he went far enough he would circle the world and 'come across the island of Zipangu' with its fabulous riches. His quest for gold took him to another small island, Cuba – which he thought was Japan – and on until finally he reached the New World, America.

The City of Gold . . . Long before Sakanoue-no-Tamuramaro marched north to subdue the Ezo, they found gold here, in 749, and began mining the Oshu mountains and panning the rivers. The gold for the entire country – to make shrines, Buddha images, shrine furnishings, decoration for temples and palaces – all came from Oshu, and so did horses and falcons; and gradually the conquered northern lands became very rich.

By the eleventh century, a hundred years before Yoshitsune, the Ezo were becoming unruly again. The governors of Oshu at that time were six Ezo brothers called the Abé lords, a remarkable bunch, according to the *Gikeiki*. One 'could make fog and mist or stay under water all day long' and all of them were 'taller than Chinese' – and much taller than the little men of Yamato. 'Sadato was nine feet five inches tall, Muneto eight feet five inches, and every one of the brothers at least eight feet. Sakai Kanja's height was ten feet three inches'.

The Abé were supposed to travel down to Kyoto every year to pay tribute to the Emperor (a considerable journey – six hours on the Bullet Train, weeks by foot or on horseback). But one year they sent a message saying that they would only go if the Emperor would pay their travelling expenses – 'the cost of the journey there and back'.

Not surprisingly, the Emperor was displeased and de-spatched a force of Minamoto warriors. They fought the Ezo 'day and night for seven years' and were all either killed or wounded. Then another force was sent north, led by the thirteen-year-old Minamoto Yoshiie, Yoshitsune's great-great-grandfather (like Yoshitsune, he began his career young). But they too were beaten.

Finally they had a bright idea. Every time a new Emperor is crowned, a new era begins, and each era has a name. (The present era, under Emperor Hirohito, is the Showa period.) Perhaps, they thought, 'the era designation might be at fault'. They rechristened the year: 'The first year of Kohei', 'Year 1 of the Peace and Tranquillity Era'. Things were simpler in those days; it was the last time anyone ever won a war simply by changing the name of the year.

It was 1058. That year the Ezo fortresses were all taken, one by one, and the nine foot five inch Sadato, 'mortally wounded, lay down for the last time on the Iwate moorland, dressed in a yellow robe'. The Emperor appointed Fujiwara Kiyohira, Yoshiie's second in command, to govern the northern pro-vinces. Kiyohira had chosen to side with the Minamoto, but in fact he was at least half-Ezo, for his mother was an Abé. He took the title 'Head of the Ezo race' and set about creating a magnificent Ezo kingdom in the north, using Oshu's gold to build a capital which would rival Kyoto.

The site he chose for his capital mirrored the site of Kyoto and satisfied the rules of classical geomancy: mountains on three sides, water – the great river Kitagami, like Kyoto's Kamo River – in front, 'purple hills, crystal streams'. The city faced to the south, its streets laid out in a grid like a giant chessboard, and the greatest artisans of the day were commissioned to work on its palaces and temples.

Artists, poets and craftsmen – masters of lacquerware, gold leaf, wood and metal work, masons, dyers, weavers – flocked to Hiraizumi. The hills glittered with golden temples and jewel-like palaces and thronged with a brilliant crowd of monks, courtiers, artists and warriors; and even the smallest of Oshu's ten thousand villages boasted an image of the Buddha, of pure gold.

The sun sets early, even on these hot summer nights. At dark, I trudged up to Motsuji temple. I left my bags in the pilgrims' hall, had some iced noodles, then went outside to explore the temple grounds.

It was dark and silent. The moon had not yet risen and even the insects had stopped chattering. I took a few steps out of the pool of light around the open door of the hall, then thought better of it. The air was thick with the ghosts of all those courtiers and warriors of a thousand years ago. I could feel them at my back, muttering balefully (as Japanese ghosts do), '*Urayamashii! Urayamashii!*' – 'Envious! We are envious!' My spine was prickling. I hurried back inside, grateful for the clatter of chopsticks on bowls and the pilgrims' voices.

Next morning, I tried again. At five-thirty I was woken by the sound of a huge drum being beaten, slowly, regularly, like a heartbeat. I put away my bedding then went out into the cool dawn air.

The drumbeat drew me to the main temple. Monks in starched black robes sat in the gloom inside, two rows of them, facing each other, backs erect, chanting. It was the Heart Sutra, as familiar as the Lord's Prayer, the deep syllables rolling out one by one, evenly spaced, as if out of the belly of the earth. A thread of smoke rose steadily from the incense burning in the cauldron outside. I wafted it over myself (for good health and long life) and threw some coins into the money-box. The boom of a great bell reverberated through the silence.

Early though it was, I did not have the place to myself. An old man was swinging the huge log suspended beside the bell – as tall as he was, and much wider – back and forth, higher and higher. He gave it a final mighty swing and the bell boomed again. His friends were yelling encouragement. 'One . . . Two . . . Three . . . Now let it go. Now pray, quickly!' He put his hands together. 'Too late,' they yelled. 'Do it again.'

Further along the path, dwarfed by towering cedars, a small figure stood alone, facing east, towards the lake which lay, still and limpid, reflecting the pale sky and the hills. She was like a puppet or a wooden doll, arms held stiffly at her sides, bowing again and again, absorbed in some private ritual. Who was she, I wondered, all alone like that? And why was she bowing here, to the lake, not to the great figure of Amida Buddha in the temple? She was dressed poorly, in black, with bare legs and thonged sandals. As I passed, she never stopped her slow, jerky movement.

Little by little crowds were gathering, shuffling along the gravel paths, drawn by that insatiable urge the Japanese have to visit every famous place in their country – just once, once is enough. Cameras were coming out, photographs being taken and – it was still only six-thirty – groups hurrying off to the next place on their itineraries, having done Motsuji in a few minutes.

For after all, what was there to see? A pleasant garden full of irises with a large lake in the middle of it, a few foundation stones . . .

I sat down on a bench and looked at the lake and the reflection of the trees and the sky. Beside me, an old priest, all in black, was lecturing a group of visitors. He had a wonderfully magisterial air, every inch a *sensei*, a 'master', 'one who knows', 'one to whom respect is due'. While the guests at the back of the group covertly looked at their watches and scuffed their feet like schoolboys, the one at the front, a portly middle-aged man in a well-cut suit, had apparently been delegated to express interest and amazement, which he did by nodding like a mechanical doll and grunting in a variety of tones.

'This lake', declaimed the priest, drawing himself up and pointing dramatically with his fan, his sleeve flapping like the wing of a great black crow, 'is Oizumi Pond, famous throughout the world. It is the heart of this garden and has, appropriately, the form of the character *kokoro* (heart).'

In Heian times – the time of Sakanoue-no-Tamuramaro, long before the wicked Abé brothers – this was an elaborately landscaped pleasure garden, playground of those Kyoto aristocrats unfortunate enough to be exiled up here to rule the defeated Ezo. Delicate colonnaded bridges crossed the lake; and all around were shady avenues and contoured lawns dotted with pavilions, where the lords, in their perfumed brocades, carried on their everyday activities – moon-viewing, tea-drinking, perfume-mixing and exchanging elegant little verses with ladies whom they were forbidden ever to see. Large painted pleasure boats like barges cruised the waters.

The wooden prows still exist and later, in the museum, I saw them, one a dragon's head, the other a phoenix. There was also Sakanoue-no-Tamuramaro's flute and two faded scrolls which showed the gardens and temples as they were in the time of Fujiwara Motohira, the second of Basho's 'three generations of Fujiwaras' and Kiyohira's son.

That was around 1130. Nearly three hundred years had passed by then and, in those more troubled times, Motohira was interested less in earthly pleasures and more in the well-being of his soul. He used his enormous wealth and the limitless resources of his kingdom to make Motsuji into a vast and beautiful temple complex, with forty pagodas and five hundred cloisters. The paintings in the museum show only a few: long low halls with multi-tiered gold roofs supported on slender red pillars and stupa-like pagodas with attenuated pinnacles, artistically arranged behind geometric hills and curly stylised clouds.

For the main image of the temple – Yakushi Nyorai, the Physician of Souls – Motohira spared no expense. He wanted Unkei, the greatest sculptor of the time, and sent him the vast and outrageous fee which he demanded: '100 ryo in gold coins, 100 eagle wings, more than 60 seal skins, 50 thorough-breds, 1,000 rolls of silk, 1,000 rolls of Shinobu Mochizuri cloth (dyed with the Shinobu dyeing stone), 3,000 rolls of bleached cotton and many other rare products from land and sea'. This was the wealth of the north – gold, eagle feathers for arrow heads, horses for warlords and messengers, silk, produced in every village in the region. And when Unkei demanded yet more silk, Motohira sent three shiploads off to him straightaway.

But the hundred years were rapidly running out. The third and last of the 'three generations' was Fujiwara Hidehira, Motohira's son. Like his father and grandfather, he managed to keep his remote northern kingdom aloof from the power struggles and wars of central Japan, and Hiraizumi remained a haven of peace and culture.

5
Summer Grasses

It was the tragic story of Yoshitsune, the young hero who fought with Benkei on the bridge, which brought Basho to Hiraizumi.

Hidehira was an old man when Yoshitsune, fleeing from his vengeful brother, arrived in Hiraizumi and asked for sanctuary. The Fujiwaras were allies of the Minamoto – and Hidehira had supplied Yoshitsune with troops, among them the brave Sato brothers. He welcomed the fugitive, gave him lavish gifts and even had a palace built specially for him – the Takadachi, the Castle on the Heights, close to his own palace, on a hill overlooking the Koromo river.

Yoshitsune's brilliant victories had made his brother, Yoritomo, master of the whole of Japan except for the Fujiwara lands – which meant, ironically, that for the persecuted hero nowhere in central Japan was safe. Yoritomo's troops were searching everywhere for him and he was so famous that wherever he went he was recognised.

By the first month of the second year of Bunji, 1186, it was too dangerous to stay around the capital any longer. Yoritomo's men were closing in and he decided the time had come to flee north to the friendly Fujiwara lands. It was a desperate plan – a long and perilous journey through enemy territory, with little chance of getting through alive. Only sixteen of his most loyal followers opted to go with him. One was the gigantic monk, Benkei; another was Sato Tadanobu. (Yoshitsune's wife also went along. As a court lady, she had never walked before – she had always travelled in a palanquin – and was so slow that she endangered the whole party.

Benkei was perpetually urging Yoshitsune to leave her behind.)

In those days, the only people who habitually wandered the roads and could travel without being challenged were yamabushi, wandering hermit priests like Benkei; added to which, it was bad form to kill a monk. So the party replaced their samurai armour with all the paraphernalia of yamabushi – huge sleeved black and white checked robes, tiny black hats, great woollen balls on ribbons, like surplices, and enormous heavy 'satchels'. Benkei, who was to assume the role of leader, carried his sword, Rock Cleaver, and a horn made of a conch shell, while the aristocratic Yoshitsune took the disguise of a porter: 'dingy white undergarments, a white hemp robe with an arrow-nock design, wide-bottomed grasscloth drawers, a persimmon-coloured cloak with an all-over design of plovers and a worn black cap pulled down over his eyes'. To avoid suspicion, the party decided that for the southern half of their journey they would say that they were Haguro yamabushi on their way home; but once they got too close for comfort to that distant northern yamabushi centre, they would claim to be from Mount Kumano in the south, Benkei's home monastery.

Instead of the usual road north through Shirakawa barrier, which would be full of Yoritomo's soldiers, they took the Hokurikudo through the desolate country along the Japan Sea coast. But Yoritomo was on the look out for them and had had new barriers erected throughout the country. When they reached a place called Ataka, they found shields and brambles blocking the road, a tower full of archers guarding it and, hanging from a nearby tree, 'some blackened objects – the heads of wandering monks'.

They had no choice but to cross the barrier – and what happened next is the subject of one of Japan's most popular Noh and Kabuki dramas – *Ataka* or *Kanjincho*, 'The Subscription List'.

Benkei strode forward and, towering over the leader of the guards, Togashi, declared that they were simply humble yamabushi, collecting subscriptions to repair Todaiji temple in Nara. Togashi was suspicious: In that case, he replied, you must have a subscription list, a document setting out the merits of subscribing to that particular temple. 'I should like to hear you read from it.'

'With pleasure,' said Benkei, unfurling a scroll from his satchel, and, making sure that Togashi had no chance to see what was actually written, he reeled off a history of the temple full of erudite theological references.

Togashi, much impressed, allowed the party to pass. But as they were going through, one of his men recognised the young porter bringing up the rear.

There was only one way in which Benkei could allay suspicion. He would have to beat Yoshitsune, for a retainer would rather die than strike his lord. He turned on him, yelled at him for causing so much trouble and for daring to resemble Yoshitsune, then grabbed a stick and thrashed him mercilessly.

There is a final twist to the story. Togashi in fact knew the identity of Benkei and Yoshitsune all along. But as a samurai he was so deeply moved by the sight of Benkei striking his master that he let them escape – knowing that, having betrayed his trust, he himself would have to commit suicide.

Many months later the fugitives reached the safety of Hiraizumi and for a couple of years lived here in peace. It was during this period that Yoshitsune and Benkei went down to Otori castle to pay tribute to the memory of the Sato brothers. Hidehira was now ninety-one, and on the twenty-first day of the twelfth month of the fourth year of Bunji, 1188, he died, first commanding his sons to continue to protect Yoshitsune.

Yoritomo had been waiting for this. He sent a succession of threatening messages to the northern kingdom demanding Yoshitsune's head. The new ruler was Hidehira's eldest son, Yasuhira, a weak and treacherous man. In spite of his promises to his father, he was keen to curry favour with the powerful southern lord, and on the thirtieth day of the fourth month of 1189 ordered a surprise attack on Yoshitsune's palace.

Yoshitsune and his eight followers (ten were inexplicably

absent) were surrounded in the Takadachi by an army twenty thousand strong. All eight performed amazing feats of hero- ism, killing hundreds of the 'eastern dogs', as Benkei called them (they were, of course, Ezo, while Yoshitsune's men were from Yamato). And not one suffered the humiliation of being cut down by the enemy. They all, when they were so badly wounded that they could fight no longer, cut open their own bellies and died an honourable samurai death.

Yoshitsune, meanwhile, sat in his palace, slowly and de- liberately carrying out the preparations for ritual suicide. It was Benkei's particular task to ensure that he was not dis- turbed. Having completed his preparations, he drew a short dagger and plunged it into his stomach in the prescribed fashion, 'so deep that it almost emerged through his back. Then he stretched the incision in three directions, pulled out his intestines and wiped the dagger on the sleeve of his cloak'. It was, as one would expect, a textbook suicide. Then, 'leaning heavily on an arm rest', he said farewell to his wife, whose death he had ordered, and ensured that she and his two children had been properly killed, before dying himself. The Takadachi was burnt to the ground.

There is a story that Yoshitsune did not die but somehow managed to escape and flee north. Old country priests like to tell you how he spent a night at their temple on his way through. Some say he became lord of the northern island of Hokkaido, others that he crossed to Mongolia, and that Genghis Khan was none other than Yoshitsune under another name. But most people prefer to believe that the great hero died, tragically, at the age of thirty-one, at Hiraizumi.

In fact Yasuhira had made a severe miscalculation. Yori- tomo, not a man noted for his sense of fair play, had been waiting for an excuse to annex the northern kingdom and make himself ruler of all Japan. A few weeks later – to avenge, he said, his brother's death – he sent an army of seventy thousand to the north and had Yasuhira hunted down and beheaded. Only a couple of Hiraizumi's wonderful temples survived the conflagration that followed. So it was that 'the glory of three generations of Fujiwaras passed like an empty dream'.

Basho's journey was in a way a pilgrimage to the places associated with Yoshitsune, this greatest and most loved of Japanese heroes. From Hiraizumi onwards he would be following his path, but in the opposite direction, cutting west across the mountains, then travelling south down the Hokurikudo towards Kyoto.

He passed the ruins of the Great Gate – a few jagged beams in an empty field – and came to the site of Hidehira's palace, the Muryokoin. At one time it had been among the wonders of the north, modelled on Kyoto's Phoenix Hall (the Byodoin at Uji), with curving golden roofs and delicate orange pillars which seemed to float above the wide lake on which it stood. But now there was nothing but fields. The hills that had gleamed with golden temples and jewel-like palaces and thronged with monks, courtiers, artists and warriors were silent, a tangled mass of trees.

'First we climbed the Takadachi', he wrote, 'and saw the great Kitagami river which flows down from Nambu province. The river Koromo, circling Izumi Castle, meets the Kitagami here, below the hill. Yasuhira's castle stood on the other side of Koromo barrier, protecting the road to Nambu and keeping the northern Ezo at bay. But alas! Of Yoshitsune's select band of loyal followers who took refuge in this castle – all their glorious deeds have turned in an instant into a thicket of grass.'

Some lines by the Chinese poet Tu Fu came to his mind: 'Though countries fall, mountains and rivers remain; spring comes to the ruined castle and new grass grows'.

'Thinking on these words, I spread my bamboo hat on the ground and wept and wept, forgetful of the passing of time.

natsugusa ya	Summer grasses –
tsuwamono domo ga	All that remains
yume no ato	Of mighty warriors' dreams

In among the grass were tiny white blossoms of *unohana*, deutzia flowers. Looking at them, Sora thought of Kanefusa, the loyal old retainer who, in the last dreadful battle, had been ordered to kill Yoshitsune's wife and children and set fire to the castle

unohana ni	In unohana flowers
Kanefusa miyuru	We see Kanefusa –
shiraga kana	Snow-white hairs

It was raining when I climbed the Takadachi. In spite of the leaden sky the heat was stifling. Clambering up the hillside in my wet sandals, watching out for puddles, I wondered what time had done to the Castle on the Heights. I dreaded finding the site of Yoshitsune's last battle crowded with tourists or packed with souvenir shops.

In the event there was no one at all. I stood under my umbrella and looked across at the empty paddy fields stretching to the distant hills, ghostly in the mist. There below me, winding along the foot of the hill, was the Kitakami, just as Basho had described, and in the distance I made out the thin line of the Koromo (the rivers have changed their courses since Basho's time). A couple of sodden white banners drooped nearby, like sad samurai war banners on a battlefield.

In a way, this journey of mine had started years ago, when I first read that haiku of Basho's. It is impossible to convey the power of it in English – the martial rhythm, the sonorousness of the words with their slightly archaic flavour. Translated literally, line by line, it goes something like this: 'Summer grass – strong men of old – aftermath of dreams'. The same power, the same primitiveness of feeling, as Anglo-Saxon poetry: 'Hwaer cwom mearg? Hwaer cwom mago? Hwaer cwom maþþum-gyfa?'

Reading and rereading the rolling Japanese syllables, I had wanted to know more about the doomed hero and his faithful band of followers who fought so bravely against hopeless odds, and about the old poet who sat down on his hat and wept, finding only summer grasses.

'From the top of this Takadachi Hill, you may view the ancient battlefield of Koromogawa and the place where Benkei fought to his death long time ago'. The amplified voice suddenly boomed at me out of the trees, destroying my reverie. Someone must have noticed me standing here and kindly decided that I was a tourist and must have information.

'No peace in this country,' I thought tetchily. For a moment I remembered cycling through the idyllic tangerine groves of Shikoku, miles from anywhere, and suddenly being assailed by unwelcome music and exhortations to physical jerks from loudspeakers concealed in the branches. Another time I was climbing the hill behind my home in central Japan when – my presence must have set off some kind of remote-controlled response – the air was filled with artificial birdsong and a recorded voice telling me the history of the place. It was as if silence was some kind of vacuum that was abhorrent and had to be filled.

Still, in spite of myself, I looked across the plain to where the wide Kitakami curved out of sight – and realised what it was that I was seeing. Just there, on that bend, was where Benkei had stood, holding back the enemy so that Yoshitsune could complete his suicide in peace.

All alone by now, his black armour stuck with innumerable arrows like a porcupine, the gigantic monk planted his halberd on the ground and stood, all eight or ten feet of him, legs wide apart like one of the wrathful deities. The enemy kept a safe distance, fearfully waiting for his next attack, but Benkei continued to stand without moving. Just then a warrior on horseback galloped past. The gust of wind caught the great monk and he crashed to the ground. Even as he fell, he seemed to lunge forward, gripping his halberd, and the enemy warriors scurried out of reach. When they finally dared investigate, they found he had been dead for some time – he had died on his feet, defending his lord even after death.

I stayed a long time at the Takadachi, looking out across the river. On that quiet hilltop among the 'summer grasses' I felt closer to Basho and the past than anywhere else I had been.

From there, the two travellers went on to Chusonji Temple. When it was built, long before Yoshitsune fled north and brought the southern wars with him, it was one of the most magnificent structures in the whole of Japan, perhaps the most magnificent – there was little in the southern capital, Kyoto, to match it. Even Yoritomo was impressed when he saw it on his one fateful expedition to Hiraizumi. They say he exclaimed at its beauty, before ordering his soldiers to burn the surrounding city to the ground.

The temple dates from quieter times, when Kiyohira, the first and greatest of the 'three generations of Fujiwaras', was creating his City of Gold, his Mirror of Kyoto, in the north. He was a pious man and a man with a vision: that his northern kingdom should be paradise on earth, a haven of peace and culture, where there was no war and the people could devote themselves to Buddhism. The centrepiece of the City of Gold was to be not a palace, as Marco Polo assumed, but a temple.

Chusonji was built in the image of Amida Buddha's Western Paradise. It took twenty-one years, from 1105 to Kiyohira's death in 1126, and when it was finished its temples covered an entire hill, a total of three hundred and forty shrines and cloisters, where several hundred monks and nobles lived and worshipped.

On the summit of the hill a golden statue of Amida sat gazing out across the plains to the east, surrounded by Buddhas, Bodhisattvas and guardian deities, all housed in a dazzling golden temple – the Konjiki-do, Golden Hall, or Hikari-do, Hall of Light. This was Kiyohira's mausoleum. His remains, and those of his son and grandson after him, were interred here.

As I sweated up Tsukimi-zaka, Moon-viewing Slope, the long cobbled path to Chusonji, I imagined how it must have been when Basho and Sora were here. I pictured them in their black robes, with their shaven pates, straw sandals (they must have got through a pair a day) and bamboo hats, pushing their way through long grass and undergrowth, up a hillside as silent and deserted as the Takadachi had been. Basho perhaps was worried, fearful that when he reached the top he would find that the Hall of Gold, like the Takadachi, was no more than 'a thicket of grass'. Here, where there had once been temples and halls full of noise and laughter and the chanting of monks, the only sound was the drone of the cicadas, twigs snapping underfoot, the swish of leaves against robes, from time to time the harsh caw of a raven. Perhaps there were foxes and badgers.

A romantic notion, I decided. It was more likely that Basho climbed a path very similar to this one, pushing through not undergrowth but crowds, as I was doing.

Tired of dodging the points of umbrellas, I stopped halfway up for a glass of water. I needed a rest. It was still drizzling and grey and as hot as ever. Hard to imagine, I thought, surveying the crowds shuffling by like London rush-hour traffic, that only a few minutes before I had been standing alone, in silence. The Japanese obsession with fame had its advantages. The Takadachi was not famous – there was after all 'nothing there' – and it was blissfully free of people.

The shopkeeper who gave me water gave me a cake as well. She had black eyes and brilliant orange lips which went strangely with her curly grey hair and checked apron. She asked where I was going. This was a new question, and a serious problem. Travelling north-south (more accurately north-east south-west), up and down the country, was easy enough – this was the route that all the people and transport took. What I had to do now was turn off, into the mountains, cut across the flow of traffic. From now on the journey would be tortuous – chugging slowly along in little local trains, hanging around stations . . . But I was not ready to start walking yet. There was still some ugly country ahead of me; and I had had my fill, in Fukushima, of walking along main roads.

Four large men, all with round heads and short bristly haircuts, were lounging around, drinking cans of beer. Either gangsters or lorry drivers, I guessed; not farmers or cloven-toed-boot men, the kind you see mending the road at midnight or clustering at the top of telegraph poles like flies on a fly paper, who always looked small and undernourished.

'She's going to Narugo,' said the woman. 'You going that way?'

'Sure,' grunted one, looking unenthusiastic. Even if they

were gangsters, they still suffered from the Japanese inability to say no.

'It's OK,' I lied. 'I'm meeting some friends.' I wouldn't have minded taking a lift with them; it would have been perfectly safe. But I wanted to travel at my own pace.

They looked relieved and offered me a beer, which I accepted (I have the same inability) and didn't drink.

'Seen the Konjikido (the Golden Hall)?' growled another. At least, that was what I think he said; it was impossible to understand much of their gruff samurai drawl.

They had.

'Just up there,' they said, and showed me the prayer books they had bought, like schoolboys, stamped and dated to prove they had been there, then pointed the way for me – straight along the path – unfurled their umbrellas and strutted off shoulder-to-shoulder down the hill.

As I came out at the top, I looked around, half expecting to catch a glimpse of a golden temple glittering between the trees or a sudden dazzling shaft of sunlight reflected from its walls. The rain had stopped and the sky had suddenly cleared and for a few minutes there was a perfect rainbow.

'The two halls, of whose wonders I had heard with amazement ("which had surprised my ears"), were both open to view and their images were on display. In the Sutra Hall were statues of the three great lords and in the Hall of Light, which is dedicated to the Three Buddhas, their three coffins.'

Here at least Basho had no need to sit down on his hat and weep. The great civilisation of Hiraizumi had not, after all, been entirely an 'empty dream'. The Golden Hall still stood, as glorious as it had been centuries before when Kiyohira built it.

'Its seven treasures should have been scattered and lost, the jewel-encrusted doors broken by the wind, the golden pillars eaten away by frost and snow – the hall itself should have crumbled and vanished beneath the grass, had it not been recently enclosed in four outer walls and covered with a roof to protect it from the wind and rain, thus preserving this monument of a thousand years for a while longer:

samidare no   For all June's rains
furinokoshite ya   It's still untouched?
hikari-do'   The Hall of Light

'*Samidare no furinokoshite ya* – For all June's rains . . .' So Basho too got wet here. I had spread a plastic bag under me and was sitting on the steps of an old wooden temple, my soggy sandals propped beside me in the sun in an attempt to dry them out. Did he have an oiled umbrella, I wondered, or did he rely on his bamboo hat? How long did a pair of straw sandals last in the rains?

There was also no sign of the Golden Hall – which, if it still existed, had by now survived nearly nine hundred rainy seasons. There was, however, a queue snaking across the concrete plateau at the top of the hill, so I joined it.

As always when surrounded by well-scrubbed Japanese, I felt conspicuously scruffy. I glanced down the line to see if I could see any other bare legs or, even better, any other toes, but mine were the only ones. I wished I could hide them somehow. Despite the recent rain, everyone else looked spruce and clean, dressed not for sightseeing, not for walking in the rain, but for a day at the office. The men, even those whose leathery old necks marked them as farmers, were in suits or shirts and ties, the women in kimonos or tights and long skirts, and everyone, even the children, had a neatly rolled umbrella.

The Hall of Light is, if anything, better cared for than it was in Basho's time, sensibly enclosed in a 'fireproof ferro-concrete shelter'. I stood on tiptoe in the concrete entrance, trying to see at least a golden roof over the heads of the crowds. Looking at the mass of bodies in front of me, I doubted if I would ever manage to reach the Golden Hall.

It was, I soon realised, a remarkably orderly crowd. It was organised into distinct groups who shuffled quickly in, stood in complete silence while a recorded voice droned out the history of the place, then, the instant it finished, shuffled on to make room for the next. I had hoped to cut across the flow; but it was impossible. It was a microcosm of Japanese society. The only thing to do was to follow the crowd.

From one side of the room came a regular thumping. Squashed into a corner were two monks, side by side at a desk, with a heap of prayer books in front of them, the same prayer books which the gangsters had shown me.

One was writing, beautifully calligraphed characters, his brush rising and falling, hovering above the paper, stretching out a line like a hair, then coming down firmly to make a fat round stroke. He looked young, very young, I caught myself thinking, to write so well – as if only old men could write well. The other one, older, with glasses, in brown cotton robes instead of blue, was stamping each book with a large stamp, energetically banging it on to an ink pad then on to the blank page, leaving the delicate imprint of a stylised red flame.

The crowd swept me on. Suddenly I was in front of Fujiwara Kiyohira's Hall of Gold.

It was magnificent – but small, just seventeen feet square: an exquisite miniature, a scale model of the Hall of Gold I had been imagining. Not a soaring Gothic cathedral, but the kind of structure one would expect of this small crowded country – a tiny elegant chamber, perfect in its detail, enclosed in a glass case. Not a symphony but the delicate tinkle of the shamisen; not the fourteen books of Wordsworth's *Prelude* but a seventeen syllable haiku. Still, I had hoped that the wild Ezo might have created something grander, more imposing.

It was all immensely opulent, just as Basho had described and Marco Polo had imagined: 'golden pillars', 'jewel-encrusted doors', roof, floor, ceiling all covered in 'fine gold to a depth of more than two fingers' breadth'. In form it was a canopy rather than a building. No walls, just a roof heavy with gold, vaulted ceilings, hefty golden beams, all propped on four thick pillars lavishly inlaid with mother-of-pearl. From the beams hung a delicate golden tracery, a lace of golden threads linked with finely wrought medallions; and all around the central plinth were peacocks and birds of paradise. Presiding over all this splendour, seated on a lotus at the centre of it, was the serene golden figure of Amida Buddha, hands folded in meditation, a halo like a golden flame curving around him.

While I looked, everyone else worshipped. They stopped for a moment, put their hands together, bowed their heads, then tossed a coin into the collection box and shuffled on. I felt a curious sense of disappointment. It was all too neat, too well ordered; there was nothing here to evoke a past age. For me the golden Buddha in his glass case was simply a work of art, nothing else.

'Excuse me . . .' The crowds parted. It was the young monk whose calligraphy I had been admiring. He came up and gave me a perfunctory bow. 'Welcome to our temple,' he said gravely. Were foreigners so rare? Or had he noticed me because I had stayed for so long?

'I think you are interested in our temple.'

Without pausing for a reply, he launched into the history of the Hall of Gold and the names of each Buddha and Bodhisattva enshrined here. He must have been in his mid-twenties; but his round shaven head made him look like a schoolboy. In spite of his wooden *geta* (clogs), a good four inches high, and his baggy blue robes, he seemed oddly out of place. What was he doing here, I wondered? There was something about him that didn't belong.

He gestured towards the altar.

'The three great lords, Fujiwara Kiyohira, Fujiwara Motohira and Fujiwara Hidehira – you have heard of them? They are all entombed here.' Their tombs were opened, he said, some years ago. All three had been mummified and lay, in an excellent state of preservation, each on a straw mat, their heads on pillows, holding beads, with a sword and a piece of gold beside them.

They were hauled out of their tombs and subjected to all sorts of indignities in the name of science. Their skin was analysed, their heads measured. Kiyohira was pronounced to have been, as he claimed, part Ezo, though his head was unusually long. Motohira, the builder of Motsuji, was five foot six, with a short neck, broad shoulders, thick chest and a big stomach, and wise old Hidehira had three cavities in his teeth.

Beside the three coffins they found a small box. In it was the head of the treacherous Yasuhira, the last of the Fujiwaras. There were holes right through the skull where a long weapon had pierced it.

I was childishly pleased at all this. So it was true – they had really existed. It was not just a legend.

The monk's story had come to an end; but he didn't seem inclined to go back to his calligraphy.

'You must be from Tokyo,' he said. I thought I detected a note of wistfulness. Certainly his tone had changed, become more intimate. He was no longer simply the temple official. 'I used to work in Tokyo. I knew many foreigners then.'

'In Tokyo?'

'In Akasaka.'

Somehow, I was not much surprised. I could picture him in one of Akasaka's bars or restaurants or strolling around its fashionable streets, dressed, like everyone else, in black, with big shoulder pads and gelled hair.

'In computer software,' he added. The words sounded strange among all this ancient splendour.

'But this is my family's temple. My elder brother was priest here. He died, so I had to give up my job and come back.'

His tone was matter-of-fact; there was no hint of regret. He would rather, I knew, have been in Tokyo. But there was no question but that he would do the honourable thing, put his duty before his own wishes.

He gave a sudden schoolboy grin. 'Sometimes this place reminds me of Shinjuku station,' he said. As the crowd caught me up and swept me out of the hall I had to agree with him.

Outside, the sun was dazzling. A man and a younger woman, both in berets, were sketching, while a woman in white wellingtons and a pinny was hard at work, smoothing the ground with a rake.

There was a shout behind me – '*Chotto matte*! Wait!' The young monk ran up to me, a packet in his hand.

'Don't forget the Golden Hall,' he said, bowed and ran off again.

The packet was of purple paper, beautifully folded, marked 'Konjikido', Golden Hall, in silver characters. In it was a delicate gold medallion engraved with birds of paradise.

Turning Inland

6

To the Country of Dewa

That evening I went in search of sushi. The crowds had all disappeared and the streets were dark and shuttered though lights glimmered like fireflies from the houses on the far side of the paddy fields.

The town was so small it didn't take me long to explore it. Even in this out of the way little place were a couple of signs reading 'Snack', outlined in red neon, in front of anonymous closed doors, concealed discreetly down back alleys. This, I knew, meant a room the size of a hallway with space enough for six customers to squeeze in, red velvet walls lined with ornate red sofas, a charming mama-san in matching red velvet, a karaoké machine, some drunken businessmen and plenty of saké – but, despite the name, no snacks (except, perhaps, for a few strands of dried squid).

Everyone, it seemed, must eat at home. But eventually, plodding along the dark highway which led out of town, I saw a lonely square of light and found a small sushi shop.

I was the only customer. The dour old chef, a cotton scarf twisted into a thick rope and knotted around his bald head like an Indian headband, was not inclined to chat. He took my order and assembled my sushi with one eye on the television, balanced on a shelf well above his head, then turned it so that I could watch it and retreated to a table at the back of the room, where he sat hunched over a ledger, grunting and chewing his pencil.

I took out my dictionary, opened Basho, spread my map on the counter and began to plan the next day's journey, trying to ignore the chatter of the television.

'Casting a long last look at the road to Nambu stretching

away to the north . . .' I knew the feeling well. From the top of the Takadachi you could see Route 4, the great north road, winding away across the plain and disappearing enticingly into the mountains on the horizon. It was tempting to forget all about Basho and his path and set off along the road, follow it for as far as it went.

But Basho and Sora went no further north, no deeper into Ezo country, than Hiraizumi. They turned back and retraced their steps in the direction of Edo for a few miles, as far as the village of Ichinoseki. Here they left the great north road and cut inland, west, towards the mountains.

Behind them the noise and bustle of the highway faded away and they trudged in silence between the flooded fields, full of young rice. That day they covered a good forty miles – an amazing distance for a man who complained of being old, feeble and in poor health, as Basho did – and at night 'stopped at the village of Iwaté'. It was the fourteenth of the fifth month, June 30th 1689.

I turned to Sora's diary. 'Weather fine', he began, and confirmed that that day they had walked from Hiraizumi to Iwaté. He described the town: 'Inn quiet, town quiet. On top of the mountain is Masamune's first castle. Luxuriant cedars, to the east is a big river. It is called Tamatsukuri River. There is a rocky mountain'. ('Masamune' was Daté Masamune, the 'one-eyed dragon' whose family, in Basho's time, were still ruling the region from their great white castle in Sendai.)

The next day, continued Basho, 'we passed Oguro-zaki ("small black headland") and Mizu-no-ojima ("small island in midstream"), then from Naruko hotspring arrived at Shitomae Barrier. From here we planned to cross into the country of Dewa'.

As I read, I had been half watching the television; and gradually I found myself getting caught up in the story. It was one of those depressing soap operas – the Japanese love three handkerchief movies – on the theme of the *kariya-ooman*, career woman, who has made the Faustian mistake of trading in a woman's only possible path to happiness, marriage, for the deceptive attractions of a career. This particular *kariya-ooman* was a glamorous creature who ran her own fashion business. But, as always, the story was not about that.

Instead it dwelt on her loneliness, her dissatisfaction – after all, how could an unmarried woman possibly be happy? You saw her in the evening, all alone in her luxury Tokyo flat, painting her nails, doing the ironing or sprawled on her bed, waiting hopelessly for a phone call from some man who, it was clear from the start, was no good. In the final scene she was standing in the rain outside a café, looking at the man, inside with another woman.

I watched with growing gloom. It all accorded rather too well with my mood. I was getting tired of my own company, of being alone in a country where you are never allowed to forget that you are a foreigner, an outsider. What was the point of all this travelling, moving from one historical monument to another, skimming the surface of the country like a water beetle across a pond?

Basho had one answer. '*Tabi wa jinsei desu*', he said, travel is human life, life is a journey – there is no other way to find yourself. All right for him, I thought sourly. He was never on his own. He always had Sora with him, sometimes a whole retinue of admirers and pupils. Though he wrote of loneliness too

kono michi ya	This road –
yuku hito nashi ni	With no one travelling on it
aki no kure	Autumn darkness

Next morning, early, I was out on the road, standing at the side of Route 4 with my rucksack. Enough of studying railway timetables, I had decided. 'The road gods beckoned', as Basho put it. I would give hitchhiking a try.

The first euphoria quickly evaporated. Hitchhiking is not the custom in Japan and most people do not recognise the thumb signal. The traffic rolled by in a steady stream. Everyone stared; but no one stopped.

Japanese roads are spectacularly ugly. This road out of Hiraizumi cut straight through the paddy fields and dwindled away into the distance, long and grey and lined with warehouses and stacks of car tyres, wires and cables looping overhead. I had found a tree to stand under, but the higher the sun rose, the smaller my patch of shade became. I wiped the stickiness and dust off my face and began to wonder if I should have taken the train.

Ten minutes passed. I was beginning to feel rather self-conscious, standing there alone with my arm out like a railway signal. Two little boys on bicycles suddenly raced past me, one on each side, yelling '*Zis-is-a-ben! Zis-is-a-ben!*' like an exorcism, pedalling hard. I watched their red satchels disappearing along the road. Were foreigners really so distinctive that they could spot one from the back? Still, 'This is a pen' made a change from '*Harro, harro*'.

Another ten minutes dragged by. There was nothing for it, I would have to use the Japanese method. Putting my scruples aside, I started to wave urgently as if I were flagging down a bus.

A black car, a Honda City, drew up immediately. The three men inside looked rather bewildered but said yes, they were taking Route 4 as far as Ichinoseki and yes, they would give me a lift. I put my bag in the back and squeezed in. I was surprisingly unembarrassed.

For a while we sat in silence. I was enjoying the luxury and the cool of the air-conditioning. Outside, grey warehouses alternated with the green of paddy fields and distant hills. There was something lonely about the landscape: empty of people, empty of animals, endlessly green. I tried to remember when I had last seen a cow. There were those two who lived in a shed beside the railway line near Totsuka, outside Tokyo; I always used to look at them from the train and feel homesick. Then there were four or five, looking thin and sad, tied up in sheds on Awaji island, in the real countryside. But otherwise – well, there was no spare land for them to graze on; it was all needed for paddy. Up on the northern island of Hokkaido, of course, where the climate and landscape were more like England, there were fields of sheep and horses. I remembered how pleased I had been to see them when I went there, after years of living in Japan. But pigs – I had never seen a pig, though there was plenty of pork around.

'Up from Tokyo, are you?' asked the man who shared the back with me. Like the other two, he was in a brown overall with a gold crest on the pocket. He couldn't have been much more than twenty, tanned and well-built. He was not bad-looking, but his teeth were grey and his thick fingers nicotine-stained.

'Seen the Giants?' I confessed with shame that I knew nothing of baseball – nor sumo either, anticipating his next question. He took a few puffs on a Mild Seven cigarette, stubbed it out and tried another tack. 'Been to Hayama? There's a good beach there – good for wind-surfing.'

'My brother went to Tokyo,' interrupted the man in the front, craning around to eye me over his shoulder. 'Moved down there a couple of years ago. You should hear him – lots of work there, good money, nice girls. I'm not staying here. I'm saving up. I'm going to go and join him.'

'Why?' I asked. 'It's beautiful here.'

'Not if you have to live here,' said the driver firmly. The other two fell silent. Clearly he was the *sensei*, and they his apprentices. 'It's hard to make ends meet. When I was a kid, I didn't ask much – just ate, and my mother made my clothes. But my kids now – they have to have new clothes every year, not hand-me-downs. They want piano lessons. They want violin lessons. It all gets expensive. You wouldn't understand,' he sighed, 'your country's rich, but we Japanese, we're poor.'

I wondered whether to argue with him. But how could I tell him that the rest of the world saw Japan as rich, when you had only to look out the window to see how poor it was?

'I'm tired.' My companion in the back was puffing on his third Mild Seven. 'Makes me tired, talking like this. I'm not used to it.'

'You wouldn't understand us, you see,' the driver explained kindly. 'You're a foreigner. You wouldn't understand if we spoke normally. We speak dialect, you see – Tohoku dialect.'

'Say something,' I begged. They grunted a few syllables. It

had been difficult enough to understand them when they spoke standard Japanese, their accent was so strong; but their dialect was like another language.

They were teaching me how to swear in their dialect when we reached Ichinoseki, where Basho and Sora had left the main highway to strike out into the mountains. 'We turn off here,' they said, and disappeared, leaving me standing at the side of the road.

I looked around in dismay. I was stranded on a concrete island in the middle of a flyover high above the paddy fields. I was also thirsty. But there was no coffee house, no shop, no shade and the traffic was going so fast there was no chance that anyone would stop. I was trapped. The only possible escape would be to walk along the edge of the highway until I came across a railway station.

It seemed pointless to hitchhike but I put my thumb out anyway.

Almost immediately, a small black van pulled off on to the dusty hard shoulder in front of me. There were angry hoots from the cars behind. The door slid open. The van was completely full, of people and children and boxes and bags, but they made room and I scrambled gratefully in, amazed at my good fortune.

Squashed beside me in the back was a large woman and two little boys. 'I'm Shiuko,' she smiled. 'These are my children. That's Mochi-san' – nodding towards the driver. 'That's my little sister beside him.'

It was a long time since I had seen such a warm, open smile – or felt so welcome. Shiuko couldn't have been much more than thirty; but there was something immensely motherly and reassuring about her. The Japanese women I knew from my years in the provinces liked to appear like children, even when they were old enough to have grand-children themselves. They painted their faces white and their lips red, covered their mouths with their hands when they spoke or giggled (they seldom laughed) and spoke in unnaturally fluting voices.

Shiuko's voice was deep. She wore no make-up and, more

startling, no stockings. Her sandals, I noticed with satisfaction, were even older and shabbier than mine. Her hair, short and thick and threaded with grey, was tied back in a kerchief, and she wore a T-shirt and an embroidered Thai skirt, a faded shade of blue.

'Milk, want milk,' whined the curly-haired little boy next to her. He was big, at least three, I thought. Still, she rolled up her shirt and he nuzzled up to her. The other little boy ('I'm six,' he said importantly) started reading riddles and I sank back contentedly in my seat.

A few miles further on we turned off Route 4 and took a smaller road inland towards the mountains. The warehouses and concrete sheds littering the side of the road disappeared and we drove west between fresh green fields. The sun was beating down out of a sky so intensely blue it seemed like a solid dome.

'England . . .', sighed Shiuko. 'How lucky you are to live in England. I've always wanted to go there. I know it so well.'

As the foothills became clearer, separating themselves from the distant mountain ranges to form distinct humps, dark green against the pale green of the paddies, she conjured up an England of misty fields and pastel skies, ruined castles, milkmaids and princes. She read English fairy tales and fantasies with all the passion with which I read Basho and reeled off the great names: Eleanor Farjeon, C. S. Lewis, *The Borrowers*, Tolkien, *Lilith* . . . Listening to her tales of princesses in towers, I wondered for a moment if the romantic Japan of my imagination, the fierce Ezo and battling samurai, were any more real. The chubby little boy suckled contentedly as she talked.

The children began clamouring for lunch. 'We'll find a temple,' said Shiuko.

I unfolded my map. In all this talk, I had forgotten to watch out for Iwaté or, for that matter, Basho's 'small black headland' or the 'small island in midstream', and we had passed them all. But at the moment I was more interested in my new friends than in Basho and his narrow road.

Mochi-san, the driver, swung the van off the road and we

careered off at top speed along a track wide enough for
precisely one vehicle, wheels slithering and squelching peril-
ously close to the muddy water brimming in the paddies. For a
while we raced around the fields, looking for a temple – I had
still not worked out why we needed to find one – then hurtled
up one of the humpy little hills and came to a sudden stop in a
glade crowded with spindly evergreens, beside a faded
wooden shrine.

First we had to pay our respects to the god. We climbed the
steps in front of the shrine and tugged on the thick plaited rope
attached to the rusty bell until it clanged and rattled, then
clapped our hands and bowed.

'He's awake now, the god,' said Mochi-san seriously. He
was slight and thin and his bare chest was hairless and very
brown. He had hair to his shoulders and a towel wrapped
around his head like a sushi chef. 'You can make a request.'

'Where is he?' I asked. I was curious about these gods that
everyone prayed to so casually. They were not jealous gods.
They didn't care, it seemed, whether you believed in them
or not: if you showed them proper respect they would grant
your wishes anyway, protect you from traffic accidents,
get you through exams, help you make money. They were
wonderfully simple gods.

'Is he in there, inside the shrine?'

'No,' said Mochi-san, 'he'll be behind it. He might be a rock,
he might be an animal, he might be a snake. But up here, I
think he's probably a tree.'

At the back of the shrine we found a majestic old cedar of
divine proportions, towering high above the other trees.
Around the awesome trunk was a fat white rope, tied with
holy knots.

Cardboard boxes and battered rucksacks, piled high, were
toppling out of the open back of the van. Shiuko pulled out a
Primus stove, a box of vegetables, some *genmai onigiri*, fat
brown rice balls, and several bowls of damp washing which
she spread carefully across the bushes. 'It'll dry in no time,' she
said. She hung damp tea towels on the open doors of the van
and we all squatted in the shade and began chopping veg-

etables for lunch. Even Mochi-san, the man of the party, helped with the cooking. There couldn't be a clearer sign than that, I thought, that these were not ordinary Japanese.

As we chopped we chatted. They had set out that morning, they said, from Mochi-san's house in the countryside north of Hiraizumi and were on their way to the village in the mountains of Nagano where Shiuko lived with her children and, from time to time, their father. He was an elusive figure. He was a poet, he travelled a lot, at the moment he was on a poetry reading tour in the States. More than that she wouldn't say. For all her strength and independence of spirit, it seemed she had been left, like every other Japanese woman, 'holding the baby'.

Not that she seemed discontented with her lot. She told me about the village where she lived, which had no electricity or gas or running water. 'It's way up in the mountains,' she beamed. 'There isn't even a road. The only way to get there is by walking. Come and stay!'

It was hard to imagine such a place in industrial Japan. She had an old thatched house and lived what sounded an idyllic life, surrounded by friends, old people who had been born there, young people like herself who had opted out of the Japanese rat-race. 'You know what they say about us Japanese: "workaholics who live in rabbit hutches". That sort of life might suit the others – but not me.'

We sat in a row along the wooden verandah of the old shrine, in the shade of its deep overhanging eaves, and ate – carrot and onion soup with dumplings and brown rice balls – then rinsed out our bowls with green tea like Zen monks, rubbed them round with a piece of yellow *takuan* pickle, ate the pickle and drank the tea.

Mochi-san spread a large map on the ground and traced my route on it. 'All along the coast', he said, running a thin brown finger up and down Route 4, 'is built up. But once you get into the mountains, you'll find plenty of places where life goes on as it always has. Around here, and here', drawing circles on the map, 'are quiet unspoilt villages. Then you'll come to' – a large circle – 'Dewa Sanzan, the three mountains of

Dewa: Mount Haguro, Mount Gassan, Mount Yudono. The Sacred Mountains, we call them.'

A very old man in a faded cloth cap and baggy blue trousers wheeled his equally old bicycle up the knoll and past our little camp, revealing not the slightest surprise at our presence.

'Are there still yamabushi there?' I was almost afraid to ask.

Mochi-san pondered for a while. 'I've never been there,' he said slowly. 'I don't know anyone that has. But I've heard that there are some living up there.'

'We'd come with you if we could,' said Shiuko. I wished they would.

It was late afternoon by the time we arrived at Narugo, the hotspring that Basho and Sora passed through on their way to Shitomae Barrier. We were well away from Route 4 by now. Each village we came to had more thatched houses and less concrete and corrugated iron than the last. The mountains, dark humps bristling with trees like enormous hedgehogs, crowded closer and closer to the road. Finally, when the road squeezed between the foot of the mountains and a narrow river, we turned off and started to climb laboriously upwards. I hadn't noticed the buildings perched on the hill above us.

Shiuko and Mochi-san dropped me in front of a cheap hotel and vanished back the way they had come; they had driven miles out of their way to bring me here. I was left standing forlornly at the side of the road, holding a scrap of paper with their telephone numbers, pondering how they came to have telephones when they had no electricity or running water.

I watched the black van disappear, then checked in to the hotel and went to have a look at my room. It was small, dingy, dark but clean and equipped with all the essentials: a wash-basin, a cupboard for bedding, a window with mosquito netting across it and, most essential of all (as far as the Japanese are concerned), a television. This one had an extra slot for 100 yen pieces and promised in exchange thirty minutes of 'adult video'.

The woman at the reception desk had frowzy grey hair and a frilly pink gingham apron. There was an electric grandfather

clock on the wall behind her and a selection of pickled vegetables for sale on the desk. I asked her if she knew which path
Basho had taken out of Narugo. 'Basho . . . ,' she repeated,
peering at me through glasses as thick as bottle bottoms.
'Basho . . . Let me think, now. I know that name. You don't
mean Matsuo Basho, do you? Poet or something, isn't he?'

Basho was not impressed with Narugo. He had nothing to
say about it, simply that he passed through ('. . . from Naruko
hotspring arrived at Shitomae Barrier'), while Sora noted that
'on the other side of the river' from Shitomae 'there is Naruko
hotspring', and added the cryptic remark, 'it is said to be the
honourable hotspring of Sawako. A Sendai tradition.'

Who was Sawako? A princess perhaps? An Ezo princess
who patronised this hotspring? Musing on this I went out to
have a look around. Given Basho's lack of interest in the place,
it didn't seem likely that there would be much evidence of his
visit. Shitomae Barrier was not even marked on the map; it
had, I was sure, disappeared years ago. I resigned myself to
another day of hitchhiking before I got deep enough into
Basho country to make it worthwhile walking.

The town as far as I could see consisted of a single long street
chiselled along the edge of the hill. Lining one side was a row
of squat concrete hotels and small dingy shops. On the other,
the ground fell away sharply down to the river, a hundred feet
below. I stood and looked at the fat pine-covered mountains
across the valley and wondered where the barrier had been.
They looked very close and very high and there were wisps of
cloud hanging low between them. High above me there was a
long-drawn-out hoot and a little red train rattled by along the
cliff.

It seemed even hotter than before. Exhausted by the heat
and sticky with sweat I plodded slowly up the road. The air
was rank with the powerful rotten egg smell of sulphur.
Sulphurous steam puffed out of the drains and lapped around
my bare legs in hot damp gusts as if there were a giant pressure
cooker just under the ground – which, in a way, there was.

There was no one around. The street and shops were
deserted; though there was an oddly expectant air about the

place, like a holiday resort out of season. I wandered into some of the empty shops, mainly to escape from the heat; I was not much interested in their stale souvenir cakes and lurid pink and green pickled vegetables. Further up the hill there was a cluster of shoe shops full of wooden *geta*, large rectangular ones for men, smaller ones for women, while the shops at the top were quite grand, neon-lit and hung with tinkling wind-bells, with *kokeshi*, limbless wooden peg dolls like oversized skittles, standing in rows, looking at me through painted slit eyes.

Narugo's *kokeshi*, apparently, are highly valued, and people come from the other end of Japan to buy them. Even Japanese friends in London, when I said I was going to the north country, told me to be sure not to miss the *kokeshi*. There were huge ones, tiny ones half the size of a fingernail and antique ones, locked in glass cases and labelled like vintage wines with dates and pedigrees. But they all looked identical to me and I didn't care for their billiard ball heads and smug little rosebud mouths.

I had, I reckoned, done Narugo. There was nothing else to see. All that remained was to have a good soak in the sulphur waters, then dinner and early to bed. My thin leather sandals didn't provide much of a cushion against the hard tarmac and my feet were aching.

By now I had come to the station. I ought, I supposed, to visit the information office. I picked up a leaflet and a map of the area, flopped on to a bench in the shade and half-heartedly unfolded them. The two characters for 'Yoshitsune' caught my eye. Had he been here then? Suddenly wide awake, I set to work to decipher the rest of the hieroglyphs.

'Legend of Yoshitsune', it began. 'In the era of Bunji, when Minamoto Yoshitsune, fleeing from the Kamakura shogunate (his brother, Yoritomo), was on his way down to Oshu, his wife gave birth to a son in the Kamewari mountains. They used the hotspring here for the baby's first bath. As the baby gave its first cry here, they named this place "Naru-ko", "Crying Child".'

The story, I remembered, was in the *Gikeiki*. Yoshitsune and his little band were almost at the end of their journey; they had nearly reached the safety of Hidehira's northern kingdom. But there was one last obstacle. They still had to cross the wild Kamewari mountains. They were trekking through this rough country – 'the wilderness', the *Gikeiki* calls it – still deep in enemy territory, when Yoshitsune's wife, the delicate Heian princess who had insisted on accompanying him on the long journey from Kyoto, felt 'the pangs of approaching childbirth'. There was no question of going down to a hostile village for help. The samurai did the best they could. They spread a fur rug under a huge old tree and she lay down there, with no one to help her but those rough warriors, and had the child.

The *Gikeiki* did not mention where this had taken place. Reading the leaflet again, I felt as if I had made a small discovery of my own. Pleased, and touched as well, I looked at the map, trying to sort out where I was from the little drawings of skiers and tennis players marking places of interest. As I puzzled over it, I noticed the characters for 'Basho' and 'narrow road'. There was Basho's exact path, just outside Narugo, marked on the map. Late though it was, I was too impatient to wait for morning and rushed off to find it.

While the main road and the shops continued upwards, I took a narrow back street steeply down the hill through a much shabbier area of town, crowded with shuttered wooden houses which straggled to an end at the river. On the other side, beyond a few token paddy fields, were the hills, the pines on their slopes thrown into relief by the slanting rays of the sun.

It was another half mile before the river disappeared into a dark crevice between the hills. This, I thought, must be the beginning of Basho's path. By now night was falling. But I wanted at least to take a few steps along it.

Hurrying along, I passed a teahouse just inside the ravine with wooden benches arranged in neat rows along the riverside. The owner, a stout old man in white overalls, had nearly finished business for the day and was hanging up big wooden shutters in the light of a single bare bulb.

95

'Where are you off to?' he shouted. I pointed along the ravine.

'It's dangerous down there after dark!'

The cliffs gleamed white behind me in the setting sun.

For a while I followed the path back and forth across the river, past rocks that looked unpleasantly like immense skulls with cavernous eye sockets, across shaky little bridges, past rapids and waterfalls, each step taking me deeper into the ravine and further from the friendly lights of Narugo. Finally I came to a tunnel hollowed into the cliff. By now I was getting scared. It was nearly dark and I was quite alone.

I fumbled my way into the blackness, looking over my shoulder at the fading light and wondering what would happen if it got so dark that I couldn't find my way back. Then my foot encountered a puddle of cold water. I took it as a warning from the gods. It was time to retreat.

The old man was still packing up and waved as I hurried past his teahouse.

Back at the head of the ravine, I stood under a street light and looked at the map again. The whole thing had been a waste of time. The path along the ravine was not Basho's 'narrow road' at all.

Crestfallen, I turned to start the long slog back into town, and saw a small wooden signpost on the other side of the road. I could just make out the characters. *Shitomae no seki*, it said – Shitomae Barrier, 200 metres. That cheered me up, though it was too late and too dark to go there.

High on the hill above, the town was just coming to life. Lights twinkled and a wailing song drifted across to the bridge where I stood. Columns of steam rose straight up into the air from all the chimneys. The shuttered houses were in darkness as I plodded back up the hill but the shops above were a blaze of neon.

The nearer I got to the main road, the louder the noise of shouting and laughter became. I had forgotten what hot-springs are like in the evening. The street was full of people promenading up and down, clattering along the cobblestones in high wooden *geta*. They were all – except me – in identical navy and white cotton dressing-gowns, printed with the name of the hotel. For women the style, evidently, was to tie them at the waist, while the men wore theirs hitched up, revealing plenty of bare calf, and tied below the stomach which bulged out in a satisfyingly masterful manner.

Country folk, I guessed, from their faces, here to take the waters. Sun-tanned old farmers with bristly crewcuts swaggered along arm-in-arm with equally aged ladies (surely not their wives), with painted white faces, black eyes, orange lips and suspiciously black or, occasionally, outrageously orange hair. The smell of sulphur was overwhelming.

Looking at them all sauntering up and down reminded me of a time a few years before when I was at the seaside with Tadao, a Japanese friend. We were staying in a *minshuku*, bed and breakfast, run by a kindly fisherman's wife who carefully avoided commenting on my foreignness but kept asking with great concern, 'Raw fish all right for you, Oku-san?' (She insisted on calling me Oku-san, Honourable Wife.) 'I can give you cooked fish if you like. Quite happy with chopsticks, are you?'

In the evening, after a sizeable dinner, I suggested to Tadao that we go for a walk along the front. 'Japanese people don't go for walks,' he said haughtily, with that disconcerting habit the Japanese have of generalising their likes and dislikes to include the entire nation. 'This isn't a hotspring, you know.'

I dragged him out nonetheless. As he had said, there were no other strollers around. We walked the length of the seafront without seeing anyone. Finally a solitary walker appeared in the distance. 'What did I tell you?' crowed Tadao. His eyes were sharper than mine. 'It's a foreigner.' Even when you have fun in this country, I thought, you do it in the prescribed way – in the right place, at the right time.

The noise and jostling were becoming intolerable. I needed to escape. I headed for the Taki-no-yu, the public bath, a small wooden building at the top of town.

I paid my money to the surly old man at the door, left my clothes in the locker room and sank blissfully into the steaming water. It was milky, slightly greenish, so opaque that I couldn't see the bottom or myself floating in it.

It was a primitive old building, with wooden walls stained dark with sulphur and a rather pleasant pungent smell of hot, damp, rotting wood. The water flowed in from outside along three huge tree trunks, halved and hollowed out, and cascaded a good ten feet into the pool with a deafening roar. I could see the stars through the slats in the wall.

I sat stock still, trying not to move. Every ripple made my skin scald. This was water to wake you up, not to relax in. My head was pounding with the heat. I would bear it, I decided, for one minute longer; after all, it was supposed to be good for you.

An old woman who had been in the tub ever since I entered the room gave me a gold-toothed smile. 'On the chilly side today, isn't it,' she yelled over the splashing. 'Yesterday was better – good and hot.'

The next day was overcast – forty per cent chance of rain, said the woman at the hotel reception desk. I was glad of the cool. I got up early, packed my bag and tramped off up the road towards Shitomae Barrier.

At the time of the Tokugawa shoguns, the border post at Shitomae was like a military garrison. It was essential to the policing of the northern territories. It stood strategically at the heart of Ezo country, where the main road crossed from Oshu, Hidehira's old kingdom, into the western province of Dewa; and the border guards were particularly punctilious about their duties.

Basho and Sora arrived late in the afternoon of the fifteenth of the fifth month, July 1st. They had walked from Iwaté, fifteen or twenty miles away. They must have been hot, sweaty, covered in dust, their feet aching after plodding all those miles in straw sandals, and looking forward to the end of the day's trek. Surely two elderly men, one a rather famous poet with letters of introduction to prove it, and both dressed innocuously as priests, would not have much trouble crossing the notorious barrier.

They may not have looked like trouble-makers, but the

guards had a job to do. 'As travellers rarely use this road, we were treated with suspicion by the barrier guards, and passed the barrier only after much delay', wrote Basho, and Sora added that they were 'refused six times' before they were allowed to pass.

By the time they got through it was nearly nightfall. They hurried on into the mountains. 'As we were climbing a big mountain the sun had already set; the house of a border guard caught our eye and we asked for lodging.'

This story puzzled me. Why didn't they go back to Narugo for the night? Perhaps it was impossible, having completed the formalities at the border. But surely it was foolhardy to press on at such a late hour. How did they know that they would find anywhere to stay? Were they not afraid of being stranded in the mountains after dark?

Basho had nothing more to say about what must have been a desperate trek, looking for shelter. He was more worried about the quality of the accommodation: 'For three days a storm raged; it was a dreadful stay in the mountains.'

nomi shirami	Fleas, lice,
uma no shito suru	Horse pissing
makura moto	Beside my pillow

As was the custom in country areas, they had to share their shelter with animals. But *uma no shito suru*, 'horse pissing', is also a play on Shitomae. *Shito* is an old word for 'piss' and Shito-mae, they say, is where Yoshitsune's new-born baby had his first one.

Shitomae was at the far end of the valley, where the plain of Oshu collides with the mountains of Dewa. From here on there is nowhere to go but up. Behind was Narugo on its hill, columns of steam rising into the grey morning sky above it, and paddy fields, an endless expanse of them, emerald green, stretching all the way down to the coast. In front the hillside extended like a wall, covered in a dense tangle of pine and birch forest, every leaf dripping, smelling moistly of earth.

The car road zigzagged steeply up. But I ignored it: today I was going to walk.

I went to look at what was left of the old barrier. There was nothing much, just a rock engraved with the name and a tea-house, closed at this hour of the morning. I hitched my pack on to my back and started up the steps cut into the hillside, following a sign for the 'narrow road to the deep north footpath'.

It was a couple of hours of hard climbing before I came out of the woods on to the top of the ridge. My legs were aching, my pack was heavy, I was hungry – but I looked around with exhilaration. It was glorious, another world up here: rough wild moorland, untamed frontier country, with real mountains, not rounded humpy ones, looming all around and clouds scudding low like mist. I had been skirting the mountains for days; now I was right in the middle of them. The track meandered off through the scrub and gorse, between bushes of stunted bamboo and pines with twisted red trunks blotched with moss.

I wished I had brought some food with me. I had seen no people since I set out, passed no villages or little shops. But I loved the bleak wildness of it – so desolate, so inhospitable, so unlike Japan.

In the distance was a frayed thread of smoke. Far ahead, almost under the dark shadow of the mountains, were three small figures, sitting in a row along the path, and the corner of a roof – Amazaké jinja, Sweet Saké shrine. I was already looking forward to a cupful.

'Want to see something rare?' called one as I came up to them. He had on thick gloves and cloven-toed boots and a baseball cap pulled well down on his head. A smoking mosquito coil dangled from his belt. He pointed to the bamboo baskets propped on the ground in front of them. They were half full of round white honeycombs, crawling with white larvae the size of woodlice.

'Baby bees,' he grinned. 'We found them up the mountain. Taking them to the canning factory.'

'What are they for?' I asked dubiously, keeping a safe distance.

'For eating,' cackled a woman with a broad homely face and a headscarf tied over a baseball cap.

There was no sweet saké at the shrine, nothing at all except a broken little shack with a worn stone image and some bottles of saké in front for offerings. Laboriously I puzzled out the Japanese on the sign outside. Yoshitsune and Benkei, it said, passed through these Kamewari mountains in 1187, on their way to Hiraizumi, and spent the night here. Benkei built the shrine with his bare hands and prayed the gods for a safe journey to Hiraizumi. I doubted whether this particular shrine was that old – or whether it would last another winter.

'Aren't you afraid, walking on your own?' called the woman.

'There's a forty per cent chance of rain, you know,' said the man.

They hitched their baskets on to their backs, said goodbye and headed off, straight into the undergrowth. No wonder they needed to travel in the safety of a group. Feeling rather tame, I continued down the path. There was something special about the encounter and I mulled it over with pleasure. They had not behaved as if I were a foreigner. They had treated me like one of them.

Finally I came out on the road. I had been walking for three and a half hours. Dark rain clouds were sweeping in lower and lower. And here, in a landscape worthy of Wuthering Heights, bleak brooding moorland enclosed in pine-clad mountains half obscured by cloud, was a tea house.

It was a cheerful place. There was a radio with music piping out of it, pink paper lanterns strung around outside and an old man lounging on the tatami, smoking and eating. I could have had grilled *ayu*, baby trout, or grilled snake, neatly coiled on spits, but plumped for tea and *miso oden*, 'the local speciality', warm slabs of grey yam jelly smeared with sweet thick bean paste.

Hanging along a wall were bunches of herbs and there were bags of dried conkers on a trestle outside. 'You put them in saké,' said the curly haired woman who had served me my tea, bustling over, 'with hozuki berries, leave it for three months, then drink it – it's good for rheumatism. Or use it as an ointment.'

Outside, a swarthy man in wellingtons was grilling up more *ayu*, speared on skewers, heads down, tails up, over a charcoal brazier. The old man strolled out and began asking him questions which he appeared to answer with great reluctance, a matchstick firmly fixed in his mouth: 'Catch the ayu yourself, do you?' – 'No, the mountain people bring them.' 'Built this place yourself, did you?' – 'No, we had workmen up from Narugo.'

The woman led me to the other side of the shop. She had a pleasant comfortable face and her red apron was creased and stiff with starch.

'These are good too.' Behind the counter were two huge medicine jars, each containing a coiled viper looking at me out of a glazed eye. They couldn't have been less than a couple of feet long and were, I think, still alive. 'Keep them under water (she didn't say how you caught them) until they've emptied their intestines. It takes a few months before they're quite clean inside. You can find out what they ate by what comes out of them. See? That one ate a mouse.' True enough, the creature had disgorged an unsavoury scrap of grey fur which was floating in the water.

'Then put them into saké. It's good for old people and people with weak constitutions.'

'It must get lonely up here,' I said. It seemed a desolate place for anyone, even someone as resourceful as she was.

'It does sometimes – specially at this time of year, in the rains. But there's usually people up to see the border guard's house.'

'The border guard's house?'

'Where Matsuo Basho stayed. It's just over the road. Haven't you seen it?'

I had never imagined he had come as far as this. He once wrote a haiku about the thinness of his legs

yase sune mo	Thin shanks! Still,
areba zo hana no	While I have them –
Yoshino yama	blossoms
	Of Mount Yoshino

It must have been the same determination that drove him on those skinny legs of his, old and weary, sickly though he was, to tramp on, deep into the mountains, long after nightfall. Yet he didn't dwell on the hardness of the climb, only grumbled humorously about the fleas and lice.

In fact the border guard's house was rather a luxurious establishment, a fine old country manor, not at all the miserable hovel Basho had suggested. It was beautifully constructed in the traditional way, all wood and straw, with sliding wooden doors for walls and a high roof with thatch a foot thick. The beams were bound together with rope and the joints slotted together as precisely as the pieces of a jigsaw puzzle; there were no nails used in those days.

It was enormous, three or four times the size of the most palatial city house. I counted six ten-mat rooms: the standard Japanese room is half the size, six tatami mats, nine foot by twelve; whole families live in two-room flats and many students spend their university days confined to one four-and-a-half mat room. And besides this there was a lower earthen-floored section, with stalls for horses, old plough shares and a huge clay oven, all under the same roof.

A very old man was asleep on the tatami, his head on the sort of pillow that Basho must have used – a solid block of wood. I crept quietly around so as not to disturb him.

Basho and Sora were trapped up here on this desolate plateau for three days. But the worst of their journey was still to come.

The master of the house told us, 'From here to the country of Dewa is across high mountains and the path is uncertain; so you should take along a man who knows the road.' 'By all means,' I said, and hired a guide, a first-rate, strapping young man, who, short curved sword at his side and oaken staff in hand, went along ahead of us. Thinking 'this is bound to be the day, without a doubt, that we meet danger', we followed fearfully behind.

As the master had warned, the mountains were so high and the forest so thick that we didn't hear one bird cry; and under the trees it was so dark that it was like walking at midnight. It made me feel as if 'dust, black as night, was raining from the clouds' (as Tu Fu, the Chinese poet, wrote). We trampled our way through thickets of bamboo grass, waded through streams and stumbled across boulders, cold sweat running down our skin all the while, and finally came out in the Mogami district.

Said our guide, 'On this road there is always some terrible incident. It was lucky that I was able to bring you through in safety', and cheerfully departed. Hearing this, even though the journey was over, our hearts pounded.

7
Pampas Marshes

When I got back to the teahouse, the enclosing ring of mountains had disappeared in the cloud and swathes of mist were wafting across the ground. It was not a day for tackling the high passes.

'Big Sister!' called the woman in the red apron when I came in. 'Going down to Obanazawa, aren't you? Uncle here will take you – he's going that way.'

It didn't take much to persuade me. Relieved and grateful, I said goodbye and *mata aimasho*, 'let's meet again', wondering if we would, and scrambled into the van.

'Uncle' (who was as much the woman's uncle as I was her big sister) was an itinerant pottery salesman. His van was packed with wooden crates which slid and banged together as we swung out across the highland. He was a jolly fellow with a broad grin and a cap perched jauntily on the back of his head, who chattered away endlessly, oblivious of the bleak magnificent landscape unfolding in front of us.

There was no more sign of life than before – no people, no sheep, just moorland covered in gorse and bushes and the shadowy hills at the edges of the high plateau. But even up here, in this harsh uninviting country, someone had hacked out a few scrubby paddy fields and a couple of times we passed a lonely farmhouse. It was a tribute to something – perhaps just to the desperate poverty of the region – that every last inch of arable land was used for rice. Not an inch of soil was wasted.

The salesman had samples, porcelain, he told me, from the kilns in Hirashimizu, which he took round from village to village, and orders which he had collected last time round.

'When I was young', he bawled above the juddering of the engine and the rattling of the pots, 'I studied hard, stayed up all night studying. Could have gone to university if I'd wanted, to university! Anyway, in the end I became a pottery salesman. Why, people ask me – why did you do that? I'll tell you. It's because a salesman's salary was so high in those days – you could make good money selling cups and bowls. For a teacher – a high school teacher, even a university teacher – the money was bad. It's the opposite now, of course. I made a big mistake!'

He told me all this chortling with laughter as if it were the most amusing story in the world and mopping his face with a checked handkerchief.

'Why not get a new job?' I asked.

He was ready with the answer. 'It's not the Japanese way. We Japanese don't leave a job just because it's not paying well. We stick at it. That's our duty.'

Gradually the mountains squeezed closer and closer to the road until there was no moorland left and we were climbing between steep hills covered in spruce and pine trees, so tightly packed it was impossible to imagine there could be any way through them. It was exactly as Basho had written, 'the mountains so high and the forest so thick we couldn't hear one bird cry'.

Finally we came right up against the mountain face. '*Natagiri Togé*,' said the pottery salesman – Natagiri Pass, the pass that Basho had struggled across with such difficulty. I caught a glimpse of cobwebby silver birch trees and stubby bamboos clinging limpet-like to the rocks, before we rushed into the long dark tunnel that bored straight through it.

In a minute we were out again – and out of the mountains, rolling downhill into another, brighter, world. The clouds were no longer around but above us, resting heavily on the tops of the hills, still brimming with rain.

We had suddenly left the autumn tints of the moorland and were back in summer again. The green all around was startling. The road ran straight across a prairie of emerald paddy fields, over streams and little bridges, through villages of grand old farmhouses, where cars passed so seldom that some little boys throwing a ball around stopped to stare and wave. I rolled down the window and waved back. The air was close, clammy, earthy, like a jungle or a Kew Gardens greenhouse, and grass and leaves spilt extravagantly on to the road.

But the mountains never disappeared completely. As one range dropped away behind us, another began to rise on the far side of the plain, the peaks faintly visible on the horizon above the haze of heat. Right the way round this gentle, prosperous country was a wall of mountains, like an enclosing barricade.

The pottery salesman dropped me at Obanazawa. And at last the rain, which had been threatening for so long, began – not a gentle drizzle but a tropical downpour, water tumbling straight out of the sky as if someone had suddenly emptied a bucket over my head. Huddled under an umbrella, I hurried off along the grey street, looking for somewhere to shelter. There were shops, plenty of them – seed shops, fish shops, clothes shops, slipper shops, several tea shops with crates of tea and cabinets full of tea pots and tea cups, and a shop with a rusty bicycle jammed in between ornate black and gold altars and gleaming gold Buddha images in cardboard boxes. Plenty of supplies for local farmers; but a strange lack of provision for visitors from out of town – no coffee shops, no restaurants, nowhere to sit out the rain. From somewhere above my head came music – the 'Four Seasons' – competing with the drumming and splashing of rain on tarmac. Looking up I saw that each lamppost all the way down the street had a loudspeaker attached to it.

Eventually I found a tiny takeaway sushi shop and ducked inside. There were two chairs and a table with a vase of plastic flowers on it. I sat down uncomfortably in my wet clothes.

'Rains stopped yet on the other side of the mountains?' The woman behind the counter was small, bird-like, and wore a green and white paper cap with 'Snack Sushi' written across the front.

'Of course, our rainy season's always late over here.' 'Over here' . . . She made it sound like another country – which, in a way, it was: *Dewa no kuni*, the land of Dewa.

'You should see it here in winter,' she added, leaning across the counter to give me a welcome cup of tea. 'So much snow you can't see the road. Two or three metres deep it is, every year, from November right through to April. We're famous for our snow – more than anywhere else in Japan!' Many of the menfolk, she said, still went to Tokyo at the end of November when the snow came, to look for work; and some of the younger ones never came back. 'There's no work for them, you see, not in the winter – though they're building factories here now. Matsumura Seisakucho, machine parts, that's the biggest. Lots of the young lads work there.'

When the rain let up, I went in search of two things – wellington boots, the first priority, and somewhere to stay.

Obanazawa was like an extension of the countryside. It began as a cluster of farmhouses, sprouted a couple of service stations and suddenly developed into a line of shops thrust into the middle of the rice fields. It consisted in fact of two roads, the second at right angles to the first, with a network of small lanes behind, which quickly petered out among the fields. There were no restaurants (except for the takeaway sushi shop I had found) because there were no tourists; and there were no tourists because there was nothing to see. Obanazawa was a functional little town, here to serve local farmers – which was exactly what the people around me were, splashing down the street in wellingtons and baggy trousers, scarves around their heads, riding down it on battered old bicycles, knees knocking the handlebars, or rattling through the ankle-deep water in little white pick-ups, kicking up a swirl of waves.

The lack of tourists was not altogether a blessing. No tourists, I feared, meant no accommodation. Near where the two roads met I saw the familiar sign for *ryokan*, inn, above a rambling wooden house, and slid open the door and went in. A woman appeared in answer to my shouts.

'Accommodation?' She looked me up and down suspiciously. 'Can't do it, dear – no doors, you see.' She moved her arm back and forth as if swinging a door open and shut. 'You need a door, don't you? Only *fusuma* here.' She gestured sliding a fusuma door back and forth.

I didn't need a door, I answered, as politely as possible – nor a bed, nor a shower. Japanese style was fine.

She shook her head firmly. 'Full up for women here,' she said; 'only room for men.'

'Is there anywhere else to stay in town?' I called after her retreating back.

'You could try Suzu-no-yu, I suppose.'

For Basho and Sora, Obanazawa, 'Pampas marshes', this fertile country on the far side of the mountains, was a haven, a place where they could rest and relax. They had been tramping the roads now for over six weeks, without much of a break, culminating in the steep and dangerous climb over Natagiri Pass, and were exhausted.

When they got here, on the seventeenth of the fifth month, July 4th, the weather was no better than when I came. It was fine, Sora wrote, when they crossed the pass. But just as they reached a village called Shogon – perhaps the very village where the children waved at me – there was a sudden rainstorm and they were soaked through. They trudged on through the mud and puddles in sodden straw sandals, hot and sticky in their black robes, and reached Obanazawa 'after lunch'. They had covered a good twenty miles that morning.

In those days Obanazawa was a prosperous provincial town, noted for its fine half-timbered houses and its heavy snows. It was one of the most important stations on the Ushu-kaido, the great road of Dewa (Ushu was another name for Dewa), and the commercial hub of the region, full of travellers and bustle. Merchants from Edo and Kyoto would come up to stay in its inns and temples, bringing with them the latest news and gossip and the cultured ways of the capital, and local merchants in their turn often travelled down south. As a result, Obanazawa became a lively cultural centre, an oasis of culture in the wild north country.

The leading light of this small cultural mecca was a man called Suzuki Seifu. He came from one of Obanazawa's oldest and most respected families and was a direct descendant, so the townspeople claimed, of Suzuki Saburo Shigeie, the only member of Yoshitsune's party who managed to escape from Hiraizumi. He fled, according to the story, as far as Obanazawa, where he settled and made his home, and, as a result, many people in Obanazawa have the surname Suzuki.

Seifu and Basho were old friends; and when Basho and Sora arrived in Obanazawa, they went straight to his house.

'Even though he was a wealthy man, there was no vulgarity in him', wrote Basho. Basho was a samurai and Seifu, despite his honourable ancestry, a mere merchant, one of the despised lower classes who soiled their fingers with money. But, like many members of his class, he had used his wealth and opportunities of travel to better himself, by absorbing samurai culture.

He was a dealer in silk, tobacco, wood and rice, and in safflower, Obanazawa's most famous product, and often went down to Edo, Kyoto and Osaka on business. (At that time the journey to Edo took fourteen days. Seifu travelled on foot or jogged along uncomfortably in a sedan chair, on the shoulders of bearers – horses were for the samurai, not for the lowly merchants.) On one of these visits, long before Basho came to Obanazawa, he had met the old poet and asked to be accepted as a student of his. He became a fine poet in his own right and published three books of haiku.

As a traveller himself, Seifu 'well understood the hardships of travel. He insisted that we stay here for several days, taking care of us after our long journey and showering us with kindness.' Playfully using some Obanazawa dialect, Basho added

suzushisa o	The cool –
wa ga yado ni shite	making of it my house
nemaru nari	I be at ease

Suddenly, after the hard weeks on the road, the travellers found themselves surrounded with comfort and luxury and congenial company. They rested in Obanazawa for eleven days, longer than anywhere else on their journey, staying partly at Seifu's and partly at Yosenji, the local Tendai temple. Here, Basho was a celebrity. It was the first time that such a great and famous poet had ever visited this distant part of the country. There were dinners in his honour, where he was served the local speciality, prepared only for great cele-brations – *naracha*, rice and black beans. The local poets were all eager to meet him, he presided over poetry gatherings almost every evening, and a man called Toyo arranged a trip on a pleasure boat for him along the river. The result of the eleven days' stay was two sequences of linked verse and many haiku.

Looking up and down the grey street with its drab little shops, there did not seem to be much left of the cultured world which Basho had found in Obanazawa. Almost directly op-posite the *ryokan*, behind a large bank, I came across a signpost at the side of the road, marking the place where Suzuki Seifu's house had stood. The house itself was torn down, I was told, a few years ago. Nearby was an imposing old building, long and low, the upper storey whitewashed, the lower one made entirely of sliding doors of dark wooden slats. Perhaps Seifu's house, I thought, looked like this. On a board along the side of the main door were the words 'Basho-Seifu *Shiryokan* (museum)'.

Despite the name, there was not a lot to see – a few empty rooms with plastered walls and tatami-matted floors, a hearth with a kettle hanging over it, some local handicrafts . . .

As I was leaving, the girl at the door looked up. She was young, serious, with steel-rimmed spectacles. 'Ah yes,' she said. 'You will want to meet one of the professors. I will make an appointment for you.' I hesitated. What kind of 'professors' could there be in this little town?

'You're staying at Suzu-no-yu, I assume.' (Presumably it was the only place willing to accept visitors from out of town.) 'I will telephone you there. You can meet one of the professors tomorrow.' I thanked her, sighing inwardly. The prospect of half a day in the company of some ancient sage was not an enticing one. Finding out about Basho was not a problem. There were any number of people eager to provide me with detailed information about every aspect of the Narrow Road – there was after all, as Horiguchi-san had pointed out, a 'Basho boom'. But what I was after was not history, not information, but something more amorphous and more alive – to get under the skin of this place and thus somehow get close to Basho himself. Meeting a dry old sage would not help me with that.

It was my second night at Suzu-no-yu, a bleak little place on the outskirts of town. With my fellow guests I sat cross-legged at the low table, picking at the dishes of raw fish and bits of vegetable laid out on the sticky plastic tablecloth. There was imitation straw matting – also plastic – laid over the tatami and flies buzzed around the food and around the neon light overhead.

'You should see it here in winter . . .' the young man opposite was saying, raising his voice to make himself heard above the television (it was a quiz show of some sort) . . . 'when the snow comes. Two or three metres deep. Lasts all winter. Great skiing.' He had been at Suzu-no-yu for months (a depressing thought); he was building a coffee shop at a nearby ski resort and had to get it done by winter.

The second guest said nothing. He was a seedy-looking character in a navy-blue suit, stained and grubby, shiny at the elbows and bulging at the buttons. A medicine salesman, confided the old granny who served us – stayed here two weeks a month and went round selling aspirins to the local farmers. 'Not a lot to say for himself,' she added.

I was back in my room when the phone rang. The girl from the Shiryokan, I assumed, with an appointment for me to meet one of her professors the next day.

'He's at the Shiryokan now,' she said urgently. 'Can you come?' It seemed a strange place and a strange time to meet an elderly professor – and rather a sudden summons.

'He's had a bit of saké,' she added. 'Hope you don't mind.'

I went as quickly as I could to the Shiryokan – after all, it would not do to keep a professor waiting. As I splashed along the dark street, wishing they had discovered street lighting in this part of Japan, I was wondering what we would talk about.

Perhaps, I thought, I should have prepared some questions about Basho.

In the centre of town, a few ancient gas lamps cast a glimmer of light on the wet road. Only the Shiryokan was brightly lit. There seemed to be some sort of party going on. As I slid open the door, I was beginning to fear I had misunderstood.

Sitting around the hearth were three figures, none of whom resembled an elderly professor. '*Nagatsu Sensei* – Professor Nagatsu,' said the office girl anxiously. She had something of the air of a lion-tamer about to put her head into the mouth of a lion – proud of her captive, but fearful that he might misbehave. He, for his part, was rather like a lion. Mid-forties, I thought, no more – far from elderly – with a mane of black hair down to his collar, flopping forward in long strands over his eyes whenever he shook his head, which he frequently did. He had a dramatic face – wide and flat, high-cheekboned, quite unlike the round, bland, blobby faces of the south.

'Welcome, welcome,' he cried, waving his arms expansively – 'We've been waiting for you – welcome to our ranks. There – sit there – that's your place.' I took the fourth place around the square hearth, while the girl knelt behind and began to pour drinks.

'We are all followers of Basho here – students and followers – of Basho and Seifu.' He introduced me to Kawashima-san – 'a fine poet and devotee of Seifu' and to Mitsuko-san – 'a famous dancer'. She smiled and nodded. As one would expect of a dancer, she was tall and willowy, with a long slender neck and head gracefully poised. Her face was extraordinary. Rude though it was, I couldn't help staring. Her hair, swept back, accentuated the angularity of the jutting cheekbones, deeply hollowed cheeks and enormous dark eyes. Beautiful – but a harsh beauty, the beauty of the north, with none of the softness or smooth anonymity of classical Japanese beauty.

Nagatsu was talking, shovelling back his hair in handfuls, gesticulating wildly. 'Basho', he was saying, 'crossed twelve countries; covered six hundred ri, two thousand four hundred kilometres (1,500 miles); and spent a hundred and fifty days on his journey. Of those hundred and fifty days, he spent the most – forty-two – in the country of Dewa, Yamagata. And of that time, he stayed the longest, eleven days, in Obanazawa.'

'He came at the beginning of July', said Kawashima-san, 'so that he could see the safflowers in bloom.' He was quieter, less flamboyant than Nagatsu, softer featured, with something warm and fatherly about him. He was a confectioner by trade and had brought *kujira mochi* for me to sample, 'whale rice cakes', thick slabs of rice pounded with walnuts and brown sugar – 'our local speciality'.

'Safflowers have to be picked in the morning, you know. One blossoms, then they all blossom together, not higgledy-piggledy – so you always see a field of blossoming safflower, never just one or two blooms.'

While the men talked, the women were silent. Mitsuko sat smiling while the girl with glasses passed around plates of food and kept our saké cups filled.

The conversation ranged from love suicides (a young couple had recently committed suicide in Obanazawa – 'Do you have a lot of love suicides in England?' they asked. 'No harakiri, no love suicides,' I answered, to their amazement) to mochi, 'rice cakes' – but *tsuchi mochi, wara mochi*, made of mud or straw, not rice.

'People are very poor up here . . .' said Nagatsu.

'You should see it here in winter,' added Kawashima.

'. . . and when times were hard, they used to make mochi of mud or straw . . .'

'Just mud, just a ball of mud or a ball of straw.'

'. . . and eat them, just to fill their stomachs. I made them once, for an experiment – and ate them, too. Not bad.' He threw back his head and guffawed.

I gaped at him, then asked, 'Nutritional value . . . ?'

'Nil,' roared Nagatsu, shouting with laughter. 'They just make you constipated.'

Later the girl with glasses brought out squares of white card, a pile of them, and they asked me to write something – about why I had come to Obanazawa, Basho, anything. I sat and looked at the white card and thought. 'O-ba-na-za-wa' – five syllables. Perhaps I could try a haiku. The rain was pounding on the roof and the wind rattled the windows in their wooden frames.

Obanazawa wa	Obanazawa –
Basho no Nihon deska	Is this Basho's Japan?
natsu no ame	Summer rains

Not bad for a first attempt, I thought. Dipping the brush in the ink, I shaped each character slowly and carefully, trying to make my calligraphy as good as possible.

Nagatsu studied the card sternly, holding it at arm's length. 'The first line is too long,' he pronounced. '"Wa" – you don't need "wa". The second line is too long too. "Ba-sho-o-no-ni-ho-n-des-ka"' – he counted them off on his fingers – 'nine syllables.'

He adopted the pose of Rodin's 'Thinker', frowning. '"*Obanazawa/Basho no sekai/natsu no ame*" – "Obanazawa/Basho's world/summer rains" – that's better.'

I took a clean white card and wrote it out laboriously. 'No good,' said Nagatsu, looking at my pinched little hieroglyphs. 'The characters have to fill the page.'

Finally – after several more attempts – he was satisfied. As I was painting on my signature, suddenly he cried out, 'Ah!' flinging up an arm. '"*Natsu no ame/Basho no sekai/Obanazawa*" – "Summer rains/Basho's world/Obanazawa" – best of all!'

'Your haiku', said Kawashima, 'means – "Here we are together; this meeting, this gathering, is Basho's world; and it's summer, and raining."'

'We are all poets in Japan,' said Nagatsu excitedly, scooping his hair back with both hands. 'We all sing and write poems to express ourselves. That is Basho's world.'

On the back of one of the cards he scrawled

Nihon no fudo	The beauty of Japan –
tomoni tazunen	Let's look for it together

His characters filled the page beautifully.

'After a haiku, two lines of seven syllables,' he explained. 'Then another haiku, then another two lines . . . Thirty-six verses in all. That is linked verse. Always four people, four people writing together, nine verses each . . . Mitsuko-san, the next verse.'

She laughed graciously and shook her head.

Kawashima thought a little, then came out with

aka aka to	Red and red
irori wo kakomu	Gathered around the hearth
yo naga kana	The night is long . . .

'It's eleven o'clock,' he explained – '"the night is long" – it's late.'

Behind us, the girl with glasses was writing down each verse.

'Basho was a poet – his journey was a poet's journey,' declaimed Nagatsu. 'Wherever he went, he gathered with others to make poems.' During his journey around the deep north, he sat with local poets composing linked verse at just ten places, most of them in Dewa; and at Obanazawa he composed not one linked verse sequence but two – 'because Dewa is a country of poets' – and of all the poets Basho met on his travels, Seifu was the best.

'Sitting here making poems together – this is Basho's world.'

That was the first of many *de-ai*, many gatherings. I left Suzu-no-yu and went to stay with Kawashima and his family above the shop – called 'Basho and Seifu' – where they sold *kujira mochi*, whale rice cakes, and other cakes.

When I arrived, his wife was waiting in the teahouse to meet me. This was a real traditional teahouse, for tea ceremony, such as you might see in the gardens of grand old mansions in Kyoto or Tokyo: a tiny hut of wood and paper, four-and-a-half mats square, with sliding paper walls, a low doorway you had to stoop down and creep through and a decorative bamboo and brushwood gate outside. It looked strange among the leek fields and cabbage patches.

'We love tea ceremony; that's why we had it built,' beamed Kawashima, full of innocent pride. In mainstream Japan, the old 'land of Yamato', people do tea ceremony because it is an accomplishment, because it is the proper thing to do, but seldom because they love it.

His wife, whisking up the bright green tea for me, was as warm and welcoming as he was. She was plump, pretty, with clear soft skin (no make-up) and the broad features that all these northern people seemed to have.

'Come and visit us in winter,' she smiled. 'You should see it here in winter – the snow so deep we have to cut steps in it to get down to the front door.'

'Twenty years ago', said Kawashima, 'the snow used to obliterate the roads completely so you didn't know where they were. You just walked anywhere – across the fields, across the hedges, anywhere – with your bags on your back. That was how it was when we were first together' – he smiled fondly at his wife – 'though nowadays bulldozers clear the roads.'

'Kawashima's father, now', said his wife, 'he was a famous traveller. Used to pack his *onigiri*, his rice balls, and off he would go across the snow.'

I stayed nearly a week in Obanazawa and would have happily stayed longer. Kawashima's wife spread bedding out for me in his study and I slept there, surrounded by scholarly works on Basho, volumes of the quarterly *History and Culture of Obanazawa*, to which he contributed, and his *nihonga* painting of Basho and Sora, in bamboo hats and straw sandals, striding across Natagiri Pass, pushing aside spiky stylised grass and brambles with their staffs. There were haiku pinned up in the hall and over the wash-basin next to pictures of Jesus (Kawashima's wife was a Christian) and pens and a pile of exercise books in the toilet, with the legend 'Thoughts, ideas, haiku – please record here'.

Sitting there one day, keeping a wary eye on the ants which scurried up and down the wall beside me, I was flicking through the top most book when I saw my name. 'July 2nd', Kawashima's wife had written. 'Lesley-san came. She is a lover of Basho and is travelling the narrow road to the deep north. We are going to cook and make haiku together . . .' and much more which I couldn't read. At the end were the words

'Welcome, Lesley-san'. Touched, I started to plan the answer I would pen in before I left.

In the evenings I helped her in the kitchen, trying to keep up or at least keep out of her way as she rushed around, an apron tied over her skirt, energetically chopping vegetables and grinding tofu with gusto, impossibly fast.

The first night she made *naracha*, rice and black beans, the dish that Basho had enjoyed when he was in Obanazawa. Kawashima came to help and they sat facing each other on the floor, taking turns at holding down the huge mortar and grinding away with the pestle.

'It's the first time I've ever seen a Japanese man in the kitchen,' I said, impressed with this domesticity.

'It's the first time he's ever helped,' she laughed. 'It's because you're here.'

Yuko, their daughter, an elegant young lady who worked in a coffee shop (so there was, somewhere, a coffee shop in Obanazawa) and drank tea with her little finger extended, had gone out.

'*Baka-na musume*,' said her mother vigorously, 'idiot daughter!' Father had disappeared by this time. 'She's off with that boy again. Wants to marry him – but he's no good. Still, I won't stop her. I won't make her have *o-miai*.

'We had *o-miai*, you know.' I knew that most people of their generation, particularly in the countryside, had had arranged marriages. But it was hard to believe it of these two. They were one of the most affectionate couples I have ever met, perpetually together, joking and teasing each other. I had always thought of Japanese couples as rather distant: the men put their energy into work and spend the evenings drinking with their workmates, the women devote themselves to their children and meet other women for lunch. Some of my women friends I have known for years, without ever meeting their husbands. But up here in the north, these stereotypes seemed no longer to apply.

'I don't like *o-miai*,' said Kawashima's wife. 'At first you don't like each other. It's terrible, having to live together. You don't agree about anything! I remember one time, we had had a row. I was scrubbing out the bath, feeling lonely and sad, and all of a sudden, through a crack in the wall, I noticed a dandelion, just one. It was summer; usually dandelions flower in spring. So I made a poem

kekkyoku wa
hitori to omou
settsu zurete
sakishi hito mo to no
tampopo no hana

In the end
When I think I'm alone,
Out of step with the season –
Here too, blossoming,
A dandelion flower.

In the end I'm alone, like this one dandelion, flowering out of season. So we're both lonely.'

Every evening, after dinner, guests arrived. Professor Nagatsu came several times. And there was Suzuki-san, a descendant of Seifu (and therefore of Suzuki Saburo Shigeie), a dignified, silver-haired man who was the head of the Basho-Seifu Shiryokan, the museum, the cultural focus of the town; and Nagasawa-san, an artist and farmer, who had made a painted scroll of all the stages of Basho's journey through Dewa. As artists are expected to, he had long hair and looked rather bohemian. 'What do you think of this?' grinned Kawashima, tugging his moustache as he introduced him. 'Don't see many of these in Japan, do you!'

Apart from myself, Kawashima's wife was the only woman. She carried out all the duties of a good Japanese wife – kept the saké cups filled, peeled peaches and sliced them, brought out plates of fresh green soya beans in their pods. But instead of creeping back to the kitchen and leaving the menfolk to their talk, she contributed as much as anyone else, closing her eyes and listening hard, quietly repeating difficult words to herself.

Sitting there trying to keep up with the conversation – especially with the jokes, which I nearly always missed – it seemed to me that these *de-ai*, these gatherings, were the nearest I was ever likely to get to Basho's world. When Basho sat down with his students and fellow poets to make verses, it must have been exactly like this. The culture of his time, which, down south, was preserved as carefully as those bottled vipers in the mountains, here, in this remote little town in the rice fields, was still alive. These people gathered to talk, dispute, discuss and make poetry for the pure joy of it. It was the last thing I had expected to find – and it was difficult to tear myself away.

Before I left, I wanted to see Yosenji, the temple where Basho had stayed for eight of his eleven days in Obanazawa. It belonged to the Tendai sect, the Buddhist equivalent of High Church. 'Basho's patrons were the shoguns and the rich', Kawashima told me, 'and he always stayed either with them, in their big mansions, or in Tendai temples – because Tendai was the sect of the rich. He never stayed with ordinary people like us.'

The temple was on the other side of town, beyond the Shiryokan. I didn't know that part and blundered around the narrow lanes, stopping every now and then to ask directions of tiny withered old women in headscarves with hefty babies tied to their backs; it was easy, among all the heady intellectual discussion around the table of an evening, to forget that Obanazawa was a farmers' town. Then a couple of little girls in pinnies – the first to give me a really long, hard stare – pointed me along a short road lined with trees and tall wooden houses.

Abruptly the village came to an end. The houses and trees stopped short and the road pitched down into paddy fields. Standing on the furthest outcrop of high land I looked across this glistening green sea, specked with dots of white – *shirosagi*, white herons, perched on the pathways between the paddies. Somewhere in the trees painfully close to my ear a semi let off a high-powered whirr, like an electric saw starting up, and out in the fields a frog was groaning like a door – a western one – creaking open and shut on rusty hinges. Dragonflies brushed gently past.

Hanging like a mirage on the horizon were the western

mountains, the mountains of Dewa – and, somewhere among them, the Sacred Mountains, the home of the yamabushi. They looked tantalisingly close, not much more than a day's walk away. But it would be a few days before I could explore them. Basho had made a detour from here, gone south through the central plain to see a famous old temple – Yamadera, Mountain Temple – and I would have to go there too.

The temple, Yosenji, was so small and unimposing that at first I walked straight past it. I turned in through the gates, housing a couple of giant guardian deities, roughly carved and painted, and a life-size wooden horse. The grounds were bustling with pilgrims, plump women and children all in white, busily sticking prayers on to the wooden walls of the shabby little temple building. It was already covered in squares and oblongs of paper several layers thick. An old man was watching them with a faintly bemused air. One by one they went up to him, bowed, spoke, then clambered into two buses drawn up under the trees. Between the buses was a small hut. I picked my way across the muddy ground to it, past a small shrine and a tombstone wrapped, for some reason, in blue plastic. It contained a stone with Basho's haiku carved down it: *suzushisa o* . . . The cool . . .

When the pilgrims had gone, the old man shuffled over to me, cigarette in hand. He was, I gathered, the caretaker of the place. 'Welcome to Yosenji, number twenty-five of the thirty-three Yamagata Kannon temples,' he said absentmindedly, as if he had recited the words a thousand times before. He had a shock of black hair streaked with white which stood up on his head stiff as gorse and a long, gaunt face, hardly lined, with high Ezo cheekbones.

He beckoned me to follow him and we went and sat in his house at one side of the grounds. I was looking forward to his tales of Basho's stay.

'Basho?' he said, looking rather surprised when I asked him. 'The temple was over there then,' gesturing vaguely in the direction of the paddy fields. 'But it burnt down, many times. This temple here was built in Meiji 8 (1876). Had a thatched roof until ten years ago. Got the tiled one put on then.'

He made tea, pressing the top of a large thermos flask to squeeze hot water into a tiny pot full of well-used green tea leaves, then poured out two cups and lit another cigarette.

'Pilgrims, mostly, groups of pilgrims,' he said. 'That's who we get here. Doing the Yamagata Kannon temples. Not in winter, of course. No-one comes in winter.'

He knelt on the tatami, his back as straight as a soldier's.

'It's tough here, you know, tough in winter.'

I was waiting for him to tell me about the snow, but instead he said, 'Forty years ago, we used to go down to Tokyo every year when the snows came. Together, ten of us. On the overnight train from Oishida. Leave at six in the evening, get in next morning.'

He looked at me hard to see if I was listening and when I nodded went on, 'Stayed in *hanba* – barracks, like soldiers.' (I was fingering my dictionary – construction camp, it said.) 'Worked as a carpenter, here and there. Sent money back to the wife and kids – it wasn't much, but there was no work at all here.'

He was on his fourth cigarette.

'It was worse before the war. We were so poor around here, people had to sell their daughters. I knew one girl who was sold. She was a nice girl. Sometimes wonder what became of her.'

I had heard this before. Most of the prostitutes of the Yoshiwara, the old red-light district in the east end of Edo, had been Tohoku girls.

'No, not the Yoshiwara,' he said, when I asked him. 'Obanazawa girls didn't get sent to grand places like that.'

Later he talked about the war.

He had been seven years in China before he was invalided home. One thigh and hip were shattered by a hand grenade and he got a bullet in the other hip. He still had pain, he said. 'Got a bit of money after the war – a thousand yen (£4 in modern currency). What use is that? A healthy body – that's the important thing!'

He was hardly aware that I was there any more, talking more and more fiercely, waving long thin arms, eyes glittering.

'In war you have to kill to avoid being killed. We're all human beings – Chinese, Japanese, English – but war is about killing. *Baka-na senso!* Stupid war!' He banged his fist into his hand. 'All those men going off, leaving their wives and children. Stupid – giving your life for nothing!'

Outside it was clouding over, threatening rain. A grey-haired old man puttered up on a motorbike, climbed the steps to the temple, stepped neatly out of his wellingtons and vanished inside. The dry 'tock tock tock' of a wooden stick hitting a wooden drum started up, accompanied by the dull reverberation of a gong. Then came the sound of an old thin voice, chanting the Heart Sutra.

8

The Temple in the Mountains

'In the domain of Yamagata is a mountain temple called Ryushakuji. Founded by Great Master Jikaku, it is a particularly tranquil place. People had advised us that we should by all means see it once, so from Obanazawa we turned off our planned route, for a distance of just seven ri.'

It was approaching the middle of July – the twenty-seventh of the fifth month, July 14th – when Basho and Sora left Obanazawa. For once the rain had stopped and they set out early in the morning, at eight o'clock, the hour of the dragon. They planned to continue westwards, deep into the mountain country of Dewa, keeping to the path (though in the opposite direction) which Yoshitsune had taken on his way to Hiraizumi, five hundred years before. But first they wanted to see Ryushakuji – Yamadera, 'Mountain Temple' – the most famous temple of the north. They had to make a long detour to get there: seven ri, more than seventeen miles, south through the Yamagata plain, then back again, before turning into the mountains.

Seifu found horses for them for the first part of the journey, as far as Tateoka. From there they may have taken fresh horses or gone on foot (I couldn't understand Sora's cryptic characters here) for another ten miles down the muddy highway, through broad rice plains. No more than a mile away across the fields, the eastern hills thrust out of the plain in a jagged wall, range upon range of them, rough crags wrapped in thick forest.

It was here, deep among these formidable peaks, in 860, that the Tendai priest Jikaku founded Ryushakuji. Basho and Sora passed the town of Tendo, then left the highway and followed

124

a path leading through orchards of green persimmons deep into the hills, and arrived at Ryushakuji at the hour of the sheep, around two-thirty in the afternoon.

'After arranging to lodge in a local pilgrim house, we climbed to the hall at the top of the hill. The mountain – rocks and boulders heaped one upon the other – was covered in pines and cedars, ages old, its earth and stones venerable, encrusted with moss – and on its topmost crag, the doors of the shrines were closed and not a sound could be heard. Edging round the cliffs, crawling across the rocks, we came to the main temple and worshipped there – and the beauty and stillness of the place brought a clarity into my heart.

shizukasa ya	The stillness –
iwa ni shimi-iru	Shrilling into the rocks
semi no koe	The semi's cry.'

The noisy semi, with a cry akin to the whirr of a dentist's drill, was silent the day that I visited Ryushakuji. Though the rain had stopped, the air was suffused with moisture and the place was steamy and dripping like a tropical jungle. I was glad for once of the rain. It had driven away the semis, but it had also driven away the people, and I had the place to myself.

I arrived grandly, by car. Kawashima, who had some business in Yamagata, drove me down Route 13, the grim highway, laden with lorries, that had once been the muddy footpath that Basho had tramped along. 'No point in walking,' he said, and I agreed with him. We turned off through persimmon groves and reached a little town, a single street stretched out all along the foot of a mountain. By now we were deep in the hills. They soared all around, high, rugged – but still somehow contained, decently clothed in forest. Only this one, hanging over the town, was wild, romantic, rocks and crags bursting exuberantly out of the trees.

At the bottom of the hill was a statue of Basho, larger than life, cast-iron, brooding; or maybe just resting, sitting on a rock, looking gravely up the hill in his robes and flat priest's cap, staff in hand, satchel on his knees. A woman in wellingtons and white work bonnet was washing it – rather unnecessary, I thought, in this wet weather – scrubbing methodically, one hand planted firmly on the sage's face.

Basho's haiku was running round and round in my head. 'The stillness . . .' – '*shizukasa*', somewhere between 'silence' and 'loneliness'. It was certainly lonely today, I thought, as I set off up the rough stone steps. (I was lucky. Usually Yamadera, Kawashima had told me, is crowded with tourists.) But silent? Despite the absence of semis and people, it was far from silent. Water roared noisily along gullies on each side of the steps, trickling, rushing, splashing down the hillside, while I toiled up, carefully stepping around yet more water lying in pools in every tiny hollow. Enormous leaves hung dripping over the path and the air smelled damp and earthy.

It was a spectacular place, wonderfully primitive. As Basho had described, it was all 'rocks and boulders', massive rocks and precipitous boulders around which sprouted a forest of pines, cherries, maples, towering cedars, closing greenly over the path in a dense moist net. Clinging to the rocks, squeezed into the crevices between them, were brilliant violets, faded hydrangeas, and an exuberance of wild flowers which I couldn't put a name to. Over the years the cliffs had been rounded and hollowed as if by waves, as if the whole mountain had been under the sea (as apparently it was once). One great overhanging crag, smooth and white and pocked with caves, had taken on the look of a huge grinning skull, with a row of tombstones, evenly planted along the front of its cavernous mouth, making grotesque teeth.

All around were images of gods – for this, I realised with a sort of shock, was holy ground; this mountain I was climbing was an enormous natural temple. Every rock was crowned with an image, sometimes several, some ancient, carved of the same rock, some newer, of concrete. There were eight-armed deities sitting cross-legged on lotuses; tall Buddha figures; and *jizo-sama*, stone images mottled with moss, red bibs tied around their necks. Tombstones, rounded and phallic or straight-sided, crowded every level space; and every smooth rock face was carved with prayers or with the names of gods.

Heaped on each rock, each image, each tombstone, was a mound of coins and small stones.

Around a corner, in a clearing, I came across a bent old crone, almost as ancient as the rocks. On a charcoal brazier made of an iron pail, she had a pan full of *konnyaku*, balls of grey yam jelly, strung on bamboo sticks, four to a stick.

'Only a hundred yen,' she croaked at me. 'Local speciality!'

On a bench nearby, two women and a man sat, chewing silently. All three were in well-pressed grey walking suits. All three had grey hair, cropped very short, wore glasses, and puffed elegantly on cigarettes in long cigarette holders. I eyed them curiously, then took a deep breath and set off up the next set of steps.

The steps continued, on and on, up and up. Were there steps when Basho was here, I wondered breathlessly, or did he clamber up the rocks?

Once I passed a young man resting against a rock; he had three crates of Coca-Cola, piled one above the other, strapped to his back. And from time to time I met a group of pilgrims or an old couple, toiling slowly up or picking their way cautiously down, carrying broad flat staffs etched with scroll-like characters. Later I asked Kawashima about this. Each staff, he told me, is a soul. What is written on it is the name of a dead person and a prayer. The mountain is a link between heaven and earth where 'the dead can meet the living and the living can speak to the dead', and many people, when they die, want their names and perhaps some of their ashes to be brought here; that way they are a little nearer heaven.

I plodded on, sweat running down my face, stopping more and more often to catch my breath. Added to the sound of my sandals on the rocks and the water rushing down the gulleys, from above came the rhythmical 'tock tock tock' of a hammer striking a bell, as if someone were making a horseshoe. A voice was chanting – '*Namu amida butsu, namu amida butsu*' – and a great bell reverberated and faded away.

Then, strangely, came the notes of a piano. How on earth, I wondered, had they managed to get a piano up here? Someone was practising scales and then began, tentatively, to play

Bach. The broken phrases accompanied me as I climbed, like background music for some film I had suddenly found myself in.

The ghostly noises made the silence more silent, the stillness more still. I thought of Basho's semi, an insect so tiny that it seems to be all voice, and of the loneliness of its single note piercing the rocks

The stillness –
Shrilling into the rocks
The semi's cry

Basho wrote another haiku a year later (in 1690), that ended with the same words

yagate shinu	Soon to die
keshiki wa miezu	But you show no sign
semi no koe –	Voice of the semi

There is something immensely poignant about the semi. It spends ten years imprisoned in its cocoon, then bursts out – but it has a life span of no more than ten days. For those ten days, it lives with all its might. It mates, lays eggs and yells as loud as it can – then dies. Thinking of this I was sad not to hear its ear-piercing noise.

koe ni mina	Did you shrill and shrill
naki-shimaute ya	Till you were all voice?
semi no kara	Semi shell

At last I came to a massive gateway, stuck with prayers. Above me, scattered across the mountain-top, were temples, dozens of them. Some were large, some tiny, perched on impossible crags or balanced crazily on stilts, jutting out over the cliff. Others were built into caves. On the far side of a plunging chasm, with only one flimsy ladder to cross it by, were caves which had been sealed up, the mouths covered with wooden lattices. Here, presumably, hermits had lived in retreat. Perhaps they still did.

'Get a job in the factory down the hill – money's better down there!'

'Can't be worse than up here!'

Voices and shouts of laughter came floating down from a wing of the main temple building at the top of the hill. Those, at any rate, were not hermits.

A final flight of steps led up to this temple which Basho had 'edged round the cliffs and crawled across the rocks' to reach. I had been expecting a magnificent structure here at the heart of the mountain. But in fact it was small and humble, rather faded and worn, built so deep into the mountain it was like a part of it, surrounded by cliffs and forest. It was the mountain that was the temple. This was just a symbol of it.

To the left was a small open room, like a shop or office. Business, apparently, was slack today. Behind the shelf of amulets, lucky charms, prayer books and souvenir chopsticks, five or six priests were sitting around playing cards. All but one had discarded their white robes and stripped down to singlets and there were bottles of saké and bowls of peanuts around the floor.

I coughed. They looked up. One, hastily shuffling on his robe, assumed a stern priestly air and sold me an amulet.

I smiled to myself. No one but a foreigner like me, I suspected, would even notice the incongruity. As far as the old farmers who came to worship were concerned, priests had a job to do, most likely the job which their father did before them. If they were holy men, that was an added bonus; but no one expected it of them.

Tacked up beside the door of the temple, a few yards away from the raucous priests, was a sign. I grinned when I read it: 'SILENTLY worship please', it said in large characters. Another read, 'No naked worshipping'. Did people really use to come here naked on hot summer days, I wondered?

I paused at the enormous incense burner to waft incense over myself (to ensure long life) and started off back down the hill. Clouds were scudding low, half obscuring the misty hills opposite, and the rumble of trains and lorries rose from the little town straggling, toy-like, up the valley below.

I had missed one thing on my way up. Near the statue of Basho was a notice-board with, written above it, the legend

'Ryushakuji – Haiku Contest'. I read some of the bedraggled slips of paper pinned to the board. Most were not haiku at all. Many were along the lines of the first one I looked at: 'Walked all the way to the top, my feet are sore, signed, Yoshi'.

One, though, was inspired. Along the lines of Basho's famous and much-maligned Matsushima haiku (*Matsushima ya/Aah Matsushima ya/Matsushima ya*), some wag, yearning perhaps for chicken kebab (*'yakitori-ya'* means 'chicken kebab shop'), had written, *'Ah yakitori-ya, yakitori-ya!'*

Into the Hills

9
'Smoke of breakfast tea'

Kawashima picked me up at the foot of the mountain and we drove off back across the Yamagata rice fields. The clouds were lifting at last and brilliant shafts of sunlight lit the hills on the horizon, leaving the plain in shadow. Black tumuli stood out here and there among the fields like giant molehills.

We left Route 13 and drove through villages of wooden houses with paddy fields in every available space – tiny square ones squeezed in between houses, long narrow ones between the houses and the road. Oblivious of the traffic a couple of yards away, an old man was hoeing between lines of rice plants. We turned down narrower streets. Old people wobbled along on ancient bicycles, all wearing hats – straw bonnets, straw sunhats with huge brims, white scarves, scarves over hats, hats over scarves. The furigami man cycled slowly by in a baseball cap, pulling a cart piled high with old newspapers, singing out a mellifluous little tune like the rag and bone men used to when I was a child

> 'Furigami kokan,
> furigami kokan,
> furi-gami,
> furi-shimbun –
> Old paper,
> old newspaper . . .'

And every now and then there was a powerful country smell: sometimes manure from the fields, usually just plain sewage from the drains and toilets.

Then the houses petered out and we came to a river, broad, limpid, coiling languidly below the level of the fields, with

small bamboos swaying on its banks and dark hills rising close
behind. Here and there were fishermen and a spindly grey
heron was standing in the shallows. 'Mogami river,'
announced Kawashima as we turned along it.

He quoted Basho: 'The Mogami river rises in Michinoku and
the upper reaches are in Yamagata. There are terrible rapids
here called Goten and Hayabusa.'

At Goten the river narrowed and frothed. With the help of a
little imagination the rocks could have been flat and evenly
spaced enough to be Go-ten, the counters you use for playing
Go.

At Hayabusa – 'peregrine falcon' – we stopped for coffee.
The coffee shop was the first building we had seen for miles, a
lonely shack at the side of the river with a half-submerged boat
tied up beside it. The mama-san brought coffee for Kawashima
and icecream for me, then pulled up a chair and sat down with
us, wielding a showy cigarette holder. She was small, stocky,
dressed like a farmer's wife in pinny and trousers; but I have
never seen a farmer's wife with hair like hers – short, spiky
and chestnut brown.

While she chatted, husky-voiced, with Kawashima (mainly,
as far as I could understand, about the weather and the state of
the rice) I was daydreaming. By now we were very close to the
western hills, the mysterious mountains of Dewa. I wondered
idly if there was a road into them, a short cut perhaps through
to Oishida. I had been cosseted for long enough. It was time to
be walking again.

Some words of Basho kept running through my head,
something he had written on an earlier journey, about ambling
along in his own time. I was trying to remember how it went.
Later I looked it up.

As I have no home, I have no need of pots and pans. As I
have nothing to steal, I have nothing to fear on the roads. I
need no palanquin but amble along in my own time, and my
coarse evening meal tastes better than meat. There is no
particular road I have to follow and no particular time I have
to set off in the morning. Each day, there are just two things I

have to bother about: whether I'll find pleasant lodgings that evening, and whether I'll be able to get *waraji* (straw sandals) that fit my feet – that's all. Time after time new sights stir my spirit, day after day my feelings are kindled.

We were skirting the foothills when we came to a crossroads. There were a few buildings – some empty warehouses, a house with a woman breastfeeding a child on the doorstep and, a little way away, the steel tanks of a saké factory. Ahead, the road continued through the rice fields towards Oishida, perfectly straight. To the left the hills were so close by now that I could make out the pine trees on their slopes. A small road wound off and disappeared enticingly between them.

'It's still early. I'll walk from here,' I said to Kawashima.

He was not as disapproving as I had expected. 'Make sure you call our Ocaasan, our Mother,' was all he said, meaning his wife.

I waved until he had disappeared from sight, feeling rather small and alone out there in the middle of the plain. Then I shouldered my pack and turned towards the hills.

The road led past a large pink plaster school and then a field of flowers, some yellow, some red, spiky like thistles, a little frayed and tattered – *benibana*, 'rouge flower', safflower. Safflower is not the important crop it used to be (in Basho's time the 'floating world' of Edo and Kyoto depended on shipments of it from the north for rouge and lipstick and red dyes) but it is still a symbol of the area. These were the first safflowers I had seen – a whole field of them, like a good omen.

mayuhaki o	Image of
omokage ni shite	A lady's eyebrow brush
beni no hana	Red safflower

At the point where the paddy fields ended there was a vegetable patch with runner beans on poles, purple perilla plants, green aubergines, cucumbers, tomatoes. A woman was watering, wearing the biggest hat I had seen yet, like a doormat tied over her head. An old man in a baseball cap dozed under a tree. Right behind, the hillside rose like a cliff, tangled in forest.

Then the road started climbing and the landscape changed abruptly. I was back in the mountains, in desolate country, tramping through the passes. The only sound was the crunch of my feet on the gravel and the whine of a semi. It didn't look as if many people came this way. The road was narrow and broken, overgrown with gorse and long grass and wild flowers, hemmed in with cedar and birch woods. All around were hills.

A road with no cars on it, in Japan of all places . . . That boded ill. Perhaps I should turn back before I got any deeper into this wilderness.

I turned a corner. In the distance was a small house at the edge of the road. Nothing but a cowshed, I realised, as I came up to it, rows of thin black cows in stalls, swishing their tails hopelessly at the cloud of flies around them.

The strangeness of it didn't strike me at first, though later I realised that they were the first I had seen since I set out on this journey. At the time, I took it as a sign of civilisation. I hurried on eagerly past a bridge and a waterfall, turned another corner and stopped with a gasp of delight. The looming mountains were behind me and I was out of the pass, on a hillside, in sunlight. Trees and tall frail bamboo swayed and rustled. Between the shifting leaves were glimpses down into the valley far below.

It was as if I had stumbled into Basho's world. Where were the wires and pylons, the factories and pre-fab houses of modern Japan? The valley was hugged by dark forested mountains and carpeted with paddy fields, brilliant green, slotting into each contour like pieces of a giant jigsaw puzzle and climbing in scallops along the lower slopes. There were farmhouses with plump thatched roofs tucked into the folds of the hills; and from somewhere a child's voice floated up through the silence.

It was a magic place. For a while I stood and looked, reluctant to break the spell. I was thinking of a haiku Basho once wrote, long before he set off for the deep north. It was dawn, 'before cock crow', and he was riding along half asleep, letting his whip dangle. Suddenly he woke to see a welcoming wisp of smoke, far in the distance.

uma ni nete	Dozing on horseback:
zammu tsuki toshi	Lingering dreams, distant moon,
cha no kemuri	Smoke of breakfast tea

The season was different, the time of day was different. But I had the same wonderful feeling of arriving, of welcome.

As I ambled down the mountainside, pausing often to stop and look around me, the valley seemed to grow more and more beautiful. It was all bursting with greenness and the water in each stepped terrace shimmered in the sunlight. Huge yellow butterflies settled on the road and for a while a dragonfly hitched a lift on my shoulder.

'This is where I stay tonight,' I told myself. But it seemed unlikely. There was no inn, no *ryokan*, no *minshuku*, nothing but farmhouses scattered along the road, on closer inspection older and shabbier than they had looked from the hillside. Among the thatched roofs were others of red or blue slate. And by some inexorable logic most of those that had thatched roofs had sad tin walls and those that still had wooden walls had garish tiled roofs.

Further along the street was a shop, the only shop in the village. Shyly I slid open the door, wondering what sort of people lived here and how they would take to a foreigner.

The woman in the shop didn't seem to see my foreignness. 'Somewhere to stay? See the headman,' she said, or words to that effect; her accent was so strong it was almost impossible to understand her. As I stood hesitating she picked up the phone and a couple of minutes later a little white pick-up was rattling down the street. I jumped in. We swung round, drove back a hundred yards, turned up the hillside and stopped outside a faded old wooden house topped with a thick head of thatch.

The headman was small, cheery, slightly stooped, with a crumpled face and bristly grey eyebrows permanently raised in an expression of good-natured bewilderment.

'I'm Kuroda.' He waved for me to sit down. His hands were huge with big cracked nails, indelibly engrained with dirt. 'We're all Kuroda here – those that aren't Hayashi, that is.' His wife, a silent, rather faded woman, served iced barley tea and, despite my protests, started to bring out dishes of food which she laid on the table: rice crackers wrapped in Cellophane, slices of cucumber, tiny pickled aubergines the size of a thumb, kernels of corn.

'Twenty households we are,' he said. 'Eleven Kurodas and nine Hayashis.'

'Are you all cousins?' I asked.

'Cousins?' he chuckled. 'No, no.' A century or two ago country people had no surnames, and when the shogun came to distribute them, people in the same village were all given the same name.

He talked and talked, punctuating each sentence with vigorous nods, and I listened, trying not to stare rudely at the gaping hole in his front tooth and musing on the cost of dentistry in Japan. Eventually, exhausted from the effort of trying to understand, I sat back and contented myself with nodding and grunting at what seemed appropriate places.

Finally we had had enough pleasantries. It was time to come to the point. 'Might it be possible to stay?' I asked. Was there perhaps a *minshuku* in the village or a family I could stay with? 'If possible I'd like to stay . . .' As he spoke I had been thinking. 'I'd like to stay four days.'

Kuroda's eyebrows shot up so high they disappeared into his thatch of grey hair. 'Four days?' he repeated, gaping in disbelief. 'You want to stay four days? But what for? There's nothing here. Of course, if you want to stay . . .' he added quickly.

The village did get visitors from time to time, up from Tokyo. But one day was the longest they ever stayed. Some came 'because the air here is clean'. Some came to climb Mount Hayama. All that was understandable. But no one ever came simply to visit the village. No one could possibly be interested in this little village for its own sake! After all, there was nothing here – no famous temples, no shrines, no pilgrimage sites, no hotsprings, certainly no hotel. The only place to stay would be with one of the farmers who took in the occasional mountain climber or itinerant worker for a little extra money.

'Anyway,' he added, forehead wrinkling, 'what will you do for food?' I didn't need meat or bread or coffee, I explained, and couldn't think of anything I would enjoy more than rice and vegetables.

Finally he was reassured.

'You can stay at Kojiro,' he said, once again the urbane village headman, efficiently making arrangements. Then, all boyish enthusiasm, 'Now I'll show you our village!'

Outside the sun was shining and the sky powerfully blue. Wisps of cloud hung deep in the valleys between the hills. Notched into the horizon, not far away, was the point from which I had first seen the village. Below, interrupted first by the road then by the river, the hillside stretched greenly away, sculpted into shallow steps packed with rice plants which rippled gently in the breeze. To the left, half hidden between clumps of trees, was a row of brown thatched roofs. I felt a million miles from the nearest main road or the nearest town – yet it had been less than an hour's walk to get here. I looked and looked. It was like a scene from an old ink painting – as near Paradise as I was ever likely to see.

I admired Kuroda-san's two ponds (one for carp, one for trout), his goat and two chickens, then clambered back into the pick-up and we rattled and bumped another couple of hundred yards up the street and shuddered to a halt in front of a rambling wooden house.

'My relatives' house,' said Kuroda-san. A little brown dog tied up outside was straining at its leash and barking shrilly as we walked past.

We had not come to see the relatives. On the other side of the house, beyond the flower beds, was a pool full of greenish water with bushes on three sides and a huge rock at the far end, as big as any of the houses in the village. It was like a wall, as smooth and moss-free as if it had only recently been chiselled off the mountain behind.

'*O-ishi*,' said Kuroda-san solemnly. 'Big Stone.' I grunted in a way which I hoped communicated amazement and awe. Perhaps that was where Oishida, *O-ishi-da*, Big Stone Field, got its name.

'"*Namu myoho rengei kyo*", it says. Benkei it was wrote it.'

Benkei? Now I really was interested. I screwed up my eyes and peered long and hard at the blank grey rock face. Eventually I decided I could see some scratches, but nothing that by any stretch of the imagination resembled the famous prayer of the Nichiren sect.

'Difficult to make out, isn't it?' said Kuroda-san sympathetically. 'Can't see it too well myself,' scratching his head. 'Can't see it at all today, in fact. You could read it quite clearly when I was young,' he concluded wistfully.

'He fasted, you see, Benkei did, fasted for seven days. To test his strength. Then pressed his knee and his hand on to the rock. He was weak, you see – hadn't eaten all those days. But he still made a dent, he was that strong. I've seen it myself with my own eyes. A big hollow, big as this' – stretching his arms out wide – 'with his knee, and five little hollows with his four fingers and his thumb.'

This was too much, even for me. Still, I was touched that even this remote village cherished legends of Benkei and that its magnificent Benkei Stone was the first thing to be shown to passing strangers. And maybe I was wrong to be sceptical. Perhaps they really had passed through here on their way to Hiraizumi.

Did Yoshitsune come too, I asked Kuroda-san. Did they stay here? Did the village exist at that time?

Kuroda-san thought hard, ruffling his grey hair with his big hand until it stood up like a hedgehog's bristles. 'Well,' he said slowly. 'It's in the *Kojiki*, you know, our village – the Record of Ancient Things. And up there', jerking his head towards the notch on the horizon, 'they've been digging, to widen the road. Dug up a skeleton. Three hundred and fifty years old.' He nodded emphatically as if that proved it.

'They're talking about building a dam up there,' he added, enthusiastic as a schoolboy. 'Up by the waterfall – came in that way, didn't you? To flood the valley.'

'Flood the valley?' He said it so carelessly I didn't understand the significance for a moment. 'So . . . you'll all have to move out?'

'It's for water. And electricity. They're flooding all the valleys.' He seemed quite unconcerned. Perhaps he simply couldn't imagine the consequences. Or, in the usual Japanese way, wasn't going to concern himself about it until it happened.

So even this last remnant of Basho's Japan was not safe. If I came back next year, the road would be wider, there might be a factory or two; or perhaps the whole place would be under water. Progress in Japan was as fast and as destructive as that.

It was night by the time Kuroda-san drove me up to where I was to stay. He turned off the headlights and shuffled on ahead, leaving me in complete darkness. The sky was a dome of stars. Hoping I wouldn't put my foot into a wet muddy paddy field, I felt my way along the side of the house. A chorus of bullfrogs was sounding off deafeningly like foghorns. Semis were shrilling, dogs were barking and somewhere unnervingly close to my feet was water, rushing.

Above all this noise, I could hear old Kuroda-san at the front door, bellowing 'Oh! Oh!'. I couldn't help smiling. While you might bawl '*Oi!*' at your wife who would come scurrying with tea or saké, visiting the neighbours, even close ones, was usually a serious matter, surrounded by protocol. You phone up first, buy gifts, then, at the appointed time, slide open the door and call discreetly '*Gomen kudasai* – Excuse me, anyone at home?' then wait hesitantly in the entrance until your host appears. Then follows a long pantomime in which the host apologises for the smallness and dinginess of the house while begging you to step up, while you apologise for the meanness of your gift and for causing him such trouble and insist that you can't possibly impose on his hospitality.

By the time I reached the door, the lady of the house had come out to meet us and was standing barefoot on the wooden floor, a good foot above the earthen area where we were taking off our shoes. She was chattering excitedly as Kuroda-san finished off his greetings, a bare *'O-sewa-sama-su'*, 'Thanks for taking care of us'.

She and I took to each other immediately. She was a strong, handsome woman with a magnificent sculpted face, broad and full, a tiny nose and huge welcoming smile – a true Ezo matriarch. She too was Kuroda-san. But I knew immediately what to call her. Of course, she was Ocaasan, Mother.

She turned on an ancient cast-iron electric fan which groaned and spluttered and blew out dusty explosions of air, then spread cushions around the table and brought tea and crackers and more tiny pickled aubergines. Old Kuroda-san, eyes twinkling, began to introduce me, regaling her with what I took to be an imagined history of my life, with plenty of embellishments. She looked at me, beamed, laughed, spoke, laughed again merrily. She had a big hearty laugh, not the cramped shy giggles of city women. But there was one thing worrying me. Whatever tongue she spoke, it was quite incomprehensible, a succession of barbarous sounds which were nothing like Japanese. I was afraid it was going to be impossible to communicate.

I retired early and sat quietly for a while in my room at the top of the house, listening to the noisy bullfrogs groaning and croaking in the fields outside. It was a big, spacious room, ten or twelve mats, with an alcove where I hung my clothes and another with a scroll of the seven jolly gods of good fortune, some wooden images (including fat Hotei with his sack) and a bottle of saké. Already it felt like home. I brushed the dead insects off the table – a hopeless task; more kept coasting down from the neon light like ashes from a bonfire – spread out my books and opened Basho.

'We wanted to take a boat down the Mogami river, so we waited for fine weather at a place called Oishida.' I was a little off course, but not much. Oishida was just the other side of the mountains, maybe an hour and a half on foot, minutes by car.

For Basho and Sora it was a six-hour trek from Yamadera, the mountain temple, back across the rice plains. They took horses as far as Tendo then trudged on, through the very same villages they had passed on the way down, and at two o'clock in the afternoon, the hour of the sheep, arrived 'at a prosperous house' in Oishida.

Oishida and Obanazawa are separated by no more than a mile or two of paddy field. In Basho's day they were twin cogs, twin hubs, in the communications network of the north. Oishida was if anything busier than Obanazawa, for it was the great port where merchants gathered to ship their rice and safflower down the Mogami river to the Japan Sea coast.

In those days there was no road across the wild Dewa mountains and the river journey was long and dangerous. It took a month for a laden boat to reach Sakata on the coast and many were lost on the way. Canny merchants spread their goods between several different boats so that if one or two sank they would not be completely ruined. Once the boats had reached Sakata, the problems were not over. The cargo was unloaded and put into storage, then left to rot for weeks or months until a ship was ready to transport it down the coast to Kyoto.

In the Oishida Minzoku Shiryokan (folkcraft museum), which I visited while I was staying in the village, there are paintings of the white straw-roofed Oishida houses along the river front and the famous river boats setting off in flotillas, square white sails swelling in the wind, painted with the symbol 'Rice' or 'Safflower' in bold black brush strokes. They look like Turkish slippers, with curling pointed prows and a flat base to carry them easily across rapids and shallows. Each had a paddle and a long pole for punting. They were basically cargo boats. The passengers had to crouch among the sacks of rice, safflower and lacquered trays and plates, and the only shelter was a straw canopy in the centre of the boat.

Like Obanazawa, Oishida was a town of inns, crowded with merchants and travellers, and it too had become a cultural centre. Basho was welcomed. He met the headman, a certain Ojoya-san, and stayed with a local poet and pupil of his, Takano Ichie, for three days until the weather cleared. There was nothing much to see in the town: no historical relics associated with Yoshitsune, no holy places or places mentioned in poetry. For most of the three days, Basho sat as teacher, guiding the local poets in his particular school of linked verse.

It must have been a long time since a poet from the capital had visited this remote outpost of culture. ' "Here the seeds of the old style of linked verse were sown, and, mindful of its flowering, we continue to practise in the old way. Our hearts are as rustic as the notes of a reed flute and we walk this road (the path of poetry) with uncertain steps, wandering confusedly between old and new ways. We need someone to guide us" – so they insisted and I left them a round of linked verse. *Kono tabi no furyu, koko-ni itareri*: Thus I brought the poetic spirit of this journey as far as this remote place.'

Takano arranged a poetry gathering at his house and with Basho guiding and a local poet called Takakuwa making the fourth member, they composed a sequence of verse. It was usual for one of the junior members of the group to record the poems. But at Oishida, as a special favour, Basho wrote them himself and left behind a scroll, now the proud possession of the Shiryokan, covered in his spindly writing.

As I woke next morning, I smelled wood smoke, 'smoke of breakfast tea', and wondered if I was still dreaming. Sunlight was dappling the tatami. I slid open the window, almost afraid that the beautiful valley too might have been a dream. There were the misty hills and terraced paddy fields, just as they must have been in Basho's time.

The semis were already shrilling and somewhere just out of sight water was rushing like a waterfall. I ran out to find it. Kojiro, my new home, was on the edge of a hill. It was a big, imposing farmhouse with gables and a broad thatched roof topped with a long beam holding the thatch in place, curved at the end like the prow of a ship. Wedged into the narrow strip of land between the house and the hillside was a pond, crowded with thin black trout, jostling against three fat watermelons tied in a net in the corner. Water – the source of the noise – spouted into it through a long bamboo pipe, then gushed out the far end and down the hillside, zigzagging through tiers of vegetables and flowers into the network of channels which fed the rice fields in the valley. There were fields beside the house too, all irrigated with channels of gurgling water.

Inside, my hostess was waiting for me. 'Look at the size of these!' she beamed, holding up three thick green celery-like stalks. It was easier to understand her this morning; I was getting used to her accent. 'Found them up in the woods on Mount Hayama. Big, eh? I'll cook them for you for dinner.' She showed me all the stalks she had collected, heaped on bamboo trays. '*Fuki*,' she said. I looked it up: butterbur, coltsfoot.

While I ate breakfast (*aomidzu*, a green, stringy stalk that was not in the dictionary, yellow chrysanthemum flowers, salted mushrooms which she had picked in the mountains last autumn and, of course, tea) Ocaasan was busy on the telephone. There were two phones, one standard and one for calls within the village, which were free. The second one also played music, night and morning, and delivered information about village events. 'Hate that thing!' Kuroda-san had grumbled the previous night when the music tinkled out. 'Wish you could turn it off!'

I listened to her chatter, concentrating hard, trying to understand. 'Philippines, Philippines,' she was saying excitedly. I realised she was talking about me. 'No, no – England,' I called. She laughed, corrected herself, then made another call. 'Australia', I heard. I gave up and returned to my meal. By the third call, I was from Ethiopia, by the fourth Italy.

It didn't really matter where I came from. I was *yoso no hito*, someone from outside the village, not really all that much stranger than the people from the next village along. Ocaasan had little notion of the world beyond the valley, let alone beyond Japan. She had never been further afield than Tateoka, the town that Basho and Sora passed through on their way to the mountain temple. Certainly she had never been to Tokyo – 'No time,' she laughed; though the woman over the road had been once, forty years ago. Old Kuroda-san, now, that was another matter. He went off to Tokyo every year, when the snows came, and stayed away till spring; he had a brother to stay with there.

But she did go on visits with the local Ladies' Group to

nearby temples and showed me a picture of herself outside one, with the women from the village, in a row, all in bonnets. Other photographs came out: two faded pictures of young men in uniform – her brothers, who died in the war, one in the Philippines, one in Russia; her son, a white scarf around his head, performing a series of dramatic postures – the annual rice-planting dance. Next I admired her three daughters' wedding photos, hefty country girls posing uncomfortably in stiff brocade kimonos and mask-like white make-up. 'My two eldest grandsons are at university,' she said in tones of awe. 'Imagine – a grandson of mine at university!'

Finally she brought out a yellowing picture of a young man in army uniform, outside a tent. 'My husband,' she said, suddenly old and small and sad. 'They sent him to Manchuria and he got ill. He was never very strong. He was in hospital six months. It's ten years ago now since he died – he was only fifty-seven. It was his stomach. Three years and eight months he was ill, then he died. People nowadays live to eighty or ninety – but not my husband.' It was almost as if she blamed him for it. She looked at the picture for a long time then said slowly, 'He died when he was only fifty-seven.'

None of the villagers had ever met a foreigner before and Ocaasan was anxious to show me off. I was equally anxious to meet them. First I had to put on a pair of her plastic outdoor sandals, several sizes too small – my strange foreign ones would never do. Then we shuffled off together around the village, unceremoniously shoving open doors, barging in and yelling 'Oh! Oh! *O-sewa-sama-su!*'

The houses were big and old and, for Japanese houses, surprisingly dirty. The tatami rooms where the family lived by day and slept at night were fairly clean, but I didn't feel comfortable walking barefoot on the dusty wooden floors of the hallway and toilet or in the greasy kitchens. There were plenty of corners which a broom couldn't reach, thick with cobwebs and dust. There were no flush toilets, of course, just a malodorous hole in a little tiled room at the far end of the corridor or out by the woodpile, where one squatted uneasily,

fearful (at least in my case) of losing a plastic toilet slipper, a
purse or a pair of spectacles into the cesspit.

The old man next door had a wasps' nest in his entrance way
and bunches of drying herbs hanging over an ancient wood-
burning stove. The beams were black with smoke. He and his
wife sat outside in the sunshine, patiently sorting coils of
coloured wires and threading plastic toggles on to them.
(Something to do with the inside of a car engine. Everyone in
the village was doing it, peering at complicated diagrams,
ripping their fingers trying to prise the wires apart. 'Not much
farming work in the summer,' explained Ocaasan. 'Can't
waste time.' And no one knew how much they were going to
be paid. Not much, I suspected.)

'My birthday today,' announced the old man. That much I
understood, though his accent was, if anything, thicker
than Ocaasan's. 'Seventy-five years old. Oldest man in the
village.'

'Ask to see the *tokonoma*, the alcove,' whispered Ocaasan.
'He'll like that.'

In the alcove, watched over by photographs of the emperor
and his family and the ancestors, a row of solemn-faced
matriarchs and patriarchs, was an extraordinary clutter of
things. The old man had a story for each. There was a stuffed
badger standing on its hind legs, wearing a cap and an apron
with *'Kotobuki'* – 'good fortune' written on it, and a stuffed
grouse; he had caught them and stuffed them himself. There
were the seven gods of good fortune, two bonsai trees he had
grown, a cask of saké, colourful dolls in glass cases which one
son had brought back from Okinawa, and a wooden bear
which another had brought from Hokkaido.

'Four sons and two daughters,' said the old man wistfully.
'All in Tokyo.'

Last year the second son came to visit, bringing the grand-
children with him. This year no one had come. The two old
people sat alone in their big thatched house.

House after house was full of grandmothers and grandfathers. Fat pale babies crawled between coils of wire and
heaps of plastic toggles while we sat sipping iced tea and

chatting. There were no young people; they were all away at work.

I met Grandad over the way, the village bear-hunter, and Grandma who kept silkworms. In the house on the corner were two more Grandads, both old soldiers, one a veteran of Manila, the other of Manchuria.

Grandad up the road, a bright-eyed elf of a man with pointed ears and tufty grey hair, still climbed the mountain every day to chop wood and tend his charcoal kiln. Hanging in a dark corner of the entrance way was a straw raincoat, almost as worn and battered as the one I had seen in Basho's hut in Iga Ueno.

'That's an old one. Wear it to carry charcoal,' he grinned.

He showed me his new one, like a bird's plumage, pale gold, thick and heavy and fresh-smelling. He had made it for himself last year, of woven rice straw. I fingered it with reverence. It was certainly waterproof – though I had never expected to meet people who still wore these things.

'I'll make you some straw sandals, dear,' beamed his wife. 'Big ones, because you're so big.'

She was right. When we all stood up, I felt like Gulliver in Lilliput. Even Ocaasan barely reached my shoulder.

I listened entranced to their tales of bear-hunting and eating bear meat, of silkworm-keeping, the rice harvest, the winter snows – 'boars rooting up the rice shoots, plagues of rabbits in the bean fields'. Here among these old people I was in a world that Basho would have recognised.

On the way home we cut through buckwheat and mulberry fields, past gardens of hollyhocks, pink and red, hydrangeas and wild daisies. We stopped beside a large shed. While Ocaasan chatted to a thin lively woman in a headscarf and pinny, I wandered in. It was hot, even hotter than outside, and musty, full of cardboard trays like giant egg boxes, hanging in mid-air.

'You don't know what those are?' Ocaasan guffawed. My ignorance of absolutely everything common and everyday was a source of huge amusement to her. 'Silkworms! Silkworm cocoons!'

They were like feather-light quails' eggs, soft and dry and brittle. The woman laughed too, kindly, then put one of the pale green caterpillars in my hand.

Basho wrote about the silkworms when he was in the region

hai ide yo	Crawl out!
kaiya ga shita no	Under the silkworm shed
hiki no koe	Voice of the toad

Once we were outside again I glanced surreptitiously at the bottom of the shed but there was no room at all there for a toad. Sora's haiku was

kogai suru	Silkworm keepers –
hito wa kodai no	Like figures from
sugata kana	Antiquity

'It was better in the old days,' said the woman. 'Used to watch the butterflies coming out. That was nice.'

'White ones,' said Ocaasan.

'Then wind the silk off. Nowadays a truck comes for the cocoons. We never see the butterflies.'

In the past, everyone kept silkworms in their houses. In the summer you couldn't move for all the cocoons. But now most people had given up.

'Lot of trouble, feeding those worms every day,' said Ocaasan. 'Young folks now, they'd rather go to work.'

Back home, we started preparing dinner. Ocaasan's son got in a few hours later. He was the village thatcher, as his father and his father's father had been. But there was not much work for thatchers any more. No one wanted a new thatched roof; they were too expensive to maintain. So he worked as a carpenter or did labouring jobs in nearby villages.

With his great cheekbones, high forehead and dark skin, he should have been riding across the Mongolian steppes, not hammering houses together. He sat at a corner of the low table in the living room, watching television, a glass in his big carpenter's hand.

'Oi!' he shouted every now and then. 'Saké!'

His wife would creep out from the kitchen with an

enormous bottle and fill his glass. She never spoke and kept her eyes averted. She wore a plain pink dress and white ankle socks and looked less than twenty; it was hard to believe she had been married ten years.

Old Kuroda-san had told me their story. When his father died, the son brought home a bride. (No one ever spoke of getting married; it was always 'bringing home a bride' or 'coming as a bride'.) But in ten years they had still not produced any children. That, I knew, was a tragedy, not in personal terms (that was irrelevant) but for the 'house', the family. No children meant the end of the family line – no one to till the family fields and, much more serious, no one to tend the ancestors' graves and make offerings to them. 'No one knows whose side the fault is on,' Kuroda-san had said, hissing through his teeth and shaking his head.

After dinner a car drew up outside and there was a hubbub of voices. Ocaasan rushed out. 'Just the relatives,' grunted the son, sipping his saké. The doors slid open and people crowded into the room.

Ocaasan's sister-in-law was first, a thin sprightly woman with a face covered in tiny wrinkles and a perpetual smile. Then came her son, Toshiyuki, and two of his children. They all lived together in the village up the road, just beyond the big stone.

Ocaasan introduced me. 'From Italy,' she said.

'England,' interrupted her son wearily.

'Shake hands with the foreigner,' Toshiyuki said to his little son. Foreigner? Among the villagers I had almost forgotten that I was one. To Ocaasan I was always 'Lesley-san'.

Still I smiled and held out my hand like a foreigner to the little boy. He looked sulky and put his hands behind his back, but his sister stepped up and timidly touched her hand to mine.

Silently the daughter-in-law spread cushions on the floor and brought out more saké and snacks – cobs of sweetcorn, pickled Chinese cabbage and fresh soya beans in hairy salted pods. There was also a bowl of large sautéed grasshoppers, complete with legs and antennae. I looked at them uneasily.

Ocaasan picked one up with chopsticks and offered it to me as if it were a special treat. There was a hush. I was going to have to eat the thing. I took a deep breath, shut my eyes and put it in my mouth.

'Lovely!' I exclaimed, picking a little black leg out of my teeth. Everyone roared. I'd passed the test; though I desperately hoped they wouldn't offer me a live one. I had meant it, too, and took another. It was sweet and crunchy, flavoured with soy sauce.

'Karushiyaam,' said Ocaasan approvingly, 'calcium'. Not much in their diet was rich in it, but grasshoppers certainly were.

Toshiyuki took a mouthful of saké and grinned. 'You can't be English. Why don't you have blonde hair and blue eyes?' He was a large, ebullient young man with a big bush of hair and a merry laugh.

'Wives – that's what we need up here,' he said. 'No one comes as a bride any more. They all go to Tokyo and marry salarymen.'

In the old days if you were told to go as a bride, off you went; everyone married whomever they were told to. But now, in these two villages alone, there were three eldest sons who were thirty and still couldn't find wives.

Down the road in Okura village, he said, things were desperate. There were two hundred unmarried farmers there. Unless they found wives quickly, the whole village would die out. A couple of years back, ten of them had decided to look abroad. They spent a week in the Philippines, where there were villages full of unmarried girls who needed husbands. By the end of the week, all of them had chosen a wife and married them and they all went back to Japan together.

None of the girls spoke a word of Japanese. But that, said Toshiyuki, was not a problem. The only person they had to worry about was the mother-in-law. And, to please her, all they had to do was cook some nice Filipino food.

All this was leading up to an important request. He leaned forward and said very seriously, 'When you go back to your country, send us some English girls – blonde ones!'

Ocaasan and her sister-in-law, Obasan (Aunt), had vanished into the next room, where they kept the family altar. Every house in the village – probably every family in Japan – had one of these huge up-ended chests, gleaming black, inlaid with gold and mother-of-pearl. Inside was a gold tablet for each ancestor, inscribed with name and dates, and on the wall photographs of Ocaasan's husband and his parents and grandparents. There were always vases full of fresh flowers in front of the altar, and bowls of fruit.

The two women reappeared, rocking with laughter, holding strips of gold paper, and gave them to the daughter-in-law, sitting mouse-like in a corner. She seemed to shrivel even more under all the attention.

'Prayers,' explained the son. 'For people who can't have children. Someone has to give them to you – they don't work if you go and get them yourself. Take them to a temple, pin them up, pray to Kannon, then you get a child. We have no children,' he added, in case I had missed the point. 'That's why they're giving them to us.'

He gulped down a mouthful of saké and said, 'Drinking saké is another way of making children. Come back next year and we'll have a baby to show you!'

Everyone roared with laughter. I smiled uneasily. As with Toshiyuki's request, I didn't know if they were joking or serious; perhaps both.

Next morning I announced that I was going for a walk; I wanted to explore some of the little footpaths that led off into the mountains.

'On your own?' gasped Ocaasan in tones of horror. 'No, no – you'll be lonely! I'll come with you.'

I wondered if she knew what loneliness was. Ever since I had been here I hadn't felt lonely once. I had had no chance to; I was never alone.

What range of emotions did these people experience? Different from ours, I suspected. For a start, they all had arranged marriages. As old Kuroda-san said, 'Myself, I like a little saké; but the wife doesn't touch a drop. That's the trouble with *o-miai*. You don't know what the other person is like, or whether you'll get on.' It was a practical, sensible way to marry – but hardly romantic. Sometimes, of course, the couple fell in love; often they just made do and perhaps never felt that kind of love in their lives.

They probably didn't miss it. They didn't seem to feel part of a couple but part of a 'house', part of a family – and part of the village. They led an intensely communal existence. Whatever they did, they did together. No one was ever isolated. The young people took care of the old people, the old people took care of the babies and they all took care of each other.

In the end we compromised. Ocaasan was far too busy to come with me; I had taken up enough of her time already. We agreed that I would go up to see Toshiyuki and his family and that she would phone to say I was on my way.

Once I was out of sight I turned off the road and walked down between rows of sweetcorn and aubergines to the dazzlingly green rice fields, noisy with trickling water and honking frogs. There were old people in wellingtons up to their knees in the water, hoeing and weeding – an endless task in the rainy season, when you can see everything shooting up day by day. They all knew me by now and stopped to wave and smile.

A white headscarf turned out to belong to Grandma from two doors down. She was stooped right over, scything grass from the verges. She straightened slowly, one hand on her back, beamed and said, 'Where to?'

'Up there,' I said, pointing to the hill on the other side of the fields. I had decided on a short detour before going to Toshiyuki's.

I had left the fields and was strolling up a stony path along the hillside when I saw a large handwritten signpost. Even with my limited Japanese I read it immediately. BEARS – BEWARE, it said. Suddenly I no longer felt like an adventure. I scuttled back down the hillside, glancing nervously behind me.

Toshiyuki had told me he had a small shoe factory in the next village, about fifteen minutes' walk away, at the far end of the valley. Toiling along the deserted street in the midday heat, I

was relieved to see that there were no gleaming factory chimneys among the flower-beds, moth-eaten thatched roofs and
tattered wooden houses.

Finally I came to a corrugated iron shed with an enormous
noise of rattling and clattering coming out of it. There was
Toshiyuki at an ancient cast-iron machine, busily stamping out
shoe uppers from a sheet of stiff black leather. He called over
his wife Junko, a rosy-cheeked, merry woman, and two girls
and an old man left their machines to meet me.

Ocaasan's daughter-in-law, I knew, worked here. I looked
around for her but at first couldn't see her. She was sitting on
her own around a corner, cutting out shoe soles and smearing
them with glue. I had been hoping that she made up for her
dreary evenings at home by enjoying herself in the day and
was sad to find her alone and silent here too. So her dominant
mother-in-law was not the only problem. But at least her
husband was fond of her. On the Sunday they went off
together for a drive and Ocaasan spent the entire day
complaining bitterly about being deserted.

Obasan appeared, a white headscarf knotted around her
head with a straw hat as big as an umbrella tied over it and
a baby – Toshiyuki's latest – strapped to her back. As always,
she was smiling, gold teeth glinting in the sun. She must have
been pretty when she was young; she had small delicate
features, quite hidden now under a tracery of tiny lines.

She took me back to her house for tea, bundling away the
bedding still spread in a heap in the middle of the main room,
and brought out photographs of her wedding to show me – a
young girl with a fresh, lovely face. 'We're all pretty when
we're young,' she chuckled. 'But you know the saying – when
you get old, you turn into a monkey.'

I supposed it was an arranged marriage, I said.

She laughed again. It was much simpler than that. 'We are
relatives, this house and mine, relative houses. Mother-in-
law, my husband's mother, went down to Kojiro, where I
lived. "Please give us Ayako," she said – that's me. So I came
up here as a bride. That was it. It was nothing to do with me
really.

'That's the way it was in those days. We didn't worry about such things. Now it's different. My daughter went off to Yamagata and married a bus-driver – not even a farmer! I thought she should have married a farmer. And my other daughter married a taxi-driver from Kaminoyama.'

Through the bamboo awning shading the window I could make out paddy fields and the slope of the mountain covered in trees, just outside.

I asked her where the road went from here. 'Nowhere really,' she said. 'Some valleys, some villages. Comes out at the Mogami river.' In effect it simply bypassed Oishida and rejoined Basho's path at the river. I had come too far now to turn back. I had to go on along the road.

It was my last morning in the village. Reluctantly I had packed my bags and was having breakfast.

'You can't go,' wailed Ocaasan. 'I haven't made bean jam for you yet!' Some village children had burst in and were playing noisily on the floor while their mothers sat drinking tea. 'What will you do, all on your own?'

She came down to the road to wave me off. She had made *onigiri*, some of the morning's rice pressed into balls, and insisted I take them with me. As I passed the village shop, the shopkeeper beckoned me in and gave me a pair of little straw boots, big enough for a doll. 'Made them myself,' she said. 'To remember us by.' Kuroda-san's wife ran down from her house with a big bag of plums and, groaning inwardly at the thought of the extra weight, I shoved them too into my bag.

10
The Gorge

I turned away from the notch on the horizon that pointed the way back to civilisation and took the road along the valley, through the village, up past the big stone and on, skirting the edge of the hill, to Toshiyuki's village and the shoe factory. The machines were already clanking and rattling busily. I took my pack off, leaned it against the wall and went in to say 'Goodbye'.

Everyone but Toshiyuki was there. They all stopped work – Obasan with Toshiyuki's baby on her back, Junko his smiling wife, the two girls, the old man, even Ocaasan's sad daughter-in-law – and came to wave me on my way. It was as if I'd known them for years, not just a few days, and I felt a pang of sadness as I walked away. But it was soon forgotten in the excitement of being on the road again with my belongings on my back, heading off towards somewhere unknown.

tabibito to	'Traveller' –
wa ga na yobaren	Let that be my name
hatsu shigure	First autumn showers

The little houses and sparkling paddy fields came to an abrupt end and the mountains closed in again. In a moment, when I looked back, the valley had vanished as completely as if it really had been a dream. There was nothing all around but trees and steep hills, long grass and wild flowers sprawling across the road. It was a perfect day for walking, like an English summer's day, cool and breezy, with snatches of cloud drifting across a sky much too blue really to be England. I tramped along cheerfully, day-

156

dreaming a little, wishing I could identify more of the flowers.

There were wild daisies, bushes covered in tiny white blossoms, huge yellow trumpet-like flowers, towering trees with shiny green leaves that might have been camellias, and flashes of purple in the grass at the edge of the road – violets.

Violets on a mountain path . . . It reminded me of one of the first haiku I ever learned and of my old calligraphy teacher in Gifu. She lived in a concrete house next to her husband's concrete dental hospital, somewhere out in the industrial flatlands on the corner of two main roads; though once you were inside it was a traditional Japanese house, all wood and tatami. Shizuko was her name. '*Shizu-ko*, "quiet child" – only I'm not quiet!' she shrieked when she introduced herself, cackling with laughter. I spent the entire week practising the haiku, trying to get every brush stroke exactly like hers, until it was impossible to forget it. Though it wasn't until now, seeing the purple violets beside the path, that I realised why she had liked it so much.

yamaji kite	Coming along a mountain path
nani yara yukashi	
sumiregusa	Somehow it tugs my heart –
	Wild violet

I used to kneel by the low table in her living-room for hours, so absorbed in grinding the ink and writing and rewriting the haiku that I never noticed that my legs were completely numb. When it was time to stand up I would have to straighten them inch by inch, closing my eyes and gritting my teeth as the blood came rushing back. I was the only adult in the class. Even the tiniest children made more graceful brush strokes than mine – though most of the time they were chattering and giggling, jarring the table just as I was in the middle of a long flowing stroke. I used to have black ink stains on my fingers for days.

There was another of her favourites which Basho had written on the same journey, in 1684:

michinobe no	Mallow flower
mukuge wa uma ni	Beside the road – eaten
kuwarekeri	By my horse!

It was a moment of enlightenment – 'like Zen', she used to say. Basho was jogging along, perhaps along a road like this, when his horse suddenly lowered its head and chomped up a white flower. Basho, startled, saw the humble flower and its beauty at the moment that it disappeared for ever.

A rustling in the undergrowth jerked me too into the present. A snake? A bird? A rabbit? Or one of the bears come down from Mount Hayama? I scuffed my feet noisily, wishing I had tied a bell to my ankle as Toshiyuki had suggested. Bears, he had assured me, had no more desire to meet me than I had them. So long as they knew I was coming, they would keep out of my way.

There was another valley on the other side of the pass, with a village, no more than a line of houses, even older and more battered than the ones I had left behind, perched on a shelf of land high above the paddy fields, the hillside soaring up close behind. The place was silent and empty, though far below in the fields were a couple of small figures, hoeing.

I walked along looking for a shop and eventually saw a tiny dark house by the side of the road with a sign swinging outside saying 'Coca-Cola'. I slid open the door. In the gloom inside was a strange assortment of goods: shelves of mountain vegetables in bottles – slimy grey stalks, green butterbur, grey horsetail shoots, and some I didn't recognise; dusty packets of crackers and biscuits; huge tins of dried milk for babies (that must be why they were all pale and fat); a *maneki nekko*, money-beckoning cat of white plaster, two foot high; and, to my relief, a fridge full of cold drinks and icecream.

I called '*Gomen kudasai*' a few times. When that had no effect I bawled 'Oh! Oh!' until a woman banged open the mosquito screening which served as a back door. She had on gardening gloves and a straw hat pulled well down over her head. I bought an icecream and she gave me a stool to sit on while I ate it.

From here the road turned into a narrow, gravelly track which climbed steeply between thick forests of cedars, chestnuts and walnut trees. I plodded on more and more slowly, endlessly up and up. The air was thick with insects – huge dragonflies darting against my face, brilliant butterflies coasting languidly, bees, hosts of flies, semis shrieking invisibly from the trees. The path was littered with dead dragonflies and semi shells.

It was afternoon by the time I reached the top of the pass. I was well above the tree line by now, in dry, barren country covered with scrub and bushes. I slumped on a rock and ate a couple of plums, grateful as much for the loss of a few ounces of baggage as for the sweet juiciness. It was a long time since I had walked so far. My feet were sore and chafed from treading the stony track in thin sandals and I wondered how I would manage another step. The mountains stretching away to the west looked higher and more rugged than any I had seen in Japan – and less hospitable. Surely no one could live here but those legendary hermit priests, I thought, wondering where on earth I would spend the night.

I heaved myself grimly to my feet and hobbled off again, on across the parched ridge and back down into the woods. Suddenly I found myself at the edge of a cliff. In front, the hillside tumbled away almost vertically. The mountains opposite were so close that I could see the trees bristling on their slopes. Beyond them were more mountains, receding, range upon range, paler and paler blue, until they faded to nothing on the horizon. Far below, squeezed between hillside and mountains, was a long narrow valley with a single road threading along the edge, dotted with toy-town houses.

The path zigzagged down the hillside into the gorge, to the tiniest, most remote village I had ever seen. I could hardly believe that this was still Japan. On one side towered the cliff where I had been standing, white limestone crags with forest overhanging at the top and a narrow river bordered with trees meandering along the foot. On the other were mountains, very steep and very high, already darkening the valley with their shadows. The village was no more than a few tattered wooden houses scattered along the lower slopes, some thatched, some roofed with red or blue slate, with vegetable patches squeezed in between, straggling upwards till they were lost in the forest. A patchwork of paddy fields filled the valley bottom, not a neat chequer-board but crammed higgledy-piggledy into the curves of the hills, all different shapes and sizes.

As I stood at the bottom of the hill taking all this in, a car, the first I had seen since I left that morning, came rattling around a corner, along the one village street and across the fields towards me. Surely, I thought, he couldn't be planning to drive up that rough mountain road?

It drew level and a familiar face hung grinning out of the window.

'Where to?' asked Toshiyuki.

I very nearly hugged him – which possibly would not have shocked him as much as I thought. I was so tired I would happily have jumped in and gone straight back to the village with him.

'Is there anywhere to stay here?' I asked. 'Do you have any relatives here?'

He shook his head.

'No problem,' he said. 'All you have to do is ask.'

He manoeuvred the car around and drove me down into the village. But the place was deserted. There wasn't even a shop.

'Which house do you fancy?' he asked, serious and business-like. 'Old one? New one? Thatched roof? Slate roof?'

'Old,' I laughed, getting into the spirit of the thing. 'This one,' as we came to a faded old farmhouse with a thatched roof.

'Good choice,' he said. 'Good and big. Bound to be a spare room.'

He marched up to the entrance and I followed behind. The door was open but there was a broom diagonally across it.

'Means they're out,' he explained. Burglars were not a worry here.

I was getting embarrassed now. I didn't want to burst into someone's house and force them to put me up.

'It's all right,' grinned Toshiyuki. 'This is what travellers always do.' He was enjoying himself. 'There's the house for you. Best house in the village.'

We drove up to a huge and beautiful two-storeyed house with a roof of moulded grey slates and heavy wooden shutters, intricately carved. I had had enough of this game by now. But Toshiyuki, ignoring my pleas, strode up to the door, shoved it open and pushed into the house. I crept in miserably behind him.

He was standing in the narrow entrance way, looking as large and bulky as Benkei.

'Oh!' he yelled. 'Oh! Oh!'

There was silence. He yelled a few more times. 'No one in,' he said, to my relief.

We were about to leave when a woman appeared out of the dark recesses of the house and stood looking down at us. It was shadowy inside and hard to see clearly, but she stood as if she were quite old, her knees bent, slightly stooped. Toshiyuki, I was glad to see, looked a little taken aback but said politely enough that he was from two valleys away, over the mountains, then gestured at me and asked if I could stay.

'Been staying with us,' he said. 'She's all right, no trouble. Speaks Japanese.'

The woman wasn't concerned about language. 'But what about food? She won't be able to eat our food,' she said. 'She'll need bread and meat, won't she? What do you think, Gran?' An even older woman, her lower back so badly bent that her face was on a level with her knees, had hobbled out to have a look at me and was sitting, legs folded under her, on the raised floor.

I was still tugging at Toshiyuki's sleeve, trying to get him to give up, when the woman said suddenly, 'I guess it's all right. She can stay.'

Feeling rather forlorn and abandoned, I waved him off. 'Don't forget now! English girls – blonde ones!' he shouted as he rattled triumphantly away.

I watched until the car had disappeared then went slowly

inside and sat myself awkwardly in the main room, wishing he had been less impetuous. Without speaking, the younger of the two women brought in tea, then set rice, pickles, miso soup and two small bowls, one containing strands of shiny black kelp, the other sautéed aubergines, on the table in front of me. As I was eating, Granny crept over and knelt close beside me, her legs disappearing under her like a concertina.

'The girl upstairs,' she whispered into my ear, as if she were letting me in on a dark family secret. 'She can't speak and she can't hear.'

So there was some kind of madwoman locked away upstairs, like Mrs Rochester in one wing of the house. I finished off the scraps of food uncomfortably, glancing around the great shadowy room with its high ceiling, blackened beams and single bare light bulb with flies circling around it, wondering what sort of place Toshiyuki had brought me to. The younger woman reappeared with two more bowls of soup and rice. The two small dishes had been for all of us, not just me. I had eaten all their lunch.

Above me, the noise of sweeping had finished. A pretty girl in red peeped smiling around the staircase and beckoned me up to my room.

A stray shaft of sunlight lit the polished wooden hallway upstairs and the large rooms off it, separated by sliding doors of thick beige paper. Through the delicate fretting over the windows I could see the village meeting house and the fire tower, a miniature Eiffel tower with a ladder up to the small platform at the top and a big warning bell. At the side of the house, directly under the window, were cowsheds.

The younger woman was watching as I opened my bag. On the top were the straw sandals that the charcoal-burner's wife had made, enormous ones for my enormous foreign feet, with red thongs – 'red for good luck' – made by Auntie over the way.

The woman darted forward, snatched them out of my hand and started poking and prodding, pushing the strands of straw apart with her knobbly fingers.

'Aren't they well made!' She looked up and gave me an

intimate smile. 'Go and show them to Granny.' Suddenly we were friends.

This new Ocaasan of mine, my new 'mother', had a face like a berry, round and brown, fringed with wiry black hair cut very short, usually hidden in a white scarf. She looked as if she had worked hard all her life. Her face was creased and weathered and blackened from the sun, her hands rough and engrained with dirt and her clothes working clothes – a shapeless cotton T-shirt stuffed into cheap tracksuit trousers. The family, she said, was called Sato; as were all the other families in the village.

'Come on!' she called. 'We'll go and get something for supper.'

She tugged on wellingtons and made me put some on too, then hobbled off on legs so bent and twisted that she bobbed along supporting herself on a stick, one hand holding her back. 'I'm only fifty,' she said, 'that's all. But my back's already all crooked!'

First we climbed to the village shrine, at the top of a long flight of rough stone steps which led straight up the side of the mountain. From outside it looked old and uncared for, the unpainted wood cracked and warped. Ocaasan tugged on the bell then heaved open the outer door and, beckoning me to follow, knelt down to pray. Inside was spick and span. In front of the altar was a big drum and some bottles of saké. Hanging from the ceiling were bright paper cranes, thousands of them, on long strings, revolving slowly in the breeze which wafted through the open doors.

'Yakushi Nyorai,' she said – the shrine of Yakushi Nyorai.

We pushed on up the hill, Ocaasan, for all her bad back, way ahead of me. I kept an eye on the little figure bobbing ahead confidently between the trees while I stumbled after, picking my way gingerly along the steep hillside, clambering across tree trunks, tripping over thick tangles of root.

Suddenly she disappeared. By the time I reached the place where I had last seen her, the bushes and branches far below were shaking wildly lower and lower down the hill as if something were falling through them. I stood bewildered, wondering what to do. I didn't even know my way back to the village to look for help and it would soon be getting dark.

Then the bushes began to shake in an upward direction and eventually she scrambled back out, bits of leaf and twig sticking in her hair. She shook the earth off some fat brown roots and dumped them in my bag.

'Look at this.' Her face crinkled into a smile and she held out a huge horse chestnut. '*Tochi!*' – a conker – 'Fancy finding one in July! Pity it's too old to eat. You keep it.' She thrust it into my pocket.

We stood for a while looking out through the pines and thick bushes down to the valley. To our right, where the mountains began, it narrowed and disappeared into the shadows of a deep gorge, walled by pale limestone cliffs. Water sparkled from tiny paddy fields carved into every available nook and shelf of flat land.

'Bears up there.' Ocaasan screwed up her eyes and stared across into the hills. 'House over the way, they're hunters. There was a huge one they caught the other year – how long ago was it now? Everyone wanted some. I didn't get any, there was such a rush. I was so disappointed! After all, it's not every day you get bear meat, is it?'

To our left, the road wound thinly along the valley.

'Shinjo,' she pointed. 'Do you know you can get there in forty-five minutes now?' The village was right at the end of the valley, in the heart of the mountains, as deep as you could get, a long way from anywhere. Not so long ago, Shinjo was half a day's walk away; and in the winter, when the snow was six or eight feet deep, everyone just stayed home.

'It's all changed now,' she said. 'Used to come up the mountain a lot when I was young. But no one makes charcoal these days; no one keeps silkworms, either. They all have cars, two or three a house. All go down to Shinjo, to the canning factory.'

A jolly little Walt Disney tune came floating up, repeated again and again, relentlessly cheery, like background music for some film I had suddenly found myself in. Surely . . . some surrealistic, little-known Fellini film. I wanted to laugh. Everything was suddenly thrust into relief – what different worlds we belonged to, how irreconcilable our perceptions were. Perhaps it was akin to the moment when Basho's horse ate the white mallow flower.

Ocaasan was oblivious to the intrusion from another world. The music grew louder and louder, then stopped and was replaced by a woman's voice, hideously amplified, reciting rhythmically like a mathematical table: 'peaches, plums, biscuits, bread, milk, yogurt, crackers, fish cakes . . .' Way below a small white van trundled slowly along the road.

On the way back we stopped at the vegetable fields to pick aubergines, cucumbers and beans, then plodded home and squatted at the carp pond outside the house to wash them.

Inside, a paunchy heavy-jowled man in a vest was sitting in the main room. All the other men I had met in the valleys were sinewy and black from working in the fields. But he was as pale as I was, soft and spreading, with hair cut so short you could see the pink scalp underneath. He yawned, stretched big flabby arms, looked at me, gave a friendly smile and turned back to the television, a bulky old-fashioned one which took up one corner of the room. He was engrossed in high volume baseball.

The three women of the house were in the kitchen while I, as the guest, had been left to be entertained by father. As I jumped up to go and help, I felt my hair catch on something sticky. I put my hand up and with a shudder closed my fingers on a strip of crackly yellow paper, curled at the edges, stuck with dead flies.

There were more flies in the kitchen, live ones, settling on the plates of food spread on newspaper on the wooden boards and buzzing around Ocaasan, who was squatting barefoot, peeling the mountain roots she had pulled up. It was one of the grimmest kitchens I've ever seen. It was huge and empty, lit by a single dim bulb somewhere high up among the blackened beams. Apart from the floorboards, which had gummed paper taped over the cracks, there was nothing in it but a rather striking tiled sink with two taps, both for cold water (one tap water, one well water), and a two-ring gas cooker.

Granny held out some wilting flowers in a withered hand. 'Can you do anything with these?' she croaked in a half whisper. Her seventy-seven years had bent her back until she was doubled over but she had a startlingly beautiful face, fine-boned, aristocratic, with delicate Ezo cheekbones and pale translucent elderly skin.

'Give them to Naoko. She's good with flowers,' said Ocaasan.

The girl in red had been stirring something on the stove. She took the flowers then smiled at me almost coquettishly. I followed her into the big bleak main room with the television blaring. We knelt silently side by side and she showed me how to trim the dead stems and leaves. Then she put the flowers one by one into a vase, leaning back every now and then, tilting her head critically to one side, frowning and pursing her lips with the air of an artist creating a masterpiece. She was as out of place here as I was. She had on a blouse and bright red skirt, clean and well-pressed, not grubby trousers and pinny like everyone else, and her pretty face was carefully made-up, more like a city secretary than a farmer's daughter.

Father shifted a little, scratched, yawned noisily and at length and called out with the same good-natured smile, 'Supper ready yet?' He turned to me, still smiling, and said, 'Good life we have out here, eh?'

He did, certainly. Perhaps I am maligning him; but all the time I was in the village, I never saw him do anything except eat, drink tea and watch television. The women were perpetually busy, weeding the rice fields, working in the vegetable gardens, cooking meals, while he sat large and immobile in the main room. It was hardly surprising he was so cheerful.

'We can't eat yet,' croaked Granny. 'We have to wait for Grandad. He's in Shinjo . . .'

She crept close beside me and added in a whisper, '. . . playing pachinko. Goes to Shinjo every day to play pachinko. We say he's at work, that's what we say. But he isn't. He's playing pachinko. He comes back on the seven o'clock bus.'

She made it sound like another of the family's dark secrets. Having met 'the girl upstairs', deaf and dumb Naoko, I doubted if Grandad either would turn out to be as sinister as he sounded. I was looking forward to meeting this rakish old man who frittered away his days and his money at the pin ball machines in the sinful neon-lit pachinko parlours of Shinjo.

Naoko was pouting and making harsh shrieking noises as if she resented me speaking to anyone else. She beckoned me to follow her and we went upstairs together.

Her room was next to mine and, like mine, large and unfurnished. Only mine, though, was plagued by the horrible *kusa mushi*, 'smelly insect'. There were swarms of them, flat pale green diamond-shaped bugs which whirred relentlessly round and round the light and dashed against the walls and against me. Whenever they hit something, they gave out a cloying sickly sweet smell which permeated the room and clung to my clothes for days. I never managed to think of a way of driving them out without injuring them.

Naoko had set up a small dressing-table and mirror on the tatami in the middle of her empty room and had her make-up arranged in rows on it. She knelt in front and painted a thin line of red around her lips, then carefully filled it in, looking at me in the mirror to check that I was watching. Silently she brought out books and pictures to show me.

She opened an exercise book and wrote 'What is your country?' then passed it to me. I took it and wrote 'England' in reply. So, slowly and laboriously, with frequent consulting of the dictionary on my part, we managed to communicate. She had worked hard at school, she told me, had even studied English and dreamed of going to America. She managed to escape as far as the huge sprawling industrial city of Kawasaki, just outside Tokyo, and worked in a factory there for two years. A few months ago, she had given up and come home. She wouldn't say why. And here she was, doubly trapped – trapped by her handicap and trapped in this tiny remote community, centuries behind the rest of Japan. I was very sorry for her. She was bright and pretty and yearned for the world outside the valley. Unlike the others, she had been there. She knew how different it was.

'Let's go to Shinjo', she wrote, in big clear child-like characters so that I could read them. She looked at me, wrote 'Shinjo – very good', smiled prettily and gave an emphatic thumbs up sign. 'Let's go and have coffee in Shinjo'.

Shinjo, Shinjo. It was like shorthand for everything that was missing from the valley. To Granny it was a dreadful den of vice, full of pachinko parlours. To Naoko it was coffee shops, department stores, beautiful clothes, hairdressers, dancing, neon lights. I didn't need to go there to know what it was like: arcades of noisy shops, plastic flowers sprouting from lampposts, big bright pachinko parlours with music blaring and neon flashing, concrete streets full of cars and buses and motorbikes, a mesh of wires crisscrossing overhead . . .

'No time,' I wrote, feeling guilty and unkind. Her face snapped shut sulkily.

Later she wrote, 'Do you have a boyfriend? I do. His name is Yoshio. He is coming this evening to take me to Shinjo.'

At seven o'clock the heavy outer door ground open. It was not Yoshio but a dignified old man in a bowler hat. He stood silently in the entrance way, very upright, like an old soldier, thin and gaunt. Showing not the slightest surprise at my presence, he went to change and reappeared in a big blue cotton *yukata*, dressing-gown.

After dinner we all sat together around the rusty stove in the centre of the room; there were no cushions to sit on. Even in the heat of summer, there were a few sticks of wood burning and an old kettle simmering on top. Something – perhaps the smell of wood smoke – made the place feel immeasurably backward and primitive, as if centuries of history had never happened; or at least had never penetrated as far as this remote valley.

I sat quietly, looking at the broad high-boned faces and listening to the burble of voices. When they spoke among themselves it was difficult to understand much at all. *N'da n'da* they went – that much I had picked up – when in standard Japanese you would say *so desu*, 'that's right'; *n'da ga, n'da bé* instead of *so desu ka, so desho*, 'is that so?', 'that must be so'.

Ocaasan and Granny called themselves *oré*, 'I', and me *omae*, 'you'. I had never heard women use words like that before. *Oré, omae* – the kind of words that gruff old farmers use, or workers in cloven-toed boots or strutting yakuza, drinking chummily together, slapping each other on the thigh, usually when there are no women about. No one had ever called me *omae* before. At first it was startling, almost shocking. Then it came to feel curiously intimate, as if I were part of the family, not someone other who had to be addressed using special polite words.

These valley people, as far as I could see, didn't have any of the vast bulk of polite language that fleshes out Japanese: different words for 'I' and 'you', for 'I am' and 'I go', 'you are' and 'you go', depending on whether you are a man or a woman, of an upper or lower class, speaking to an inferior or a superior. All those little social niceties that are embalmed in the language and somehow prevent a foreigner from ever becoming part of the society, simply didn't exist here. I felt more at home, less foreign, than I ever had anywhere in Japan.

Grandad took a mouthful of saké and turned sternly to me. 'You find a nice man and settle down,' he said. It went against the natural order of things that I wasn't married. 'Young people today don't have enough will to marry', speaking slowly to make sure I understood. 'And then what happens to the parents? There's no one to perform the funeral, that's the danger – and the line is broken.'

I smiled and nodded.

'Where are you going from here?' he asked.

'Dewa Sanzan,' I told him. 'The sacred mountains. Mount Haguro.'

He had been there, he said. Five or six times. The first time, he was fifteen; he had walked it in two days. I listened with excitement. So the sacred mountains were only two days away . . . I was impatient to be on my way.

He had gone with a group of friends. Five or six together. Five or six, five or six – like an incantation.

'How many in your group?' he asked. I had been dreading this question.

'Only me,' I answered. 'I'm going on my own.'

'Surely not! Not on your own!' He shook his head heavily, not so much in disapproval as sheer disbelief. What was the world coming to?

Father insisted that I leave them my address in England and I wrote it out in capitals very clearly. He took the paper, looked at it, turned it upside down, scratched his head, grinned hugely. 'You expect me to copy all those squiggles when I write to you?'

I was amazed. Everyone in Japan, I had thought, learned English, or at least the Roman alphabet, at school. There was English everywhere – shop signs in English, T-shirts and carrier-bags and notebooks with English on them, television adverts peppered with English . . .

Father was bent over an exercise book, still grinning. Licking his pencil and wrinkling his forehead like a school boy, he set about laboriously copying my hieroglyphs, writing the L back to front and the W upside down. Naoko was shrieking with impatience. She snatched the pencil and wrote quickly, then passed me the book. There was my address, neatly written, and under it, in Japanese, 'Please write to me from England!' I promised I would.

Back in my room, I was getting ready for bed when my hand closed round the conker in my pocket, round, hard, corrugated as these brown Ezo faces. (As I had suspected, no 'Yoshio' had appeared.) I took it out and put it on the table.

In the autumn of 1688, the year before Basho set off for the deep north, he made a short journey to the village of Sarashina deep in the mountains of Kiso, in central Japan. He wanted to see the harvest moon over Mount Obasute, a remote and desolate peak where, according to the stories, people used to take their old mothers and abandon them to die. The sight of the autumn full moon here was said to be particularly beautiful and moving.

He had two travelling companions: his friend and pupil Etsujin and a servant whom another friend, Kakei, had sent to help out along the steep and dangerous mountain road. Both, as it turned out, were completely inexperienced travellers, and as a result 'everything was disorganised and back to front, and many amusing things happened'.

They had started into the mountains when they met an old priest – the very one who later on disturbed Basho's concentration so much with his chatter that he couldn't write a poem. He was about sixty, 'with nothing interesting or amusing about him', and was plodding painfully up the narrow path, stooped under a heavy load of luggage. Basho's companions felt sorry for him and heaped his luggage on to the horse. As a result, Basho had to travel precariously perched on top of a huge swaying pile. It would, of course, have been unthinkable for the great poet to give up his horse to the old priest, even though he was fifteen years younger; he was after all a *sensei*, a master.

They journeyed higher and higher into the mountains. 'Beetling crags and wierdly-shaped peaks piled up one on top of the other way above our heads; to our left, far below, at the foot of a ravine which looked a thousand *hiro* (fathoms) deep, a great river rushed; there wasn't a single square *shaku* (foot) of level ground. Perched up on my saddle I was far from calm; nothing but danger and frightening moments following one after the other.'

Basho was so nervous he got off the horse and let the servant ride instead. Even on foot he was afraid and dizzy by now with the altitude. They edged along a mountain path with so many turnings it was called the Forty Eight Bends and scrambled trembling with fear across a rope bridge suspended high over a gorge.

kakehashi ya	Hanging bridge:
inochi wo karamu	Clinging for their lives
tsuta katsura	Ivy and katsura vines

The servant was completely unaffected by all this. Once he was comfortably settled on the horse, he started to nod off, as Japanese travellers do. Basho, plodding along behind, watched in horror as his head dropped lower and lower and he swayed dangerously first one way, then the other, as if he would topple off any minute and plunge over the side of the cliff. 'Many times he nearly fell off; just watching from behind I was terrified.'

Eventually they reached Sarashina without any dreadful accident. That night the sky was clear and they were able to see the full moon. 'Truly I felt to the full the sadness of autumn'.

On the ground was a conker. *Tochi*, horse chestnuts – which the fine aesthetes of Edo, the pleasure-loving people of the 'floating world', never looked twice at – were food for the mountain people. What more fitting souvenir (*miyage*, local product) to bring back from these wild parts? So Basho took it back to Kakei, the kind friend who had lent him the servant.

Kiso no tochi	Kiso horse chestnut
ukiyo no hito no	For a man of the floating
miyage kana	world
	My gift . . .

11

Down the Mogami

I woke early and heaved open the wooden shutters. Outside it was still cool. Mist hung low in the valley, parting here and there to reveal a great gnarled rock, a clump of dark twisted pines, a glimpse of ghostly white crags looming over the paddy fields, wisps of cloud curling at the foot.

In the silence the plaintive strains of an *enka* drifted across the fields. Somewhere not far away, hidden in the mist, a woman was singing, one of those sad sobbing ditties that Japanese love so much. A small figure in blue, head swathed in a white scarf, hurried past in front of the meeting house. Further along, children in pinnies and grubby trousers were playing in the road. It was so medieval, it wouldn't have surprised me if two figures dressed in black like priests, with straw hats slung on their backs and staffs in their hands, had appeared around a corner, scuffing along in their straw sandals down the valley towards the river.

I would happily have stayed a few more days. But I had loitered long enough. It was time to rejoin Basho. From here on there would be no more interruptions. I wasn't going to stop again until I reached the sacred mountains.

Early though it was, everyone else had been up for hours. My breakfast was waiting on the table, covered in a wire mesh to keep off the flies: rice, miso soup, *aomidzu* (a green celery-like wild vegetable) and a brown gooey mass which slithered from the bowl into my mouth; it turned out to be the fat brown root which Ocaasan had dug up on the mountain, grated raw.

'Going by bus, aren't you?' said Ocaasan. I had told her I was going to walk, but she still hoped I would see reason. 'You can go on the eight o'clock with Grandad.' He was off to Shinjo as usual, to 'work'.

As the road curved around a corner and the house vanished from sight, I turned for a last look. They were all standing watching and waved and bowed when they saw me stop. There was Granny in her pinny, all bent; pale grinning Father with his big stomach; Ocaasan with her brown berry face; and Naoko hovering behind, elegant in her red skirt, waving feverishly. That was the trouble with all this travelling – having to say goodbye.

okuraretsu	Now being seen off
okuritsu hate wa	Now seeing off – the end of
Kiso no aki	all this?
	Autumn in Kiso

– or in my case, summer in Mogami.

Still, I was excited to be on my way and set off in high spirits, my back nearly as bent as Granny's under the weight of all the *onigiri* (rice balls), home-made *mochi* (rice cakes), pickles and plums which they had insisted I take. A few minutes later, the bus overtook me with a roar. Through the window Grandad gave a regal wave.

Then I was on my own. The road wound off, clinging to the edge of the mountain, following in and out along its curves.

Every now and then I came to a tiny remote village, nothing more than a few tattered houses perched forlornly on outcrops of land high above the fields, with thin cows tethered, cropping the scrubby grass. Some of the houses looked as if no one had lived in them for years. The roofs were falling in and grass and lilies sprouted from the thatch. There were no shops, of course. But in each village there was a fire tower and a tumbledown shack with the characters for 'Meeting House' written on the rusting iron wall.

Mainly there was nothing to see but stepped paddy fields and steep wooded hills soaring up on each side of the valley. The rice must have been about a foot high, glowing green, and the wind which rushed up between the hills sent long ripples across it like waves. Down in the fields some peasants in straw hats and wellingtons were weeding. Somehow they no longer seemed alien now, but like the people that I knew.

Gradually the valley grew wider and the hills lower and the road began to wind uphill. The top of the pass was marked by a small wayside shrine, two rocks one on top of the other. In the lower one was an indentation, a natural basin brimming with rain water. Someone had left a rusting tin ladle laid neatly across it. Some characters like a prayer were carved on the upper one.

I sat on the grass and looked back at the valley, wishing I could have stayed longer. Water was splashing noisily along irrigation channels on each side of the road and a semi was shrilling in the rocks. Then I heard music, a tinny little tune somewhere in the distance, coming closer and closer. Finally I made out the words: 'Ladders, washing poles, ladders, washing poles', again and again. A blue truck bristling with ladders and long broom handles – the second vehicle I had seen that day – appeared over the top of the hill and trundled off down the valley the way I had come.

Reluctantly I picked up my pack and trudged off. Ahead was an endless sea of rice, broad and flat, greenly rippling. The mountains on the horizon looked as far away as ever.

But now there were shops. First there was one, all alone at the side of the road, an old wooden house badly in need of rethatching, with sacks of seeds and rice stacked outside and flower pots tied together in bundles. Inside were dark shelves with a few dusty packets of crackers and biscuits and a fridge full of icecream and cold drinks. Then came more and more until there was a whole village of them, even a bicycle shop and a chemist's, lined-up along the road with the sparkling paddy fields just behind, stretching away to the horizon.

I was tramping through one of these small villages, feeling the sun on my head and wishing I had a hat like everyone else, when a woman on an outsize tricycle pedalled slowly by, calling out 'Where to?' as she passed. She had a round button face and a warm smile and baggy country clothes – a long loose pinny, baggy brown trousers and a white scarf knotted round her head. On the back of her tricycle was a wire basket with a large blue bucket wedged into it.

'Furukuchi,' I called back.

'On foot? It's a long way,' she shouted. She was well ahead by now.

Fifteen minutes later we met up again. She was on her way back, the lid of the bucket propped in the basket. I asked what she had had in it.

'Tofu,' she smiled, stopping this time – beancurd. She had been up since four in the morning, preparing a special order of it 'for those people there,' gesturing to a large house set back from the road among trees. 'They're having a party.'

'Not from the Philippines, then, are you,' she added. It was a statement, not a question.

Rather mystified, I agreed that I wasn't.

'Knew you weren't Japanese,' she beamed, pleased with herself. 'Thought you must be one of those Filipina brides. That's why I said hello. But your Japanese is too good. "Good morning", "Good afternoon", "Thank you", that's all they can manage. Friendly girls, though.'

I was still puzzling over this half a mile later when I came to a signpost. There was the name of the village – Okura, where unmarried girls were so rare that they had had to send to the Philippines for brides.

On the other side of Okura, the road began to climb. Below, the paddy fields spread into the distance like a giant chessboard of brilliant green squares outlined in darker green, as flat as a well-tended lawn. A narrow river meandered between sandbanks on the far side of the plain. I stopped to rest and gaze at the pale line of mountains on the horizon. Which, I wondered, was Gassan, the highest of the three sacred mountains?

I struggled on. It was well past midday and the sun was blazing.

At the top of the hill, in the shadow of a grove of pine trees, was a coffee machine, offering hot and cold drinks. I suppose at another time it might have seemed incongruous, this gleaming metallic obelisk in perfect working order, in the middle of remote countryside. But today it seemed quite natural, quite appropriate, just what one would expect to find all alone at the top of a hill – and delightfully Japanese. I put in my coins and the machine rewarded me with a little tune as I took my Vitamin C Juice (properly chilled, of course) and a woman's voice thanked me politely for my custom.

Around the next corner, on the other side of the grove, was something stranger. It was a huge painting of the moon, enormous and pock-marked, and some planets against a black sky full of stars. I pondered it for a while, then trekked around it (it was the size of a small house). In fact, it seemed, it was a screen, like the screens the Okinawans build in front of their doors to ward off evil spirits. Behind it was the entrance to a forlorn holiday camp of concrete chalets with alternating red and blue slate roofs, huddled between the woods and a field full of rice. Then I noticed a sign: *Tsuki sekai*, 'Moon World', in yellow neon on blue, and underneath two smaller signs, 'Rooms Available' (green) and 'Rooms Full' (red). 'Rooms Available' was lit up.

Of course. It was a love hotel, probably used quite innocently by young farmers and their wives – maybe even some of the people I knew – when the perpetual presence of their parents became too inhibiting. Despite the grim exterior, the interiors of the chalets, I was sure, were as gorgeous as any other love hotel: plaster statuary, a fountain perhaps, a revolving bed with mirrors above it and red velvet drapes, a pink spangled bathtub, 'adult videos' and a karaoké machine in case the lovers became bored before their two hours were up.

By now – five hours after leaving the village – I was nearly at the river. Another turn in the road and I had my first sight of it, high and brown, rolling ponderously between wide banks, dark forested cliffs soaring behind.

samidare o	Gathering the rains of June
atsumete hayashi	Swift rushing –
Mogami gawa	Mogami river

Then it disappeared and the road plunged into a shanty town of decaying tin shacks, littering the hillside right to the river bank. This, according to my map, was a town, dignified enough to have a name. Though, looking at the torn walls, flimsy as cardboard, and rusting roofs, it was hard to believe that anyone lived here. I walked slowly, tired now and saddened by the squalor. I guessed that it meant I was not far from the main road. My private escapade along some truly narrow roads was over.

Down a side turning between the tin roofs, I caught a glimpse of stone pillars. They stood guarding the edge of the water, two of them, massive and imposing, wide at the base and tapering towards the top, with four faceted sides – evidence that at one time the place had been more important and prosperous than it was now. They must once have flanked a boarding pier, though now there was no sign of it, not even steps down to the river. The road came jaggedly to an end above a precipitous drop to the pebbly shore and the sluggish brown river, a good thirty feet below.

Beside them, engraved on an old wooden signboard, faded but still legible, was the name of the place: Motoaikai. I deciphered the characters, suddenly full of excitement. Purely by chance, I had stumbled on the precise place where Basho boarded the river boat to go down the Mogami.

I sat down on a rock beside the pillars and opened Sora's diary. Basho didn't mention the long trek to Motoaikai. He left his readers to assume that the two travellers took the boat from the great river port of Oishida. As I pored over Sora's antiquated Japanese, I was remembering the lively evenings around the table in Obanazawa; it had been only a few days ago, but already it seemed like another world.

'Don't forget', Kawashima had said, helping me with the difficult sentences, 'that it was five years before Basho wrote the *Narrow Road*. He sorted through everything that happened on the journey and selected the most interesting and poetic things. That's why he doesn't mention Motoaikai. It's a poetic creation, not an accurate record.' Though, he added, shaking his head over the old poet's perversity, the travellers should have taken a boat from Oishida; it would have been the best place to board.

Basho and Sora were held up for three days at Oishida. On the first, wrote Sora, there was heavy rain. 'Tired, so wrote no haiku', he added. On the second it rained a little in the evening, on the third it was cloudy in the morning and brightened up after the hour of the dragon.

The following day was the first of the sixth month by the old calendar, July 17th 1689. The two travellers left Oishida early in the morning and took horses along the Amida-do, the broad 'Amitabha Road'. They ambled past Obanazawa, through a long valley to Funagata, then across a wooded pass and down to Shinjo, the metropolis full of coffee shops and department stores where, three hundred years later, Grandad was even now slotting coins into a pachinko machine. At that time too Shinjo was a sizeable city, *jo ka machi*, a castle town, with a community of poets. The travellers arrived in the evening and went to stay with Furyu, a pupil of Basho's.

They rested here a couple of days. The local poets, excited at the chance of pitting their wits against the famous master from Edo, flocked to meet him. They spent the afternoon together, composing a round of linked verse. Sora meanwhile was delegated to collect permits for the next section of their journey.

Finally I came to the words I had been looking for: '3rd. Weather fine. Left Shinjo. One and a half ri, Motoaikai'. I was right. It was the same characters that were written on the signboard. At that time this jumble of tin shacks, tumbling down the river bank as if someone had discarded a lorry load of boxes, had been an important port, a boarding station for the Mogami. Here – perhaps just here where I was sitting – the travellers showed their permits, then scrambled down the steps to the river and clambered into one of the long wooden rice barges. There was a big group of them by now: Basho and Sora in their black robes, some of the Shinjo poets, even a couple of Zen monks who joined them for the boat ride.

After one and a half ri, they reached Furukuchi, the village that I was headed for. Here there was a barrier. Everyone had to disembark and present their papers to the burly guards, who checked them thoroughly before allowing them to change on to another boat to cross into the territory of the Sakai lord, Saemon. One of the group, Heshichi, had forgotten to get a permit and despite their pleas, they had to leave him behind.

Basho described their journey: 'With mountains overhanging to left and right, in the midst of dense foliage we went down the river. We took a boat used for transporting rice, called a "rice boat", apparently. Shiraito no taki, White Thread Falls, tumbled through spaces between the young leaves, Sennin-do, the Hermit's Hall, stood on the bank facing the water. The river was swollen with the rains and our boat was in constant peril.'

I was hoping I might find one last remaining rice boat still plying up and down the Mogami. Closing my books, I jumped up, went as close as I dared to the edge of the drop and peered over. There were a couple of small boats tied up down there, half-submerged, but no sign of any boatman; and certainly no high-prowed barges with billowing white sails and passengers perched on sacks of rice.

It was foolish to be disappointed. The boats fell out of use years ago, in Meiji 34, 1901, when the railway came. Oishida too declined, from an important commercial and cultural centre to a backwater, with little left to recall the crowds of poets and travellers who used to hang around the teahouses. When I saw the town, it reminded me for some reason of Ilkley – long grey streets festooned with wires, plastic flowers dangling from lampposts, small dingy shops with grey cardigans and pleated skirts, fifty years behind Tokyo fashions. It took me a long time to find the town's one coffee shop. It was neat, clean and half taken up with a model of a rice boat, with paddle, huge square sail and cabin roofed with straw.

I picked my way through the broken tin roofs to the main road, Route 47, which runs alongside the river, and looked around gloomily. It was not a place for walkers. The Mogami is no less important now than it was in Basho's day; but the goods which used to travel by water are carried by road or rail. A huge lorry rolled by, then another, then another, an endless convoy rumbling along at the base of spectacular limestone cliffs thatched with thick forest. I thought wistfully of the silent white crags I had left that morning.

There was only one way to travel. I flagged down two salesmen from Sendai, who drew up in their sleek car. They were like creatures from another planet, immaculate with soft pale faces and laundered suits, each with a folded hanky peeping out of his breast pocket, chatting smoothly in standard Japanese, not the barbarous dialect I was used to. I sat uncomfortably in the back, suddenly conscious of my stained dusty clothes and grimy hands, as they took me the last eight kilometres to Furukuchi.

At Furukuchi I bought a ticket for the river boat. There was nothing left of the old barrier or the burly guards, no hint of where poor Heshichi had waited for the Shinjo poets to pick him up on their way home.

'All this way . . .' murmured the smiling clerk in the ticket office, referring, I was sure, not to my long walk that day but to my presumed long journey from unknown foreign parts. He gave me a leaflet. 'Mogami River Basho Line', it read. 'Your personal adventure. Follow the path of Basho and Yoshitsune'.

'Wait a minute,' he said, and disappeared into the recesses of his office. He returned with a tiny wooden doll, a *kokeshi*, like the ones I had seen in Narugo but no bigger than my little finger nail.

'*O-miyage*' – a souvenir. I put it into my bag along with the horse chestnut.

To reach the boats I had to cut through a group camped on the steps, tucking into enormous rice balls. To each side stretched the grassy river banks, inviting and empty. But here they all were, squeezed together, jogging elbows on the hard concrete.

The boat bobbing at the bottom of the steps was like a barge or an over-sized punt, long, narrow and alarmingly frail, with nothing but a single line of planks between us and the water. I stepped in gingerly, took off my shoes and sat down on the straw mats, between a large family who looked like local farmers and a young couple.

On the Narrow Road

At one end, manning the outboard motor, was a picturesque young man with a huge grin and magnificent cheekbones, who might have stepped out of a Hokusai cartoon. He was dressed to fit the part in a straw coolie hat and wide-sleeved blue happi coat and perched in the stern on skinny black legs, his feet, in black cloth *tabi*, spread wide apart.

The weathered old boatman squatting at the other end was equipped with a microphone through which he kept up an incessant commentary.

'Lady at the end there – what is your country?' he boomed once we were under way. All heads turned towards me.

'England,' I answered.

'And those,' waving at my battered old sandals neatly arranged with the others at the edge of the straw mats. 'What do you call those?'

'Sandals.'

'English sandals, that's what she said – English sandals, ladies and gentlemen, sandals from London! *Kawatteiru, ne!* Different, aren't they! Strange, eh! Sandals from London – what a rarity! Take a good look at them. First time we've ever had sandals from London on this boat.'

To my relief, no one but him showed the slightest interest in me or my sandals.

The boat slowed with a surge of water. 'Look to your left please,' called the boatman. A figure with a camera and tripod, silhouetted on a rock high above, waved and shouted.

'Smile.'

Everyone looked, everyone smiled. We accelerated again.

'Y2500 a copy. Pick them up at Kiyokawa.'

£10 a copy seemed a bit steep. But everyone except me, I was sure, would buy one. After all, there was no point going anywhere if you didn't have a photo of yourself to take home afterwards. Otherwise how would anyone know you had really been there?

The family had spread boxes of food – rice, pink pickled plums, cold grilled fish, a mound of simmered chrysanthemums – on the mat in front of them and were eating. Beside them, an intense young man, brushing long strands of

182

oily hair out of his eyes, was filming the unchanging wall of forest along the edge of the river. 'Excuse me,' he muttered, pushing to the other side of the boat and focusing on the identical wall of forest on that side.

Ahead of us the water was so shallow that you could see the rocks just below the surface. Grinning madly, the young boatman accelerated hard. The boat lurched forward and the bottom ground across the rocks as if it was about to tear apart. The girl next to me shrieked. She was far too smartly dressed for this journey, in white stockings and a tight black dress, heavily made-up, every hair in place. Her swarthy man friend had on an immaculate pin-striped suit and sunglasses and his hair was permed into tight curls. I wondered if this was a 'punch perm', a sure sign of a *yakuza*, a member of the Japanese mafia. His shoes were at the far end of the boat so I couldn't check if they were white and pointed, another giveaway. But I glanced at his thick beringed hands to see if he had a little finger missing.

'To your left, ladies and gentlemen, you may see Kutsu no taki, Horseshoe Falls,' droned the old boatman, swaying gently back and forth as he recited his lines. 'It is said that Minamoto Yoshitsune rested here on his way to Hiraizumi. Here his horse stamped its hoof into the ground and a spring of clear water gushed out.' The waterfall glistened thinly in a cleft between the cliffs.

Every now and then on the far side of the river I caught a glimpse of Route 47, an endless line of cars and lorries trundling silently across a tall delicate bridge straddling a gorge or emerging from a tunnel burrowed into the mountainside. The road, according to the boatman, was not completed until 1930, long after the railway. Looking at the solid rock wall with its thick forest, I couldn't imagine how they had ever managed to chip and blast a way through.

We glided past an enormous hole scooped out of the cliff face, with pines and willows hanging out crazily above it, bare roots dangling.

'To your right you may see Benkei's Cave, excavated by Musashibo Benkei with his bare hands,' intoned the boatman.

He waved to his left and declaimed with equal gravity, 'On that rise over there stands the railway station.'

Beyond Benkei's Cave a long shelf of land jutted out of the water in front of the cliffs, dotted here and there with little houses with plump thatched roofs. There was no road along the spit and the only way to reach the houses was by boat. The villagers, said the boatman, lived by collecting wild plants from the mountains behind. 'This area is particularly famous for its delicious ferns,' he added. There was a chorus of grunts as if that piece of information was of much more interest than all the stuff about Yoshitsune and Benkei.

'Shiraito no taki, White Thread Falls, tumbled through spaces between the young leaves, Sennin-do, the Hermit's Hall, stood on the bank facing the water . . .'

I had been watching out eagerly for Sennin-do, the Hermit's Hall. As we swung round a curve, I caught a glimpse of steps leading from the water up to a stone torii arch, marking the land beyond as holy. There, half overgrown with vines and weeds, hidden among the trees, was a small wooden building like a shrine, tightly shuttered, with a rope of twisted straw placed firmly across the closed doors. We slowed and turned in towards the bank, the boat rocking gently in the swell. I hoped we would stop but instead we drifted slowly past.

'Sennin-do,' intoned the boatman. 'Founded by a priest named Hitachibo Kaizon, a follower of Yoshitsune. Here is enshrined the god of boats and water.'

The family were packing away their empty lunch boxes and the girl in black studied her face in a mirror, touching up her lipstick, while her friend put a film into his camera, rings flashing in the sun.

Hitachibo was one of Yoshitsune's closest companions. He joined him when the young hero was still a lad, fought in his three brilliant campaigns against the Heike and was one of the band of sixteen who fled with him to the wild country of the north.

Like Benkei, he was a warrior monk, and the two often fought side by side. He hailed from Onjoji, the great Tendai temple in Otsu on the shores of Lake Biwa, near Kyoto, where the monks were considerably more famous for their endless skirmishes with the monks of neighbouring Enryakuji than for their pious ways. He himself, though, was something of a holy man, a master of esoteric Buddhist practices and the intellectual and scholar of the group. According to some he had magic powers and the enemy were particularly in awe of him.

But he had one fatal flaw. Once when the fugitives were on the run, struggling across the snow and ice of Mount Yoshino, starving and exhausted, they stopped to rest at a place called Sakuradani. One of Yoshitsune's retainers who lived nearby sneaked up with boxes of food for them – 'fruit, wine, rice and other food'. But just as they were about to eat, they heard voices. A hundred and fifty armed Yoshino monks were charging down the mountain towards them. Hitachibo was the first to flee. Instead of protecting his lord, he leapt up and took to his heels, the other warriors close behind.

Yoshitsune and Benkei were left on their own. Calmly they collected up the empty boxes and threw them over a cliff, then buried the food in the snow – as samurai it would hardly do to rush off in a panic. Then, without a glance behind them, they strode off.

Years later Hitachibo betrayed his master again. By then the group had reached Hiraizumi. It was the morning of the last great battle, when twenty thousand men attacked the Takadachi. But instead of eighteen followers (there were two new ones now), Yoshitsune had only eight. Says the *Gikeiki*, grimly: 'Hitachibo and the other ten retainers, who had gone to pray at a neighbouring mountain temple that morning, had never returned. Such conduct is better passed over in silence.'

After his lord's death, they say, Hitachibo returned to this forlorn spot where he passed the rest of his days as a hermit, performing penances and praying for the dead.

'We are nearly at the end of our journey,' said the boatman. 'Now I will sing for you.' As we drifted past the silvery threads of Shiraito Falls, he closed his eyes, threw back his head and sang a slow sad folksong, of the old days, when the boats loaded with safflowers sailed down the Mogami. He sang another, with a lively melody, one of the songs that they dance to in August in Yamagata. Everyone began to clap in time to the song. Even the gangster put down his camera and the oily-haired young man, carefully inserting his video camera into a leather case, clapped too.

I spent the night at Karikawa. The road up from the river dwindled away across the plain between shadowy walled houses jutting up like islands in a palely green sea. It was hard to imagine anything as flat as that rice plain. It stretched as far as I could see, right to the horizon where the sun was setting. Silhouetted against the blazing sky, the line of darkening mountains looked as far away as ever. But now I was sure that those were the sacred mountains. Tomorrow I would be there. Tomorrow, perhaps – if they still existed, if there were any to meet – I would meet the yamabushi.

After the remote villages I had been staying in, Karikawa seemed a great metropolis. Along the main street was a row of shops – a fishmonger's, two chemists, a bank, a bicycle shop, even one stocked with electric fans and televisions, the bright neon inside lighting up the dark street. I turned down an alley towards the station. The only light was a sign, glowing green above a doorway: 'Spur – Coffee House'.

Inside the cramped little room was a counter, some white tables and chairs and a powerful, all-pervading fragrance which seemed somehow familiar. A muscular bearded young man with a towel wrapped around his head was bent over a table heaped with dry leaves and twigs.

'*Irasshai irasshai!* Welcome!' he called without looking round. 'What'll you have today – chamomile, sage, rosemary, thyme, lemon balm . . .' He straightened, turned, saw my face. 'Your country . . . ? England, it must be!' A huge grin spread across his face as if he couldn't believe his luck. 'In that case – surely – you must know Suttons – and Thomson and Morgans!'

He rushed behind the counter and pulled out a battered Suttons seed catalogue, holding it out to me with both hands as reverently as if it were a rare and valuable tea bowl.

'Fourteen years I've been studying English herbs,' he chortled. 'Best collection of herbs in Japan – just out there, in my greenhouse. Seventy different varieties. These are my books. Problem is, I can't read English.'

He brought out manuals of herbs and stacked them on the table – an ancient Culpepper bound in leather with yellow crackly pages, volumes on the medicinal properties of herbs, a couple of Latin herbals, even one in Greek with fine line drawings.

'This one,' he said, pointing to a drawing in the Greek manual. 'Been trying to get these seeds for years. You must know what it is' – as if the mere fact of being English, a compatriot of Thomson and Morgans, meant that I held the key to some secret herbal knowledge.

The clue was the beard. As soon as I saw it, I knew that he was either an artist (unlikely – artists have droopy moustaches) or *kawatteiru*, 'changed', different, other, like my sandals. In this country conformity is prized; and the way you look is the way you are. Everyone, to show that they are like everyone else, is clean-shaven. This jolly, bouncing, bearded fellow, bursting with good health and muscle, was clearly not like everyone else.

'What'll you have, anyway?'

He took four jars from a shelf and started stuffing handfuls of herbs into a teapot, talking non-stop.

'Used to work in Shinjuku – in Manna, you know Manna?' Manna was a little natural food café in Tokyo, on the wrong side of the tracks, full of *kawatteiru* people.

'When I was young. Came back, of course – we all do, don't we. Have to look after the old people. Same in England, I expect.'

In England, I told him, people didn't usually live with their parents.

He looked at me with that familiar Japanese expression of disbelief. In this at least he was just like everyone else.

'But who looks after the old people?' he said in shocked tones. 'You have to take care of the old people.'

A bit later some girls dropped in, not at all the kind of girls I had expected to see in this remote country town. They sat around a table, reading comic books and giggling. They were all dressed-up for a night at the disco – rather wasted in this little coffee shop. One had orange hair teased into a shaggy pile, plenty of make-up and a tight black satin skirt.

'Look at these,' she shrieked to the herb man, heaving her skirt up to reveal a pair of glittery gold stockings secured just above the knee with elastic and an expanse of pale fleshy thigh bulging out above.

'All the girls like me,' he chuckled gleefully after they had left. 'They all come here. There's nowhere else to go.'

One girl, in a long white dress, was left, sitting quietly at a table, filling plastic bags with thyme leaves.

'Going to Mount Haguro, are you?' she asked.

'Stay with us,' the herb man butted in. 'All the Haguro pilgrims used to stay with us.' In the old days, before people began making their pilgrimage to Haguro by car, they always stayed here in Karikawa and walked up to Haguro in the morning. 'They had to stay at our inn – ours is the only inn in town! Famous people stayed here too. In those days we were rich.'

The girl in white had been to Haguro several times.

'If you want to meet yamabushi,' she said gravely, 'stay at an inn called Miyatabo. There may be some there.'

She considered a while, then added, 'The real yamabushi are called *matsuhijiri*. That's who you should meet.'

That night there were twigs of thyme floating in my bath.

The Sacred Mountains

12

The Gateway

I was the only guest in the inn that night and the only pilgrim on the road next morning. I was miles now from the great noisy thoroughfare of the Mogami and walked along in silence, my feet crunching the gravel and the dead dragonflies and semi shells that littered the path. Once a car roared past me and turned off across the rice fields. I watched it sail away, slowly getting smaller and smaller until it turned into a black dot and disappeared over the curve of the horizon. Immeasurably far away tiny cars shuttled back and forth across the plain; and here and there a small becalmed village protruded from the green.

I would have been thankful for a lift. It was my third day on the road and I was drained of energy. As I toiled along I was suddenly conscious of the heat, the humidity, the weight of my pack. There were new, inexplicable pains in my legs. The back of my calves ached and a blister appeared unexpectedly on my big toe.

At least, I reflected, I could be practically certain I was walking the same path that Basho took. There was no other way he could have come. This was the only road from Karikawa to Haguro. This gravel I was treading may have been earth when he was here, but still my feet were touching the same ground that his had. There was something that pleased me about that.

The road pushed punishingly uphill and eventually left the Shonai plain and snaked through shadowy spruce forests and orchards of green persimmons up into mountain country; though even here wherever there were a few yards of level ground the tough gorse had been hacked away and rice fields planted.

I was passing a scattering of houses that promised a village when I saw a sign at the side of the road. I stopped to spell it out, pleased that I could read the characters: *miya*, 'shrine'; *ta*, 'rice field'; *bo*, 'pilgrim house' – Miyatabo. So I had reached Togei, the village at the foot of Mount Haguro.

Sitting in the coffee shop the previous night, talking to the girl in white, I had written 'Miyatabo' conscientiously in my notebook; but I had never expected to find it. Now, looking at the sprawling concrete building, I was disappointed. The girl was not as well-informed as I thought. This was just a pilgrim hostel, a particularly large and ugly one, not at all the kind of place where I would be likely to find a wandering hermit priest. Still, I took off my rucksack, patted my hair, smoothed my clothes and went in.

There was a small fierce woman at the reception desk. She leapt to her feet when she saw me and swept me out again, then stood at the top of the steps, scowling down at me, arms folded, barring the way.

'Excuse me,' I faltered, conscious of how disreputable I must look and of the sweat stains spreading across my T-shirt. 'Actually, I had heard . . . I was wondering . . . if there were any yamabushi here.'

Even as I said it, it sounded absurd, like a child knocking on a door and asking for Santa Claus. I realised that I hardly even knew what a yamabushi was.

'Yamabushi? Wrong time of year for yamabushi,' snapped the woman, making them sound like a fruit out of season.

It wasn't the response I had been expecting. On balance, it seemed encouraging; and worth trying again.

'I heard . . . that is, someone told me . . .' Perhaps what I needed was a contact, an introduction, a name to drop. 'The people in the inn in Karikawa sent me.'

The woman softened.

'Only farmers here at this time of year,' she said. 'Try at the top of the mountain. They're yamabushi up there. In fact', brightening as she thought of a way to get rid of me, 'you can stay at the Saikan. I'll phone up now and make sure they have room.'

At the top of the village was a huge torii arch, marking the beginning of the mountain itself. It was the biggest I had ever seen, twenty or thirty times as tall as I was. I stepped through thoughtfully, conscious that I was crossing on to sacred ground.

Beyond was a pool and a waterfall and some pilgrims splashing and shouting. On a rock were three fierce stone deities and a collection box with their names on it: White Dragon; Blue Dragon; Black Dragon. There was a slender red bridge to cross and then the climb began.

There are stone steps all the way up Mount Haguro, flight after flight of them, interspersed with long cobbled paths which disappear off into the trees. Every time you heave painfully to the top of a particularly steep and treacherous flight, the steps all broken and worn from centuries of devout footsteps – every time you think that this must be the last – there is another path stretching off interminably in front of you.

Climbing through the forest of cedars which spreads endlessly across the mountainside, I might have been in a cathedral. On each side of the path great tree trunks soared like the columns of the nave and shafts of sunlight filtered through the leaves as if through a stained glass window, speckling the ground with light. Not even a semi shrieked in the silence. I had never seen such vast and ancient trees – these same trees must have populated the forest in Basho's day – and around the oldest and biggest ('Grandfather Cedar, one thousand years old', it said on a plaque on the trunk) was a thick rope hung with sheaves of holy paper. Nearby was a weather-beaten old pagoda, the same faded brown as the tree trunks and almost invisible among them.

kono sugi no	In that age
mibaeseshi yo ya	This cedar was a seedling:
kami no aki	Autumn of the gods

All along the way, wherever there was level ground, in a glade beside the path or on a shelf of land at the top of a flight of steps, there was a moss-covered rock carved with prayers, a family of life-sized stone images, a wooden temple with dragon heads sprouting from the beams. One small temple was perched on a rock looking out over the trees to the Shonai plain miles below. Around the back an old woman stretched on a bench in the shade, snoring gently, a straw hat over her face and a lunch box tied in a purple scarf at her feet.

I looked at the temple, suddenly amazed. How on earth had they managed to build it so high on the mountainside? Did they carry the wood and rock down to the village, carve it, then hump it back up again piece by piece? Or did they somehow construct it here on the mountain?

Later I came to a tap and metal cup at the side of the path and stopped to wash the sweat off my face and sip some water. I looked up and noticed a small faded sign, pointing along an overgrown path which disappeared off around the hill: '*Oku no hosomichi*' it read – 'narrow road to the deep north'.

I followed it round for half a mile or so, to a grassy meadow full of dragonflies, deep in the woods on the slope of the mountain. There was a lily pond along one side, the still surface covered in smooth round leaves, and flat rocks scattered across the grass as evenly as stepping stones or counters on a draughtboard. A raven cawed in the stillness.

I strolled through the grass to a large rock, to sit down. Then I saw the inscription: *Minami dani*.

Minami dani – South Valley. In Basho's time there was a temple here – it must have filled the narrow glade – and the stepping stone rocks had supported the heavy wooden scaffolding, raising it above the marshy ground.

'On the third day of the sixth month (July 19th), we climbed Mount Haguro. We enquired after a man called Zushi Sakichi, who arranged an audience for us with Egaku the Ajari, the acting high priest. He permitted us to lodge in the sub-temple in South Valley, treated us with great kindness and entertained us most hospitably.'

Basho and Sora didn't stop at Karikawa but hurried on the

last three and a half ri (8½ miles), along the edge of the Shonai plain and up into the hills to Togei, the village where the woman had told me that yamabushi were out of season. They arrived at the hour of the monkey, around tea time, and went straight to the house of Zushi Sakichi.

Zushi was a Togei man, a dyer by trade, and a poet and great admirer of Basho's. He welcomed his distinguished guests then guided them up the stone steps to the top of the mountain, and presented them to Egaku, the acting head priest of the whole Haguro religious complex.

I came across a picture of Egaku when I was staying at the top of the mountain. He looks an immensely dignified character, dressed like a bishop – which in effect he was – in heavy brocaded robes of red and gold, richly embroidered, with a stiff cowl rising to a point behind his head. He has a mild, rather gentle face, and long pierced earlobes, and is sitting in formal posture, cross-legged, holding a string of white prayer beads with a closed fan laid on the ground in front of him – the very posture in which he must have received Basho and Sora.

The two poets, on the other hand, after nine weeks on the road, must have looked exceedingly shabby. Basho, by his own account, had only the clothes he stood up in, 'plus a paper coat to protect me in the evening, *yukata* (for sleeping), rain-wear'. Perhaps his followers presented him with new robes from time to time, just as they kept him supplied with straw sandals. Egaku, in any case, welcomed the travellers graciously and invited them to stay in his own temple, the Jion-ji in South Valley.

In the evening, enjoying the cool breezes which wafted across the glade high on the mountain, Basho wrote

arigata ya	Blessed
yuki o kaorasu	With the fragrance of
Minami dani	snow –
	South Valley

By the time I reached the Saikan, the Pilgrims' Hall, it was late afternoon and beginning to get a little cooler. I stood in the huge entranceway, shouting '*Gomen kudasai!*', 'Excuse me', into the silence. There was no response. I took off my shoes and stepped up.

In front of me stretched acres of tatami matting, like a vast empty palace, with nothing but wooden pillars to mark where one room ended and the next began. Each room was laid out as if for a feast, with rows of tiny square tables, ankle high, set with chopsticks and dishes of food, and a flat cushion at each place – but no sign of cooks or guests.

I padded through the deserted rooms, calling out '*Gomen kudasai!*' until finally I heard an answering '*Hai!*'

'Yes, we have room for you. In fact, you're the only guest,' chuckled the old caretaker. He was slightly stooped, with wisps of grey hair straying across his freckled head, and at one time must have filled the oversized suit he wore, spotlessly clean but fraying at the cuffs. He led me along a maze of corridors, the floor creaking under our steps, to the furthest corner of the enormous building.

'This', he said, ushering me into a small room, completely empty, 'is your room.'

I was beginning to feel distinctly uneasy about spending the night alone in this eerie place, with the only company the caretaker, a very long run away down dark echoing corridors. I had been expecting a cosy little inn, perhaps no more than a single mat in a room packed with pilgrims. All this space – the luxury of a room to myself – was not at all luxurious but positively threatening. I wished I was not *hitori*, on my own. I wished, like every sensible Japanese traveller, I had a group.

Still, it was a beautiful room. It was the size of a tea room, 4½ mats, 8 or 9 foot square, with two rough plaster walls, broken into alcoves. In one was a hanging scroll with a poem on it, in one a rickety shelf, in a third a pair of tiny doors covered in white paper. I slid them open but there was only the wall behind. Each alcove was framed with a slender tree trunk, plumb with the wall: a cherry with glossy mottled bark; another, picturesquely twisted, stripped to show the pale knotted wood.

The other two walls were hardly walls at all but flimsy glass doors, pushed right back so that every tiny gust of cool air could blow in. I sat for a while dangling my legs outside. A couple of yards away were cedars, huge horse chestnuts, hydrangeas still in flower, fronds of cow parsley surrounding a small round pond. Then came a line of forest and far below, the green of the Shonai plain with darker green dots marking, I imagined, clumps of trees. Cloud shadows glided slowly across. In the distance the river Mogami glittered, disappeared as a cloud passed, glittered again. Beyond it was the pale cone of Mount Chokai. I must have been walking there that morning, though it looked like another world. The leaves rustled and the windows rattled in their frames.

Footsteps echoed along the corridor. The caretaker heaved open the wooden door and stumbled in, grinning, his arms wrapped around a large cushion, a flask of hot water and a lacquered tray with a teapot, a tin of tea and a small cup jiggling on it. He dumped the cushion in the middle of the floor, put the tray in front of it and went out again, sliding the door shut behind him.

It was dusk when I climbed the last stone steps to the top of the sacred mountain. There was a second huge red torii gate there, overshadowed by giant cedars. I stepped through it into the grounds.

There were temples everywhere, large squat ones with spreading eaves and dragons coiling around the pillars and rows of tiny ones, for lesser gods, lined up against the forest. One was dedicated to some kind of shoe god. There were shoes laid out in neat pairs on its steps and heaped in a jumble beside it – wooden *geta*, straw *waraji*, thousands of them, spangled high-heeled sandals, boots, galoshes and cheap leather shoes like the ones that Toshiyuki made in his shoe factory. Another, said the bespectacled old priest inside, was for the souls of dead babies. Behind it was a grove of sad stone images, all decked in red caps and bibs, and forests of bright plastic whirligigs, spinning in the wind with a subdued clatter.

Dominating the place was the largest Shinto shrine I had ever seen, a vast wooden building intensely red with a gigantic thatched and gabled roof which towered above the cedars. At the top of the steps which ran across the front, white-clad priests hovered, tiny against the dark recesses behind.

Most of the temples were closing, though there were still plenty of pilgrims around. Young acolytes, all in pristine white, glided from shrine to shrine, closing the heavy shutters. One was tidying the incense cauldron, stuck like a pin-cushion with half-burnt joss sticks. Carefully he brushed the ashes away until there was not a speck on the sand underneath, then swept it up into a perfect cone, a miniature Mount Fuji.

A faded woman in red hurried up to him, trailing three identical spiky-haired boys, one big, one medium, one small. She had come all this way, she said, specially. She had a relative who was ill. She wanted prayers for him. Was it too late?

'Finished for today,' said the young priest sternly. 'Anyway, you have to make an appointment. Ask at the main shrine.'

Then I saw the yamabushi.

There were two of them, leading a group of pilgrims, old country women with white jackets over their dark dresses, farmers' wives on a day's outing. They looked exactly as yamabushi should. One was young, the other old and grizzled with a wonderfully weathered, ruffianly face, a real mountain man. They strutted along on impossibly high wooden *geta*, in baggy bloomers gathered at the knee, flowing black and white blouses and small black hats like miners' lamps tied to their foreheads, each with a staff and an enormous conch shell under his arm.

'Evening,' said the younger one with a grin and nod as they passed. They both had mirrors hanging on their backs.

I walked on, pondering. The girl in white, with her talk of 'real' yamabushi, had sown doubts in my mind. These two surely, were not 'real'. 'Real' yamabushi were holy men hidden away in caves, performing difficult ascetic practices, not parading across the mountain-top dressed up like Benkei in a Noh play. These were fancy-dress yamabushi. Perhaps this was what the great warrior monks had come to. Perhaps they did no more these days than shuttle groups of pilgrims around the holy places.

'*Oi – Oneesan!* Big Sister!' A man with a droopy moustache and black beret was sitting under an enormous cedar, surrounded by paintings of writhing black dragons, outlined in gold.

'I'm an artist,' he said superfluously. Like the yamabushi, he fitted his part perfectly, from his stubbly chin and long hair tied in a knot to the string around his neck. He couldn't have been anything else. He stretched an arm down beside his chair, produced a bottle of whisky and took a mouthful.

'I'll write a poem for you. I'm famous, you know. Sofu's the name.'

Two bulky men in rather skimpy suits had stopped to watch. 'He's famous,' echoed one.

Sofu-san contemplated the row of brushes arranged on the table in front of him and finally selected one.

'What did you say your name was? Lesley? Rei-su-ri? Here you are: the Song of Climbing Haguro.'

He covered a square of white card with thick black brush strokes, ending each line with a flourish, then held it out at arm's length and read:

'A lady (*rei*-dee) from England,
From a great distance (*su*) come to this mountain,
Carrying this ideal (*ri*), now in her thirties.'

'The last line, you understand', he added grandly, as if it was obvious, 'refers to the Five Necessities.'

'The five necessities?'

He counted them off on his fingers, impatiently: 'Health, house, food, sleep, water', wrapped the card in tissue paper and gave it to me. Then he took a long sheet of paper and painted a thick curving stroke on it, brushed in glowering eyes, fangs and claws and, with a few rapid strokes, a dragon appeared.

'I'm sixty-three,' he boasted. I had thought he was twenty years younger. 'Fourteen years I've been sitting here, doing this job.'

From far away, somewhere down the mountain, came the moan of a horn, long and sad. It was un unearthly, primeval sound, like an alpenhorn or the enormous horns the Tibetans blow – or a conch shell perhaps.

'Want to know about the yamabushi, do you?' he said. 'Want to meet a *matsuhijiri*? Harada-san, talk to Harada-san. He's the top yamabushi. Snow festival, fire festival – he knows all the rituals. And he can heal – he can heal sick children. I'll arrange it for you. I know everyone. Come and see me tomorrow.'

As I hurried back across the darkening temple grounds, a man passed me. It was the old yamabushi, dressed like a farmer now in shirt and shapeless grey trousers. He was still wearing *geta* and carried his conch shell in one hand and an umbrella in the other.

I shivered a little. It was surprisingly cool on the hilltop.

suzushisa ya	The coolness:
hono mika tsuki no	Pale three day moon
Haguro yama	Above Mount Haguro

In Basho's time, Dewa Sanzan – the Three Mountains of Dewa – was the holiest place of the north. Mount Haguro was the gateway, the most accessible of the three mountains. At the top was a vast complex of magnificent temples and monasteries where Tendai Buddhist monks lived and worshipped, while the yamabushi inhabited caves on the mountainside and cloisters, nearly four hundred of them, down in the village of Togei. Here they performed the mysterious rites and practices of Shugendo.

For Haguro was one of the country's four yamabushi centres, where acolytes were initiated into the mysteries and trained in the secret yamabushi rites; and the Tendai monks too practised Shugendo. Pilgrims came here in their thousands to worship the mountain and absorb some of its sacred spirit.

For Basho it was the culmination of his weeks of travel and he wrote with great excitement of what he found

Here the Tendai practice of *shikan* (insight meditation) shines as bright as the moon, and the doctrine of *endon yuzu*

(perfection through adherence to Buddhist law) glows like a
lamp.

Cloisters stretch row upon row where devotees carry out
the Shugendo disciplines with immense zeal. The power of
their austerities makes this a holy mountain and a sacred
place, which fills men with admiration and awe. The wonders of this mountain are beyond measure: surely its
prosperity will last for ever!

Basho stayed a week in South Valley as the special guest of
Bishop Egaku and there were feasts and poetry parties in his
honour. On the second day of his visit, the fourth of the sixth
month, he and his group went up to the main temple at the top
of the mountain for a poetry gathering. Sora, always a down-
to-earth fellow, was as interested in the magnificent food they
were served as in the poetry.

Food was scarce up in the mountains and although Basho
and Sora stayed with the wealthiest people of the area, still
they must have had to subsist on the mountain people's diet:
wild plants, preserved foods, beans, buds, shoots, the occasional insect. There was no fish this far inland and not much
rice.

'Fourth. Weather fine', Sora recorded in his diary. 'At midday we were invited to the main temple to dine on "cut soba".'
Mount Haguro's fat brown buckwheat noodles were famous,
served not in spaghetti-like strands but chopped into small
pieces, with bush clover chopsticks to eat them with.

A few days later, Bishop Egaku and his retinue came down
to the temple in South Valley. After a meal of *somen*, chilled
wheat noodles on ice, and plenty of the famous local saké,
Basho, as master poet, was called upon to compose the first in
a round of linked verse. 'Sora', wrote Sora, 'managed to
compose four verses.'

But the purpose of this visit to the sacred mountains was not
simply to compose poetry. The heart of the mountain and its
oldest shrine was Gongen. Basho and Sora went twice to
worship there, first purifying themselves by fasting half a day.
'The shrine was founded and this mountain opened by the

Great Master, Saint Nojo,' wrote Basho. 'But no one knows in
which period he lived.'

Nojo Daishi, Great Master Nojo. It is said that when he came
to the land of Dewa he brought with him the seeds of the five
kinds of grain – rice and wheat, barley and buckwheat – and
taught the people how to cultivate the soil, how to make things
with their hands, how to heal illness. So he was known as
No-jo, 'man of skills', cleanser of illness.

I was wandering around the museum in Haguro one drizzly
morning, waiting for the sun to come out, taking half an
interest in the tarnished old images and yellowing scrolls,
when I saw a painting in a corner and stopped short. There
was something disturbing about it, and so hypnotic that it was
difficult to move away.

It was a medieval scene, three figures on a stylised mountain. The whole top of the mountain was a throne with a figure
in brocaded robes sitting on it, fingering prayer beads – a
priest, perhaps, or a king. Blossoming from the arms and back
were dragon heads with roses in their teeth. Below, on the
lower tier of the mountain, were two wild hermit-like figures
with long hair and loincloths, one fanged, his hand over his
ear, the other a woman, covering her mouth.

But it was the topmost figure that gripped me. He had the
face of a magician, not a holy man – a face out of a nightmare,
swarthy, hardly human, with glittering eyes and a long mouth
clamped shut in a grimace of power or unholy knowledge. It
was Nojo's face I was looking at.

He was born with the face of a bee and before he was
canonised his name was Prince Hachiko, 'Bee Child'. 'He is
said to have had an ugly face' said the painting's inscription
innocently. 'He had no forehead; his hairline and his eyebrows
met. His mouth stretched as far as his ears and his nose hung
down across it. His whole face was twelve inches long'.

It took me some time to piece together Hachiko's story.
Everyone – the old artist, the curator of the museum, the
priests in the temple – assured me that he really lived, he was
a historical figure, not a legend; and I saw his grave in a pine
grove on the side of the mountain. But no one could explain

why he had a bee's face. 'Inbreeding', suggested Sofu-san. 'All his austerities', shrugged the curator. Clearly it was not a matter worthy of discussion.

He was a man of Yamato, of course, not an Ezo. He was born in Nara, an Imperial prince, the third son of Emperor Sushun who died in 592; and his birth is recorded in the *Nihongi*. It was a time of powerful religious changes. Buddhism had just spread to Japan from China and, on the other side of the world, St Augustine was about to bring Christianity to Britain.

When he was a young man, Hachiko, for some reason, was banished. He left Nara and the Imperial family, became a monk and crossed to the bleak Japan Sea coast where he set sail for the north. He had sailed round the Noto peninsula and was near the island of Sado when his boat hit a rock and began to fill with water. At that moment a huge abalone floated up miraculously from the sea bed and sealed the hole so that he could reach the island in safety.

Somewhere near Tsuruoka, well to the north of Sado, Hachiko heard music. He looked towards the land and saw a rainbow with music playing and eight maidens dancing.

'What is this beautiful place?' he asked.

They replied, 'This is the beach of this country's god. East of here is the mountain of the god.'

He disembarked at a place called Yura and the eight maidens led him into a cave. It is still visible from the sea, apparently, and local people say that it leads all the way from the coast to Mount Haguro.

At this point the story becomes rather confused. Somewhere along the way Hachiko became separated from the maidens and a large three-legged crow appeared to guide him. He guessed that it must be a messenger from the gods and followed it across mountains and valleys, through dense forest, to Mount Haguro. (Ha-guro means 'black wing', like the wings of the crow.) It was 588, the year of the horse, when he 'opened' the mountain and founded Gongen on the summit. Then he went on to Mount Gassan which he opened in the year of the rabbit, and Yudono, the innermost mountain, the most sacred of all, in the year of the cow. He lived in these mountains for the rest of his life, performing austerities and teaching the yamabushi practices, and died at the age of ninety-one.

'Mount Haguro', said the curator ponderously, 'is the gateway, the entrance to the sacred mountains.' We were sitting in his office drinking tea and eating dry rice biscuits while flurries of rain swirled through the trees outside. The windows and doors were clamped shut and it was stiflingly hot. I sat fanning myself, feeling a pool of sweat forming under me on the metal seat.

'First you come to Haguro. Everyone can come and worship here; it is not difficult to climb Haguro. Then you climb Gassan – that's more difficult. That's where they do the toughest austerities. And finally you reach Yudono, *goshintai*, the *kami sama*: the god. It is the holiest place in Dewa Sanzan. Pilgrims come here barefoot. It is forbidden to speak of what you see here, or to write about it or photograph it.

'Matsuo Basho.' He frowned at me over his glasses. 'You will remember the words he wrote at Mount Yudono: "According to the rules for pilgrims, it is forbidden to reveal to others what is in this mountain. Therefore I stop my brush and do not record it".'

He glanced heavily at his watch. A woman in an apron was clearing away our cups.

'They say that if you do a lot of austerities', he added as I shuffled to my feet, 'you live to be very old. There are men of eighty or ninety who climb around the mountains like young boys. But they will never tell you what their practice is. It is all secret. Those who do it are not allowed to reveal it. The only way you can find out is by doing it yourself.'

I found Sofu-san, the old artist, at his table under the giant cedar, a large sheet of polythene stretched over his head like an awning, filling sheets of paper with black dragons outlined in gold.

'Ah – Oneesan,' he greeted me, waving his brush.

We chatted for a while. I was waiting for him to tell me about the meeting he had promised me with Harada-san, the old *matsuhijiri*, but he said nothing. Finally I asked him. He looked at me as if the idea was completely new to him, tilted his head to one side, sucked his breath through his teeth, weighed up the question.

'Impossible.' He shook his head. 'He's too busy. Anyway, he's deaf. You wouldn't be able to talk to him. And he's old now, more than a hundred. Doesn't know what's going on. Doesn't even know his own family.'

He picked up his brush again.

It was all beginning to seem hopeless. Every time I thought I was getting close to the yamabushi, they slipped away. Perhaps it was wrong of me to try and probe their world. It was too secret. I had learnt at least that they existed, that there were people who preserved the yamabushi traditions and lived as they had when Basho met them. It looked as if I would have to be content with that.

Sofu-san sat back in his chair, took a mouthful of whisky, looked at me seriously through steel-rimmed spectacles. 'Want to meet a yamabushi, don't you? Well, I'm one,' he said, tapping himself on the nose.

I smiled doubtfully. He was joking, of course.

'That is to say', he persisted sternly, 'I did the yamabushi training, eight years ago. I'll tell you.' He adjusted his beret, took on the air of a professor. I recognised the style. Japanese intellectuals too sport berets and long hair.

'It began on August 24th – always does, every year. Lasts seven days. We all put on yamabushi clothes and walked around the mountains – up Gassan, down to Yudono, wearing straw sandals. Straw sandals – think of that! And only two meals a day, all vegetarian. Vegetarian! Can't even imagine that, can you? Seven days without meat! How would you like that?' He gave me a sudden grin. 'Rice broth and vegetables, every day. None of this, not a drop.' He flourished his whisky bottle. 'And no shaving,' patting his stubbly chin.

'Worst of all, all we had was one or two hours' sleep a night. They kept waking us up to do prayers. That was what I wanted most – sleep, and decent food. We all had to squash into one room – a hundred and twenty-four of us there were, that year – and burnt *togarashi* and sat still for three hours.

Weren't allowed to move or talk or make notes. That happened two or three times. In the daytime we walked in the mountains, the whole group together, round the three sacred mountains, and chanted yamabushi prayers.'

He frowned and started to unfurl another roll of paper.

'That's all,' he said. 'That's all I can tell you.'

'Can women do it too?' I asked, remembering the curator's words: *the only way you can find out is by doing it yourself.* 'Could I do it?'

For all the superficial strangenesses – burning *togarashi*? Surely that was a kind of pepper – it sounded curiously familiar and immensely Japanese, this disciplined pursuing of enlightenment; for that was what I took it to be. And, of course, not *hitori*, not contemplating one's navel, holed-up in a cave on one's own; but marching round energetically in a group. Very business-like, very Japanese, with strict *senseis*, teachers, to make sure no one fell asleep and everyone worked hard.

I would have liked to ask him, too, this faintly comic figure with his beret and droopy moustache, why he had done it and what he had gained from it. What happened when they sat in that room and burnt *togarashi*? How did he feel? But I suspected he had already told me too much.

He was painting again. A crowd began to gather around the table. I picked up my bag.

'Oneesan!' he called. 'Go and see Hayashi-kun. In the mountain guides' hut. He's the one you want to talk to.'

That evening I went to the Gassai-den, the vast Shinto shrine at the top of the mountain. When bee-faced Hachiko founded it and when Basho visited, it was a Tendai Buddhist temple, Gongen, 'the incarnation of Buddha'. But in the Meiji period, the late nineteenth century, the sacred mountain was declared by law to belong to Shinto, the religion of the Emperor, not Buddhism. The Buddhist temples were burnt down and the Gassai-den took the place of Gongen.

I climbed to the verandah at the front of the shrine and stood watching the pilgrims clapping their hands and tossing coins into the cavernous collection box. The building was no more than a scaffolding of plump red struts and pillars supporting the vast thatched roof which soared into the darkening sky, with only its shadowy inner sanctum enclosed by walls. Hunched above us, malevolent black goblins with gleaming gold eyes propped the roof beams on their wooden shoulders.

Figures shuffled around in the gloom inside. The evening service was about to begin.

I asked if I could watch from the verandah, expecting to be told it was secret, I would have to leave.

'Come inside,' replied a young priest. 'Come and sit with us.'

Rather taken aback at this special treatment, I climbed over the barrier and knelt respectfully on the tatami, trying to be inconspicuous, wishing I knew the protocol.

It was eerie sitting in this vast empty place. When my eyes got used to the gloom I realised that it was populated with images: three huge human figures – perhaps the gods of the three mountains – looming out of the darkness with banks of candles flickering in front of them and barrels of saké stacked nearby; a life-sized white plaster horse; swirling tableaux with carved palm trees bursting out of the woodwork; and a three-legged crow perched on a beam. In front, the pale tatami made a stage, with three closed doors of beaten gold – the inner sanctum – as the backdrop.

After a while, young priests dressed in white filed silently in and arranged themselves in ranks, like the chorus in a Noh play. Then came two high priests, stern-faced and aloof, dignified in brocades and tall conical hats. One, in green robes, was waving a paper whisk. He came and waved it over me while I sat awkwardly with hands together and head bowed.

Offerings were brought and taken away and there were lengthy prayers addressed to the closed doors. Every movement, every gesture of the priests was neat, precisely choreographed. It was as if the ritual would be invalidated and the gods refuse to respond if one finger were wrongly placed. The second high priest, in brown, beat thunderously on a huge drum, the acolytes chanted in a deep monotone and from the verandah came the ragged claps of worshippers and the dull clatter of coins falling into the collection box, providing syncopation.

At first I was the only person in the audience. Halfway through, a latecomer rushed in, his starched blue skirts rustling, and sat down next to me. While I sat bolt upright in respectful silence, he shuffled, crossed and uncrossed his legs, yawned noisily.

As soon as the service ended, before I could creep away, he spoke, his voice startlingly loud in the vast shrine: 'What is your country?' He had a sensual face above his priest's robes – fleshy, specked with sweat, with full lips, a bristly moustache, oiled hair. Something about the way he looked at me made me uncomfortable.

Reluctantly I trailed after him across the tatami stage, in front of the holy of holies, into the recesses of the shrine, to a smoky living-room full of cushions, with a television blaring. I stood awkwardly in the doorway, certain that I was not meant to be here. Here were the young white-clad acolytes, no longer dignified or mysterious, lounging around like schoolboys, chatting, smoking, reading comics, watching the judo on television. They all sat up quickly when the older priest strode in, straightened their robes and put away their comics. He sat at the end of a table, summoning me imperiously to a cushion beside him.

Lighting a cigarette, he began to talk in slow clear Japanese. I realised with some relief why he had brought me here. I was a foreign visitor. I needed to be informed. I took out my notebook.

'These are sacred mountains and many gods live here. This shrine houses the three great deities of the mountains: Idehano-Mikoto, Lord Trough-in-the-Waves, the god of Haguro and spirit of the country of Dewa, which is Ideha; Tsukiyomi-no-Mikoto, Lord Reading-the-Moon, god of Gassan, Moon Mountain; and Oyamatsumi-no-Mikoto, Goddess-of-the-High-Mountain, who lives in the waterfall on Mount Yudono.

'Everything is a god. The gods are everywhere, not only here. There are gods in the trees, in the rocks, in the mountains, in the mirror in front of the inner shrine, in the shrine itself. The doors of the shrine are always kept shut. But I can tell you what you would find if you opened them: nothing. The shrine is empty. It contains the god; but it is not the god. Just as water needs a cup to hold it, so the god needs a vehicle, a container.'

I was listening hard, impressed with the words but not with the man who spoke them. He looked at me. He had an unpleasantly direct gaze. I shifted back a little and nodded that I understood. Some of the young priests had gathered round, as if at the feet of the master, and were scribbling earnestly.

I caught myself daydreaming, wondering what this oily arrogant man would be in another culture – in England, for example, or Tokyo. A salesman? No, something more ambitious, a managing director perhaps, or a politician. Here he had done well. He was respected, powerful; he told me later that he appeared on television as a spokesman for the shrine. But, like bee-faced Hachiko in the museum, he was not a holy man. He had an important job to do and he did it well.

He stubbed out his cigarette, lit another and pushed back a long strand of oiled hair.

'The aim of the yamabushi is to take the spirit of the mountain into themselves. They live on the mountain, eat the mountain plants, breathe its air, drink its water, become one with it. They go to all the shrines of all the gods who live on the mountains and worship at each one. So the gods are content and ensure the peace and prosperity of Japan.

'Our gods are very powerful. You may not realise how powerful they are. You will have seen the bell outside.'

I nodded. It was enormous, big enough for a man to stand under. It was cast in bronze, six inches thick, embellished with dragons, and hung from huge wooden beams with a thatched roof over it and a tree trunk to strike it with.

It was a gift, the priest told me, from the shogun to the nine-headed dragon god of Haguro, for saving Japan.

In 1281, less than a hundred years after Yoshitsune and his eight followers fought their last battle at Hiraizumi, Kublai Khan was preparing to invade Japan. His grandfather, Genghis Khan – whom many Japanese were convinced was none other than Yoshitsune under another name – had already swept across most of Asia and half of Europe with his ferocious Mongol horsemen, burning cities and laying whole countries waste. Now Kublai had made himself ruler of China – and was determined to add the little island of Japan to his conquests.

The Japanese had already had a taste of the savagery of the Mongols. A few years earlier, a vast armada had landed on the beaches of Kyushu, in the south. It was the first time Japan had ever been invaded and the first time the samurai warriors had had a foreign enemy to fight. They prepared to do battle according to the usual protocol. They strutted out on to the battlefield, issuing challenges and shouting out their rank and pedigree. The Mongols, however, had no time for formalities and to their utter astonishment began bombarding them with arrows and fireballs before they had even finished their speeches. Somehow, with great losses, the Japanese managed to drive them away. But they knew that it was only a matter of time before another invading horde arrived.

Now, while Kublai assembled his fleets, the Japanese prayed. Day and night, every temple and shrine in the country rang with the sound of gongs and bells and clouds of incense floated heavenwards. Monks recited sutras and incantations and conducted services endlessly and the Emperor wrote in his own hand to his ancestors, begging for help.

Then 150,000 Mongols in 4,500 ships landed on the coast. For seven weeks the samurai warriors held them off, but they were rapidly weakening and it looked as if the Mongols would overrun the country. In desperation the shogun turned to the most powerful deities in the land. He had a messenger sent post-haste to the distant northern mountains to petition the dragon god of Haguro.

That same night the sky began to darken. A violent typhoon blew up over the sea where the Mongol ships were anchored. It raged for two days and by the end the entire fleet was wrecked. The armies guarding the coast were jubilant. They named the wind which the god had sent *kami-kaze*, the divine wind.

'But that was all a long time ago,' I said. 'Are there still yamabushi now?'

'I am a yamabushi,' said the priest grandly. 'We are all yamabushi here. Shinto and yamabushi are the same.'

A yamabushi? I looked at him. For a moment I saw him in a suit and tie, persuading me to buy stocks and shares – or to vote for him.

He relaxed and lit another cigarette. The young priests in white closed their notebooks and went back to the television. The lecture was over.

'What do you think of Mount Haguro?' he asked.

'I'm impressed,' I replied. 'I think it's a very spiritual place.'

'And me?' He gave an unexpectedly wicked grin, as if he could read my thoughts. 'You think I'm spiritual too?'

'Not in the slightest,' I laughed.

There was a passageway lit by dim lamps all the way from the shrine back to the Saikan, the Pilgrims' Hall, on the hillside below. I ran down hundreds of echoing steps, along warrens of dark corridors, and ended up in my small room in the farthest corner of the ancient building.

I no longer had the Saikan and its vast empty spaces to myself. The first night I had huddled under my bedding, trying not to listen to the creaks and groans of the old building, telling myself firmly that Japanese ghosts were kind and harmless. If one did appear, I desperately hoped it would be an *o-baké*, one of those goblins which look like a furled paper umbrella with a single eye, hopping along on one high *geta*. Rather that than a mournful *yuré*, drifting wispily along the wall, long black hair hanging in wet strands, long white hands drooping like a begging puppy, moaning 'Envious, envious'.

The next night, to my relief, I heard rowdy shouts and laughter coming from the next room and found a group of pilgrims lounging on the tatami in their dressing-gowns, with flasks of saké and the half-eaten remains of a feast scattered across the small tables in front of them.

The Saikan was supposed to be famous for its vegetarian food; but I was disappointed by it. In the morning when I went out I would pass my dinner, all prepared and laid out on two tables, covered with a mesh to keep the flies off. By evening it was always every bit as dry and unappetising as I expected. Every evening one of the plates contained a whole grilled fish, looking at me out of a shrivelled eye. I never ate it and night after night the same fish appeared.

'Why don't you come with us?' said the pilgrims. They were leaving at two the next morning to climb Gassan. There were two girls up from Tokyo, some local men and two Shinto priests to guide them.

I intended to climb Gassan and to see Yudono, the holy mountain; but I wanted to wait a few days and do it on the same day that Basho had. And, as Basho had done, I planned to stay one night on Gassan.

'Waste of time!' they clamoured. 'Up to Yudono and back to Haguro is one day's walk. You could be back in Tokyo tomorrow – or at a hot-spring.'

As pilgrims do, they settled down to drink and tell ghost stories.

'Speaking of ghosts . . .' leered a large florid man, looking knowingly at me – saké had made him bad-tempered and his northern accent made him nearly incomprehensible – 'that little room you're in – that one really is haunted. Everyone knows.' The others guffawed and I went uneasily to bed.

Later I woke up with a start. Not far away something was moving, slowly and heavily dragging itself across the floor. I lay rigid, petrified. Undoubtedly it was an *o-baké*, heaving along on its single sandal. I could think of nothing I wanted to meet less than an oiled paper umbrella with a single eye and lay panic-stricken, wondering how on earth I could flee, and where to. It was horrifyingly close now, right in the next room.

It was several minutes before I realised with a shudder of relief that the grating sound came from one of the drunkards next door, snoring loudly and regularly.

Each day more and more pilgrims arrived. They spent the evening eating and drinking and went off to bed early. Around five – sometimes as early as two – they would all wake up with an enormous noise of chattering and laughter. Half an hour later they were gone and I would turn over and go back to sleep. They never stayed more than one night.

'Year after year they come, always the same day,' mumbled the old caretaker. We were sitting in his office, watching television. 'See? They've already booked for next year.' He ran his finger down the page. 'Suzuki-san . . . Twenty years now he's been coming. Always July 15th.'

'July 20th . . .' He was slowly turning the pages. 'Yes, season begins then. From July 20th we're always full. August – busy time, very busy. September – getting quieter.' He was almost talking to himself. 'By October there's no one here. November 12th – that's when the *matsuhijiri* come.' He breathed the information as if it were quite insignificant.

The *matsuhijiri* . . . I began to listen hard. Somehow I had never expected the trail to lead back to the Saikan; and I had never thought of consulting the shambling old caretaker.

'Of course, we're busy then. You should see the food we make for them!' I wished he would make some of it for me.

'They're not allowed fish or meat, you see. Buddhist food, that's what we make, vegetarian. At the end of the hundred days, we have a feast here – forty-six courses, imagine! Forty-six dishes each, for every guest!

'That's where they stay, the *matsuhijiri*, in that room over there. That's where they do the winter prayers and services.'

That was all he had to tell me. Once again, I was out of season. The *matsuhijiri* came here in the winter. There was no one here now. Once, I noticed that someone had left the door to the room open and peeped inside, wondering what mysteries I would see. But it was simply a large empty room with a tatami floor and a small shrine.

13
The Yamabushi

It seemed as if the yamabushi were forever going to elude me. Then, following the old artist's advice, I went in search of Hayashi-san and the mountain guides' hut.

By now I was a familiar face among the little community on the hilltop. The leathery-faced women selling *tochi mochi* (lovely nutty cakes of rice and horse-chestnuts) waved and bowed whenever I wandered by, the photographers who lounged around idly waiting for a customer asked how I was getting on, and even the disdainful shrine maidens in their red and white regalia, selling postcards, prayer books and amulets for protection against everything from exam failure and bankruptcy to ill health and traffic accidents, nodded to me.

The mountain guides' hut was not, as I had imagined, hidden away somewhere among the soaring cedar forests on the mountainside. It turned out to be a flimsy wooden house I had passed many times before, on the other side of the grounds, beyond the huge red-pillared temple and the dragon pond and the streets of little shrines, each with their devotees lighting incense and tugging bells.

Outside the hut was a crowd of men, telling jokes, shouting with rowdy laughter. Leaning out from inside, resting his elbows on the sill, was a man with a beaming round face and head shaved smooth as an egg.

'Hayashi? That's me.' It was the younger of the two yamabushi I had seen a few days before.

He was startlingly big, almost a giant among these stunted farmers. If he hadn't been a yamabushi – I smiled at the thought – he would have done well as a sumo wrestler. He had the same bloom of health, the same bulk, as a young trainee who has yet to get started on the famous diet, who has not yet turned into a moving mountain. He wore voluminous white robes. His magnificent shaven head tapered to a slight point and his suntanned face was as smooth and plump and unwrinkled as a baby's.

He eyed me quizzically with the self-assured gaze of a *sensei*.

'I, er . . . that is . . . Sofu-san . . . I'm interested in the yamabushi.' I was inexplicably overawed, at a loss for words.

'You won't learn anything up here,' he grunted, unsmiling. 'Come and stay down in the village. You can stay at my place. I've got a coach-load of pilgrims coming in from Fukushima, but we'll clear a room for you. Come this evening.'

He turned away. He was, I reflected, probably younger than I was. But his air of authority made me feel like a child.

As I turned to go, one of the other men hailed me. Most of them I recognised; but this one was new. He was a long, languid fellow in a cheap green suit with a sallow face, rather unattractive, and hair slicked back.

'Want to know about the yamabushi, Oneesan?' he said. 'I'll take you to see the mummy.'

'It's all right,' said another man – I must have looked doubtful. 'You go along with him. He's a guide. It's his job. He's a priest.'

As this unlikely priest led me along the hillside, the sound of a conch, long drawn out, mournful, followed us down between the trees.

The mummy resided in great splendour in a temple on the far side of the mountain. But before we could see it we had to admire the temple treasures and listen to the lengthy discourses of a beaming old priest in a short-sleeved shirt and shoe-lace tie, with a piece of gold brocade around his neck. I was relieved not to be alone with the man in the green suit. We had had an uncomfortable conversation as we sweated down the hill, in which I talked politely about how interesting it must be to be a priest and he grilled me on my age, marital status, and whether I liked Japan and Japanese men. His face, I decided, could best be described as horsy; and I didn't like his narrow eyes.

The temple had a barbaric, somehow pagan feel to it. It was old and dusty and the wooden floorboards creaked under our feet. We crept past women kneeling in the candlelit darkness, chanting in unison and beating little drums. The altar, said the priest, fanning himself, was only open once every sixty years and it was our great good fortune that we were able to see it. Or so I understood; as he droned on, my attention wandered more and more. There were flies everywhere, buzzing soporifically in the heat.

We ambled down the shadowy corridors, pausing to examine the ancient blackened images and be told their histories. They were the strangest, most eccentric bunch of deities I had ever seen. Instead of Kannon, the thousand-armed goddess of compassion, there was a wild-eyed god with a scaly fish's body coiled around a gold sword, its blade thrust deep into his mouth, rising out of a sea of writhing blue plaster waves. 'The sea god,' said the old priest, smiling benignly. And where the Buddha should have been, sitting serenely on his lotus leaf in the place of honour, was a small hunched figure with a skull for a head, slumped like a rag doll in its glass case.

The priest began his speech. 'This is the mummy of Ido Horiya of the city of Tsuruoka.'

I looked at it. Was this all? Was this what I had come all this way to see? I had been expecting something large, dignified, impressive, revelatory, like an Egyptian mummy. Ido Horiya of Tsuruoka was dressed like Bishop Egaku in the painting, in brocade robes and cowl, bright red, with a gold-encrusted head-dress balanced grotesquely on his lolling skull. He had one withered eye and skin the colour of parchment, stretched as taut as leather across his skull, and there were veins standing out on his hands. He was so tiny and shrunken it was hard to believe he had ever been a man.

The horse-faced man in the green suit put his hands together and bowed, then lit a candle and an incense stick. I put my hands together too, without much enthusiasm.

'He was born two hundred and twenty years ago, became a

yamabushi at the age of twenty-six and observed all the austerities strictly. Then he decided to follow the way of the mummies. At sixty-two he became a Buddha while still alive.

'Now I will tell you his diet. He gave up all sustenance – rice, meat, fish, vegetables – and ate only foods which would preserve his body: horsechestnuts, acorns, ginko nuts, hazelnuts, walnuts, chestnuts.' The priest was smiling proudly.

'You mean . . .' I needed to have him repeat it. 'He turned himself into a mummy while he was still alive?'

'Of course. It was common.'

Somehow, to me, it didn't make him any holier; simply stranger.

Self-mummification, it seemed, was a central part of the yamabushi training. It was mainly local peasants who did it. They spent years holed-up in caves or hermitages, praying and chanting and living on nuts and berries, sometimes bark or pine needles, gradually starving themselves until they were so dessicated that they were literally nothing but skin and bone; all the flesh had withered away. Then they stopped eating altogether. When they were near death, they were buried in the lotus position and given a bamboo straw to breathe through. When the straw collapsed, it was a signal that they had stopped breathing. They were disinterred and installed in state in a temple. There was another in the temple down the valley and several around Mount Yudono.

Thus, said the priest, they became Buddhas without dying – though Ido of Tsuruoka looked pretty dead to me. In any case, they had escaped the decomposition of the flesh. And through their austerities they had acquired such spiritual power that worshippers could gain immense merit simply by praying to them.

'Are there still people mummifying themselves?' I asked, and was disappointed when the priest shook his head. No, there were no shrivelled old men tucked away in caves on the mountainside, halfway to becoming mummies. Self-mummification, said the priest, was outlawed a hundred years ago, at the beginning of the Meiji period. He sounded rather sorry.

Back on the hilltop, there was music coming from the big shrine – the strains of a flute, the dry clack of two sticks being knocked rhythmically together. Pilgrims were kneeling inside and in the shadows, on the tatami stage in front of the closed doors of the inner shrine, one of the shrine maidens was performing a slow complex dance.

'Expensive,' observed the man in the green suit. When I raised my eyebrows, he added nonchalantly 'the more you pay, the more blessing you get.'

That afternoon I packed my bag and clambered back down the 2,446 stone steps, along the cobbled mountain paths through the cedars, to the village of Togei. I had time to spare and strolled along the main street, admiring the fine old houses.

They were huge, sprawling, shadowy manor houses of dark wood with sweeping thatched roofs, gracefully curved, hidden behind stone walls or thick hedges. Mysteriously, each had an enormous coil of rope and what looked like a hank of hair hung under the heavy gables. In front of some were small families of stone images, dressed in red bibs and caps. And for a gate each had a torii arch hung with straw tassels. It was almost as if I were walking through a village of Shinto shrines.

But surely that was it! Togei really was a village of shrines, a yamabushi village, as it had been in Basho's time. I remembered the woman at the concrete Miyatabo, just down the road, telling me that there were no yamabushi here, only farmers. At last, I suspected, I had the answer. Farmers and yamabushi were the same. Sometimes they wore farmers' clothes and looked after the rice fields; other times they put on yamabushi costumes and climbed around the mountains. The point was – and it struck me as peculiarly Japanese – that when they put on yamabushi clothes they were not dressing up; they became yamabushi. They *were* yamabushi.

I walked through the village, excited at the prospect of staying in one of these ancient brooding houses, a true yamabushi house, like those that Basho knew. But Hayashi's house, when I found it, turned out to be a disappointment. It was the only house in the village which was not old. It was a spruce modern house with a tile roof, stainless steel window frames and a car park.

Hayashi was waiting for me when I arrived. He was playing the farmer now, dressed in dungarees rolled up to reveal big muscular calves, though still, with his bulk and shaven head, unlike any farmer I had ever seen.

'Training starts tomorrow,' he said as I took my shoes off. 'Up at five, please, for the service – you'll hear the big drum. Then I'll give you yamabushi clothes and we'll go and stand under a waterfall.' He grinned hugely when I said I was not ready for such a sudden immersion in the yamabushi world.

'Obaasan will look after you.'

He hustled me off to the enormous kitchen where some women were kneeling on the floor, chopping up vegetables – cucumbers, aubergines, pumpkin, butterbur. At the stove was a small, round woman in a white pinny. She had a bucket full of crabs, claws waving wildly, which she was cramming into a pot of boiling water. She shoved in the last then banged down the lid and turned, smiling, to greet me.

'Eat with us tonight.'

She had her son's smooth, plump face and the comforting manner of someone who has taken care of hundreds of pilgrims as well as bringing up children and grandchildren. Tied to her back, bawling loudly, was a miniature clone of Hayashi, with the same large beautiful face and a head nearly as bald.

There was a desperate banging from the saucepan and a pink claw emerged, signalling hopelessly. She picked up a large bowl and slammed it over the lid and the clattering subsided.

Then I had to see the house. Hayashi strode off energetically down the long corridors, sliding open doors on to large empty rooms and announcing 'Twenty mats', 'Thirty mats'; which meant, I gathered, room for twenty or thirty pilgrims, all squashed together. I scuttled along behind, murmuring appreciation and admiration. Everything was brand new, scrubbed, spotless. The freshly stripped cedar of the walls and ceilings still had a faint woody smell and the tatami smelled of fresh-mown hay.

'Newest house in the village,' he said with great pride. 'Built four years ago, when our first child was born. Sleeps over a hundred.'

I was curious about this charismatic young man. Where had he come from? What had made him a yamabushi? What was he searching for? It seemed an extraordinary way of life for a young Japanese man, in the twentieth century, to have chosen.

But he wasn't giving anything away. He was quite happy to play the genial host, the official representative of the yamabushi. If it was information I was after, I had found the right person. He told me about the yamabushi festivals and about the week's training session they did in August (in Basho's time, apparently, it was a month; in Hachiko's, seventy days). Young people, old people, teachers, office workers, came from all over Japan and were yamabushi for a week, trooping around the mountains in baggy checked blouses, straw sandals and small round lacquer hats, clambering up and down waterfalls, blowing their conch shells from the top of tottering pinnacles of rock, until all the thousands of deities had been properly venerated.

Then we went to the shrine room, not brooding and atmospheric but large and sunny. Hayashi showed me the big iron hearth where he did the fire ceremony, cluttered with candles, bottles of saké, prayer books and a huge drum with ornate gold flames meeting in a triangle above it.

'This is how we make the ceremonial fire.'

Silently he took three sticks of wood and fitted them together in a triangle, balanced another three on top, then another three, then stacked wood all around like a teepee.

'That's how we do it in this house,' he said gravely. 'The other houses do a square.'

Hanging on the wall were two large conch shells and bundles of white ropes, tied in intricate knots. He separated one out and hung it around my neck.

'Now you are a pilgrim,' he grinned, adding seriously, 'these mountains are sacred; wear this for purification.'

Finally I could restrain myself no longer.

'I wonder if . . . Could I ask . . . Why did you become a yamabushi?' I said, trying to temper the rudeness of the question by the politeness of my words.

You don't ask 'Why?' in Japan. You watch, listen, learn, admire, appreciate and occasionally ask 'How?' – 'How do you make the ceremonial fire?' 'How do you wear the white rope?' – but never 'Why?' Only uncivilised foreigners ask, in their brusque, direct way. And the Japanese usually don't know the answer.

'I'm the eldest son,' he said coldly, as if the question hardly warranted an answer. That was all. No overpowering transcendental experience to set him on the path, no burning sense of spiritual quest. It was much simpler than that, much more down to earth. His father had been a yamabushi, the sixth from the top – he relaxed now that he was providing information again – and had kept the records and allocated jobs. His grandfather had been a yamabushi; and so had his great-grandfather and countless generations before him. He had had no choice in the matter.

But that did not mean he had no sense of vocation. He was totally committed, in the way that most eldest sons in Japan put all their energy into the family business, whatever their personal inclinations.

'It's a job.' He grinned again. 'We have eight hundred pilgrims a week here in July and August, three bus-loads a day. That's how we live. But it's a hard way to make a living. Most people in the village have other jobs as well. Teacher, work in the post office, that kind of thing. I'm the only full-time yamabushi. My wife has to work, though. And Obaasan looks after the fields.'

His wife, it seemed, worked in a factory in Tsuruoka, making *tochi mochi*, the brown rice cakes I liked so much.

When I met her later that evening I was puzzled again. She was a pretty woman, immaculately made-up. Her eyelids were purple, her lips pink, and she padded fastidiously around the tatami in tight skirt and stockings. She seemed made for the city. I could imagine her as a tour guide (she had been one, in fact), a waitress in a coffee shop or a mama-san in a bar – but not as the wife of a yamabushi. They were the oddest couple I had ever met.

Meeting her, I wondered if I had got him completely wrong. Perhaps he really was just an ordinary fellow with a job to do. Perhaps the charisma, the magnificence, was all in my imagination. I doubted it though.

'I'll tell you a story about Akaibo, the famous yamabushi.' We were in the shrine room still. 'It's not a very nice story . . . You've heard of Mogami Yoshiaki and Muto, of course. Well, it was about three hundred years ago. They had a fight. One of them – I forget which – ran away and Akaibo gave him sanctuary. Then the other one came chasing after him. You know what Akaibo did? He cut open his own belly, just like that, pulled out his intestines and threw them at him. That beat him off. He was the greatest yamabushi of all. So his festival is the day before we begin our week's training, on August 25th.'

When Yoshitsune and Benkei came this way eight hundred years ago, on their way to Hiraizumi, they wanted to make a pilgrimage to the top of Mount Haguro, to pay their respects to the dragon gods and pray for safe passage. Benkei, the gigantic warrior monk from Mount Kumano in the south, planned to take initiation into some of the secret northern yamabushi techniques. But Yoshitsune's wife, the delicate princess who had walked with them all the way from Kyoto, was about to bear a child – the one that was born at Narugo and died at Hiraizumi. So while Yoshitsune waited with her at the bottom of the mountain, at Kiyokawa, Benkei climbed on his own.

Halfway up, he decided to send a signal to Yoshitsune that he was safe. There was a huge rock nearby, six foot high. He picked it up with one hand, as if it were a pebble, and lobbed it way out into the air in a wide arc so that Yoshitsune would see it. It landed ten kilometres away, at the foot of the mountain, and lodged there, upright.

And there it stands to this day, apparently, on the Tsuruoka road, just outside Togei. Carved on it are three names – Kannon, Amida, Seishi. Kannon is the goddess of compassion, Amida the Buddha of the Western Paradise. No one knows who Seishi is.

I wanted to see this stone and set out next morning to walk down through the village, between the huge dark shrine-like houses, past the concrete Miyatabo, towards Tsuruoka.

There was something mysterious about the Benkei stone. The old people I asked all spoke of it as a local landmark and gave me precise directions.

'Benkei's stone?' quavered an old woman sweeping the gutter. 'Just down there, before the park, in a garden. It's huge – you can't miss it.'

There were no stones on the way to the park, nor in the park itself. An old man in a cap directed me back the way I had come. 'It's in the garden of the sixth house from the park, back towards the village.' I counted back six houses and peered into the garden. But there was no enormous stone carved with names.

In desperation I asked in all the nearby houses. The pinch-faced young women with babies tied to their backs had never heard of Benkei or his stone. Finally one called to a cadaverous old woman. 'Benkei's stone, Granny,' she yelled.

The old woman pondered, then said slowly in a hoarse whisper, 'Yes, it used to be here, didn't it? I think it's disappeared.'

I had more luck with Benkei's cooking-pot. Where the road through the village curved, a path covered in moss led to an old wooden temple which housed a pair of huge straw sandals the size of a man and smaller ones in mouldering heaps in the corners. Outside were three stone images in large flat turbans, grimacing fiercely: neither Shinto nor Buddhist, but deities of some other, more primitive, cult.

'This is the *Kogane-do*, Gold Hall.' At my shoulder was a thin, bespectacled young man with a shaven head, all in black like a crow. 'Dates from the time of Prince Hachiko.'

He had the fierce glittering eyes of Hachiko himself. He was the priest of the Buddhist temple across the road and his family had been the village priests for generations.

'We are Tendai yamabushi,' he said severely, glaring at me through wire-rimmed glasses as if he suspected I had already been corrupted by the other party. His shaven head was not

223

domed like Hayashi's but flat and stubbly and flecked with sweat.

'Our Tendai way is the yamabushi way. Tendai and yama-bushi are the same! Those priests up the hill, these farmers down here – they're just fancy-dress yamabushi. Those rites of theirs – Shinto, that's all they are, just Shinto, new-fangled stuff. We Tendai priests are the only ones who keep the authentic yamabushi practices.

'As for the *matsuhijiri*', he went on scornfully, before I could get a word in, 'as far as I'm concerned there are no *matsuhijiri*. A hundred years ago, before Meiji, the word '*matsuhijiri*' meant something. They were holy men. They had attained *satori*. They were enlightened. Nowadays all they do is perform ceremonies.'

He showed me an enormous rusting cauldron, big enough to sit inside, in the gateway of the temple. 'Made of iron sand. Dates from the Kamakura period, about 1190' – the same as Benkei.

'Musashibo Benkei carried it into battle on his back – that's the legend. Boiled his soup in it then picked it up and drank out of it.' He smiled loftily over his glasses as if to say, of course, you and I don't believe that kind of thing, do we.

That evening I went to visit Umebayashi-bo, 'the Ume-bayashi pilgrim house'. It was a beautiful old house, one of the oldest in the village. I dubbed it the 'yamabushi temple'. It had the air of a temple, but neither Buddhist nor Shinto. There was something pagan about it. Perhaps it was the luxuriant curve of the thatch, the eccentric way it wrapped the gables and protuberances of the house, or the oddly ornate torii gate or the small extra shrine in the grounds.

In the daytime there were no walls at all, only the roof. The wooden panels were pushed out of sight and you could see shadowy figures moving around against the pale paper screens inside. As I walked in through the gate the shadows were lengthening and a young woman was sliding the wooden walls back into place.

After dinner I went to sit with the family. Two plump

children were playing on the tatami. An old man was kneeling
behind them at a low table, adding up rows of figures.

He bowed, then peered at me through thick glasses. He was
tall and gangly, like a stork, with a wing of greying hair, neatly
combed, on each side of his shiny domed forehead.

'I am a *daihafuji*,' he announced. The young woman set a
cup of tea in front of me, murmuring a formal welcome. 'I
completed the hundred days. It was twenty years ago, when I
was forty-nine. I knew I would be a *matsuhijiri*. All the Togei
men are. Nowadays old men do it. But I wanted to do it while I
was young and vigorous.'

So I had found my *matsuhijiri* – this mild old man, with his
long schoolmasterly face and absent-minded air. I had almost
forgotten I was looking; which was probably why I had
managed to find him.

He shuffled off and came back with a thick scrapbook
labelled 'Matsuhijiri: Hundred Day Diary', put it down on the
table under the harsh neon light and began turning the pages
with his long bony fingers. The two children scrambled to
look.

Page after page of yellowing photographs showed two
dramatic figures striding regally through the forest or across
the mountainside, carrying staffs, in flowing white robes, high
gaiters and tall black head-dresses. They were magnificent.
They looked like high priests or kings, or, with their bristly
beards, which grew longer by the page, like wild men of the
mountains, Afghan bandits. Sometimes they were alone,
sometimes followed by a train of yamabushi, all in white,
shading them with huge umbrellas, like a pair of princes in
procession.

The hundred days began after the harvest festival, on
September 24th.

'It's like going into hibernation, like a bear,' chuckled the old
man.

The children romped off to the television and the young
woman crept away. I sat quietly while the old man talked.

'In those days there was a second floor in the Saikan, the
Pilgrim Hall. That was where we stayed, in a room up there.

We weren't allowed fish or flesh and we couldn't shave or cut our nails or our hair. Do you know how I kept my nails short? I rubbed them on the stone steps, the ones that lead up the mountain.

'First thing in the morning, we had to wash ourselves with spring water, from Gassan. I'd throw buckets of cold water over myself, like this.' He waved his long arms around.

'Then we did exercises. I didn't mind at first. But later on, when winter set in, it was hard. The worst thing of all – you couldn't have guessed if you hadn't experienced it – the very worst thing, when it was cold, was turning the pages of the prayer book. It made a sudden cold wind. That was the last straw! And the coldness of the pages.'

The three sacred mountains and the villages nearby are dotted with shrines of all the gods who live there. The *matsuhi-jiris'* job was to pray at every shrine.

'When we got to each shrine we blew our conches. We paid homage to the god with our six senses and purified ourselves. Then we prayed for the Emperor and for all the people of the world – may they all be happy.'

He showed me the shrines, page after page of them, listed in a small black prayer book.

'I've no idea how many there are. We say they are like the branches of a tree, endless.

'In the evening we used to kneel for three hours at a time at the shrine in our room in the Saikan, without moving. My legs went completely numb. We were supposed to concentrate, not be listening to noises. But I kept being distracted by the sound of mice running around.

'By the end of it, the two of us were like brothers.'

The final pictures showed the two men, heavily bearded by now, clambering through deep snow up the stone steps of Haguro. 'It was at the end of November that it snowed – that was the hardest time, walking around the mountains in the snow.

'When I finished, I felt – well, that's it, I've done my hundred days. If I'd had longer, I could have done it better.

'We're graduates now.' He unfolded his long legs, beaming

mildly through his glasses. 'We got a certificate. We don't have
to do the August training. We have a meeting every year, all
the *daihafuji*. It was May 13th this year.'

He clambered to his feet and brought down a framed picture
from a shelf. It was like a school photograph, rows of very old
men, all stern-faced, all in their white *matsuhijiri* robes, out-
sized now, with red prayer bags around their necks.

The little boy pushed in.

'Grandad! There's Grandad!' he shouted.

14
To the Holy Mountain

On the eighth, we climbed Gassan. Hanging necklaces of white mulberry paper on our bodies and wrapping our heads in bleached cotton hoods, we followed a 'Strong One', a mountain guide, up on to the mountain . . .

'Never climbed Gassan myself,' said Obaasan. We were sitting quietly in a small room beside the kitchen, well away from the activity, fanning ourselves, drinking lemonade and popping green soya beans out of their pods into our mouths. It was raining outside and exhaustingly hot and clammy.

'When I was a girl, women weren't allowed on the mountain, or on Haguro either. Only men. The mountain is a goddess, you see. So she's jealous of other women. That's what they used to say, anyway. Even now, if a young couple go walking on the mountain, they get separated, because the mountain is jealous. It's different nowadays, of course. No one bothers about that sort of thing any more. You get all sorts of people on the mountain: men, women, they all climb. But I never have.'

She was a bit like a mountain herself – solid, round, reassuring, immensely calm and sensible. I wondered how it felt to be the daughter, wife and mother of a yamabushi. The handsome little boy strapped to her back was scowling with concentration and fighting to escape. She loosed the cords and he toddled off, then ran back and began pummelling her with his fists. She stroked his fuzzy head.

'So cute but so bad,' she said, beaming fondly. 'Just like his father was!' In a few years, he too would be striding the mountains in voluminous white robes, blowing conch shells and standing under waterfalls.

228

By now the kitchen was full of helpers. They arrived at four in the morning, long before I was awake, prepared breakfast for the guests, then set about chopping and slicing sackfuls of vegetables and stirring huge saucepans on the stove. By afternoon the red lacquer trays stacked on shelves beside the kitchen door – one for each guest – were laden with little plates and dishes of food; and the floor was covered in plastic bowls full of sliced cucumber and tiny pickled aubergines.

Around six o'clock a huge bus would draw up in the car-park and Hayashi-san would stride out to greet the new arrivals, regal in his white robes. His wife had given up her job in the *tochi mochi* factory in Tsuruoka and emerged in the evening to serve everyone, padding around the tatami in her tights, an apron tied over her elegant skirt. She did a good job as the mama-san of the house, keeping saké cups filled and swapping banter with the male guests and even the young lad who squatted in the entrance way selling souvenir pickles.

The holiday season had begun and the house was getting fuller by the day. My peaceful eight-mat room had been requisitioned (it was, of course, a waste for me to sleep alone in a room that could sleep eight), and I had been transferred to Obaasan's room, where I slept alongside her and Hayashi's four-year-old daughter. Actually, I discovered, there was a spare room upstairs. 'But', said Obaasan, 'we couldn't put you in such a big room all by yourself. You'd be lonely!'

Basho and Sora made their pilgrimage up Mount Gassan and down to the hidden sanctuaries of Mount Yudono on July 24th, the eighth day of the sixth month, 1689.

They had spent the previous day fasting and worshipping at Gongen shrine in preparation. On the morning of the eighth, their fifth day in South Valley, they got up at dawn. Instead of wearing their dusty black robes, they dressed themselves in the traditional white clothes which pilgrims always wear to climb the mountains. They wound cotton strips around their heads like turbans and put on 'necklaces of white mulberry paper', like the one which Hayashi had given me, for purification.

Ahead of them was a gruelling journey. They were going to

take the path which bee-faced Hachiko had beaten out nine
hundred years before, across 'three leagues of grass, three
leagues of forest, three leagues of rock', a climb of 20 miles and
more than 6,000 feet, to the bleak windswept summit of
Gassan.

Gas-san: Moon Mountain. From inland it looks gentle and
feminine, curving above the surrounding mountains like the
full moon; but from the sea it is wild and forbidding, a
formidable barrier between Haguro and the sacred inner
shrine of Mount Yudono. Anyone that wants to stand in the
presence of the god, anyone that wants to worship at the inner
shrine, has no choice but to battle up its rugged slopes. It is
a trial to be overcome, a test, an initiation.

It must have been a fearful journey for the frail old poet. 'We
climbed through cloud and mist', he wrote, 'over ice and
snow, for eight ri, twenty miles, until we thought we must
have crossed the barrier of the clouds and were treading the
very path of the sun and moon!'

For the first few miles at least, the slope was gentle enough
to go on horseback. One by one they passed the stations
where pilgrims stopped to rest: Kowashimizu, 'strong
clearwater spring'; Hirashizu, 'level spring'; Takashimizu, 'high spring'. Along the way, they gathered bamboo
grass to make their bedding for the night; for there would
be no vegetation higher up on Gassan's barren slopes. They
had lunch at a mountain hut at Midagahara, 'increasingly
steep moor'. Then, stumbling along on foot with only their
staffs to help them, keeping close behind their guide, they
struggled up rockier and rockier paths, across steeper and
steeper slopes.

'By the time we reached the top, frozen and barely able to
breathe, the sun had set and the moon was shining. With
bamboo grass for a bed and fine bamboo twigs for a pillow, we
lay down and waited for the light.'

'Your first time is it?' asked Suzuki-san. 'It's my fifth. July
23rd, that's when I come – today's July 23rd. And I always stay
at Hayashi's.

'It's raining. Bound to rain tomorrow,' he added gloomily.

'Rained last year too. Terrible it was – terrible climbing in the rain!'

Hayashi came and sat down with us, holding a large shallow bowl of saké. 'Here's to a good climb tomorrow,' he said, adding airily, 'Took a group up there yesterday – look how brown I am!' His broad chest and shaven head were even browner than before. He downed the saké and showed me the inside of the bowl. Brushed in gold on the red lacquer surface was Basho's haiku on Gassan

kumo no mine	Cloud peaks
ikutsu kuzurete	Endlessly crumble away –
tsuki no yama	Mountain of the moon

At last I was going to climb Gassan and see the sacred shrine at Yudono. And I was going in the approved Japanese fashion: with a group. I was no longer on my own.

My group had arrived not long before in a large bus, had bathed, put on blue and white dressing-gowns and arranged themselves along the sides of the shrine room, men along three sides, women along one, backs to the wall. Hayashi's wife and the other women had distributed trays of food, Hayashi had made a speech and they had all begun to eat when he beckoned me over to be introduced.

He put me next to Suzuki-san, an amiable, rather faded man of about fifty, with wispy thinning hair. I looked around at the ranks of identical dressing-gowns. Who were all these people? Without clothing to distinguish them, it was impossible to tell whether they were company directors or road workers. The whole shrine room, bright and neon-lit, was a hubbub of chattering and laughter, people shuffling from group to group, plonking down cross-legged on the tatami, passing round huge dishes of saké.

'Farmers they are, most of them, from Fukushima. I am too,' said Suzuki. From Fukushima – that explained why it was so easy to understand him. I no longer had to struggle with the outlandish Tohoku dialect. 'Silkworms, that's what we grow, mainly. Mainly silkworms. Silkworms, rice, mushrooms.' He shook his head gloomily, hissing through his teeth. 'Bad time to go away right now,' he said. 'Too busy. Busy time of year.'

One of the dressing-gowns on the other side of the room detached itself from the group and swaggered towards me. It contained a muscular pug-nosed young man with bristly hair, who sat himself down directly in front of me, legs crossed, looked me in the eye and said fiercely in English, in a staccato monotone, 'How old are you?'

I shifted back a little. In my country, I said, it was not polite to ask ladies their age.

'No no, not in Japan either,' said Suzuki anxiously. Apparently this was the trouble-maker of the group.

The newcomer (Endo-san was his name) pushed his face closer to mine and tried again. 'Which do you like better, lice or bread?'

'Bread,' I said in Japanese, all innocence. 'In my country we don't eat lice, or fleas either.'

He gaped. Suzuki-san shifted uncomfortably. Then, fortunately, another man came over and sat down shyly next to me. He had a round rosy schoolboy's face and hair flopping over his eyes.

'May I speak to you?' he asked earnestly. 'I would like to know many things about your country. Do you have mountains in your country? What sort of plants do you have in your country?'

Endo-san had reached the limits of his English.

'If I learn one new English word a day for a year,' he said loudly, addressing the whole group, 'I will learn three hundred and sixty-five words.'

He turned back to me.

'It is raining very hard,' he snarled. 'How do you say *o-ame* (heavy rain) in English?'

I would have preferred not to have been reminded of the rain and thought uneasily of slippery rocks and muddy paths.

Next morning I was awakened by the boom of the big drum in the shrine room. It was five-thirty. I pushed back my bedding, rushed to the window and slid it open. The rain had stopped, though the sky still looked threateningly overcast and the ground was sodden.

Hayashi had given me a thin white jacket and a blue cotton strip to wear around my neck, with 'Dewa Sanzan Worshippers' Group' printed down one side and 'Mount Haguro, Hayashi-bo' on the other.

'There'll be a lot of groups on the mountain,' he said. 'This shows that you belong to the Hayashi-bo group.'

It turned out he was not climbing with us. 'No time,' he said. He stood statuesquely in the car-park as the bus backed out, then raised his conch shell to his lips and blew a long melancholy note in farewell.

The first eight of Gassan's ten stations we were to pass by bus. While most of last night's revellers sprawled in their seats, Suzuki-san, who had put me in the front so that I could see the view, stood up and addressed the group.

'Last night it rained but now it's stopped. The weather is perfect, perfect for climbing, nice and cool. It'll be good on the mountain. Don't forget, don't start drinking . . . Hands up, who's already had a drink?' A couple of hands flickered up. It was not yet six-thirty. 'Don't start drinking until you've finished the climb, not before!'

The young lady guide took the microphone. 'Good morning everyone . . .' she began.

Kowashimizu, the fourth station; Hirashizu, the sixth; Takashimizu, the seventh . . . One by one they slipped by. The towering cedars which clustered the lower slopes were replaced by woods of spindly birch trees, their trunks an unearthly white in the morning light, and thick ferns and bushes of blue hydrangeas.

'Do your best, Mr Driver,' chirped our cheerful young guide as the driver edged the bus around a particularly tortuous bend. 'You had a good time last night, you had plenty to drink, now do your best, please.'

We swung past two dark figures standing motionless, looking out across the mountainside, ghastly in white shawls and garish red caps. Half-asleep, I gaped at them fearfully, wondering who they were and what they could be doing in this desolate place. Then, with relief, I realised that they were made of stone.

Finally we were above the level of the trees. Rough moorland specked with yellow flowers covered the flank of the mountain. Everyone was clamouring '*Saiko, saiko!* The weather looks great!'

The sky was clearing. Behind us, way below, was the squat tree-covered peak of Mount Haguro, then the hazy green of the Shonai plain and, far in the distance, soaring above the clouds, the white cone of Mount Chokai, 'Fuji of the north'.

'It suddenly sent out a great puff of smoke five years ago, after sleeping for a hundred and fifty years,' said someone.

'There's the sea!' yelled someone else; but I couldn't see it.

The road ended at Midagahara, the eighth station, where Basho and Sora had stopped for lunch. From here on, as they had done, we were to walk. We bundled out, shivering in the sudden cold, pulling on sweaters under our thin pilgrim jackets, wrapping white scarves around our heads.

Suzuki-san seemed to have taken charge of the group. He counted heads before we all set off, balancing our way along narrow wooden boards across the marshy ground.

Why, I wondered, was I the only one carrying anything?

'We've got nothing to carry. We're not rich enough,' growled Endo-san. He had definitely taken a dislike to me and I vowed to avoid him for the rest of the climb.

By now we were clambering across rough stones like the bed of a waterfall. Ahead of us the path cut a narrow swathe across the endless sweep of the gorse, zigzagging around the boulders that scattered the slopes, turning abruptly every now and then into a steep staircase of giant rocks. Everyone else seemed to be in a great hurry. They tramped off, heads down, white scarves fluttering like flags, never looking round, never looking back. I was quickly getting left behind.

'If you go too slowly, you get muddled up with the next group.' The earnest young man from last night was right behind me. He gazed absent-mindedly into one of the beautiful trumpet-like yellow flowers.

'We call these flowers *nikokisugi* in Japanese. Do you have

234

them in your country? They say there are lilies up here too. And bears. And foxes and badgers. And you can hear the voice of the nightingale.'

I paused, realising suddenly how silent it was. Of course. There were no insects: no semis whirring interminably, no cicadas whining. Behind me, another man, whom I had not noticed before, stopped too.

We caught up with the rest of the group at a small shrine near the ninth station. A priest, dignified in spectacles, black hat and brocades, was chanting, while the pilgrims, suddenly subdued, put their hands together and bowed their heads. Among them stood great stone images, incongruous in red mob caps and flowery kimonos.

'Do you know, this is the very same path that Matsuo Basho trod?' A tall lean figure in climbing boots and gaiters was striding along beside me while I scurried to keep up. He had a gaunt tanned face and close-cropped fringe which reminded me of pictures of Henry V. 'Amazing to think that, isn't it?'

I looked around at the long line of pilgrims clambering across the rocks with their staffs, all swathed in white, clothes flapping in the wind, bells tinkling. They could have been the same people that Basho climbed with. Beyond them the flank of the mountain rolled away, rocks stippling the green of the gorse, falling for miles until it disappeared into clouds. Patches of snow glistened in the hollows. Mount Chokai, blue in the distance, looked higher than ever. Nothing at all had changed here on this bleak mountain since Basho's time.

I turned back. The rest of the group had disappeared. Only Henry V was standing, patiently waiting. It was his job, I guessed, to round up stragglers.

'Why are they in such a hurry?' I complained. 'Why don't they stop to look at the scenery?'

'That's the Japanese way,' he grinned. 'And they've got a bus to catch.'

I had assumed that he too was a farmer from Fukushima, though his accent seemed stronger than the others. No, he said, he was a local man, from Togei ('Tongei', he pronounced it).

'I'm the patrol,' he explained, using the English word 'patrol'. 'I climb Gassan every day.'

Every day. I tried to imagine it as I stumbled across the rocks. No wonder he strolled along so confidently, like the 'Strong One' who had guided Basho and Sora.

'It's my job. I keep the path clean and make sure no one picks the flowers. This is my rubbish bag. See? No rubbish on the path, is there?

'These pilgrims, you know, they come every year, most of them. Their fathers came, their grandfathers came . . . And they always stay at the same *shukubo*, the same pilgrim house.'

The villagers, he said, collected money throughout the year so that they could send representatives. And even though for these silkworm farmers this was a busy time of year, still they always came. Some came every year, always on the same day. Some came every two or three years, alternating with their wives or mothers.

'Why?' I puffed, panting along from rock to rock behind him. 'What do they come for?'

He looked at me as if he did not understand the question. He could tell me easily enough what happened. But 'why' was something he had never thought about. He pondered for a while.

'Religion,' he grunted. 'Yes. Religion.'

Higher up the hill, two figures had propped themselves against one of the huge boulders which lay tumbled around the gorse and were waiting for us: Takeda-san, my earnest friend, and a second man, the one I had noticed before.

'Religion . . .' I persisted. 'Meaning . . . ?'

I had to ask several times, in different ways, before he finally said, 'Well, they pray, I guess. For their families, maybe. For the village. For health. Silkworm farmers pray for healthy silkworms. Rice farmers pray for a good harvest.'

But now we had reached the snow. Ahead of us the path was blocked by a huge sheet of it, a great frozen lake spreading across the hillside for several hundred yards. The heat of the ground was gradually eating away the edge, so that it jutted out high above the grass in a sharp ledge which looked treacherous to me.

'Do you have snow in your country?' queried Takeda-san as I prodded it cautiously with my toe, wondering how firm – and how slippery – it was. As I took an unsteady step, feeling the surface give under my feet, the nameless man, who had been behind me, took my hand and led me across. He had a rough, farmer's hand.

'Gassan shrine!' crowed Patrol-san triumphantly, pointing to a small grey building on the peak of a pyramid-shaped hillock. We were climbing steeply through a barren moon landscape of black volcanic rocks scattered eccentrically across the mountainside, some big as houses, other smaller ones lovingly piled into heaps. At the foot of some of the heaps were coins and small images. Way below us, wisps of cloud drifted across the slope.

As he shepherded the three of us up the final slopes, the rest of the group, perched on the rocks above, yelled encouragement. Suzuki-san was looking anxiously at his watch.

Gassan shrine, six and a half thousand feet above the rice plains of Shonai, is like a small fortress, surrounded by high black walls to protect it against the weight of the winter snows. As we joined the line of pilgrims to go through the torii gate – not a gaudy red one but three slabs of plain black rock – into the holy area, there was a sudden hush. The banter and laughter stopped. We put our hands together and stood, heads bowed, while the high priest, resplendent in green robes and high black hat, chanted a blessing and shook his wand of white paper strips over us. He gave us each a scrap of paper, cut like a paper doll into the shape of a kimono or a priest's robe and written with a prayer.

'Rub it over your body,' whispered Patrol-san. For purification, I assumed, rubbing the paper down my arms and aching legs and casting it into the stone font.

In silence we approached the shrine itself, the heart of the holy mountain. We stood before it, heads bowed, hands together, and chanted in unison, Patrol-san leading the chanting in his deep baritone.

The sound of our voices hung for a moment in the still mountain air and the tiny bells that hung from the pilgrims' belts tinkled faintly. A coil of smoke from the incense cauldron spiralled upwards. Then there was a dry clatter, as a coin which Patrol-san had tossed on to the roof leapt from tile to tile and finally lodged in the drainpipe. Suddenly everyone was whooping and yelling, hurling coins on to the roof and jostling to drink the sacred saké which two jolly priests squatting inside the shrine were serving up.

'Half an hour for lunch,' said Suzuki-san. 'No more, mind!'

I had thought of spending the night up on the mountain, as Basho had done. But now I was here, in this bleak landscape of dusty black soil and jagged black rocks, I felt less inclined to. Besides, I wanted to stay with my group. I added a stone to the top of one of the small piles, made a wish and went to join the others for lunch.

'The sun rose, the clouds melted away, and we went down towards Yudono.' After a cold uncomfortable night on their bamboo beds on the mountain, Basho and Sora woke at dawn and hurried up to the shrine on the summit. They were hoping to see *Raiko*, 'the coming of the light'. On certain days, when the weather was right and clouds were massed like cottonwool beneath the peak, you could see your shadow reflected there, haloed in a shimmering ring of red, as the sun rose. It was said to be a profoundly religious experience, like a vision of Amida Buddha himself, approaching in a fiery halo to welcome the spirits of the dead.

But that morning they were disappointed. The clouds lifted quickly and there was no Raiko.

As they started down towards Yudono, they passed 'a hut known as Kajigoya, the Swordsmith's Hut'. Basho recorded the story of the twelfth century swordsmith who lived there

A swordsmith of this country (Dewa), selecting this place for the mysterious power in its waters, here purified body and mind and beat out swords which finally he inscribed with the mark 'Gassan' – and they were prized throughout the world. I thought of that famed Ryosen Spring (Lung-chuan, the 'Dragon Spring' in China), where they used to temper swords, and of Kansho and Bakuya of old. (Kan Chiang and his wife Mu-yeh, as their names are pronounced in Chinese, were, apparently, famous swordsmiths of the Wu dynasty.) The devotion needed to master any path is far from shallow, I realised.

'Of course, he didn't really make swords up here.'

Patrol-san was telling us the same story that, presumably, Basho had heard from his guide, the 'Strong One', as we stood, shivering in the cold, looking out over the hills that rolled towards Yudono. Beyond were the mountains of Dewa, peak upon peak of them, stretching away, paler and paler blue, until they dissolved into the sky.

Appearing and disappearing, etched along the curve of the hill, was a thin white line, the path which we were to follow. It looked a long way, further than I had expected. Snow patches dappled the green slopes and from the holy mountain itself, invisible somewhere below us, a plume of cloud swirled up. Almost beneath our feet, it seemed – though in fact it must have been several hundred feet below – was the tiny roof of Kajigoya, the swordsmith's hut.

'He didn't bring all his tools up here. It's too far. He just came up to pray, and made his swords lower down.'

Suzuki-san grunted thoughtfully in reply.

High above, a bird was singing a clear thin song.

'It's a nightingale,' said Takeda-san. 'Look – up there. Do you have . . . ?' I groaned inwardly and prepared to tell him that there were indeed nightingales in my country but that they did not sing in the daytime.

So we began the long descent to Yudono. Standing on the summit of Gassan, I had been congratulating myself that the journey was over. I had done it. I had reached the top. But in fact the worst of it was still to come.

We plunged for miles down a precipitous staircase of boulders the size of small houses, scrambling from rock to rock, slipping and sliding across the shale. Once again I soon fell to the back of the group. An old character in a pilgrim jacket and straw hat, who plonked himself down on a rock every few hundred yards for a cigarette, lent me his staff and after that I managed to keep up. But I still stopped often to rest, my legs quaking.

'Your knees are laughing – that's what we say in Japanese,' said Takeda-san once, very seriously. 'What do you say in English?'

A few minutes later, as I edged down a particularly steep and frightening slope, he was waiting for me again and asked breezily, 'What is the best way to learn English?'

It was hot again and getting hotter the lower we went.

Basho and Sora took this same path. Following along behind the 'Strong One', they scrambled down the mountainside in their white robes, exactly as the pilgrims on the slope ahead of me were doing, then tramped on, across the hills, along the path I could see in the distance, down to Yudono, to the holy shrine, and worshipped there.

For them that was only the beginning of their day's walk. The only way back from Yudono was to retrace their steps; there was no road to the inner shrine in those days. They turned around and clambered back up the steep face of Gassan, hauled themselves all the way back up these dizzying slopes, and were at the shrine at the top in time for lunch. Then they marched back down the twenty miles of Gassan's long flank. Komyobo, a yamabushi from South Valley, was waiting for them at Kowashimizu, the fourth station, with food. Finally, well after nightfall, they reached South Valley again – 'exceedingly tired', wrote Sora.

Thinking of that extraordinary journey, I stopped to look up at the jumble of rocks I had just scrambled down. I didn't intend to scramble back up again, no matter what Basho had done.

Then I felt a hand on my back. That same nameless man, who had helped me across the snow, was right behind me. I supposed I must have stopped too suddenly and he had stumbled into me. All the way down the hill he had been behind me, ready with a hand whenever I reached a steep part, walking slowly when I walked slowly, quickly when I walked quickly.

I had chatted to him a few times, at first simply to escape Takeda-san and his endless questions about 'my country'. This man, it seemed, was not interested in my country. In fact, I finally realised with considerable surprise, he was interested in me.

I was surprised too, and rather ashamed, at my own re-action. I had hardly spoken to the man. I hardly knew what he looked like – he was always behind me. Yet here I was, covertly smoothing my hair, wondering if it was windswept, wishing I had a mirror.

'What have you done with your children?' A jaunty old fellow, staff in hand, had overtaken us and was springing down the rocks, pausing every now and then for me to catch up.

'I don't have any,' I said.

'But you must have. You're forty, aren't you?'

I denied it vigorously. He grinned broadly.

'I'm sixty-two,' he said with great pride.

For all his years, he was like a mountain goat, very thin, very lithe, with a face like a pixie's, deep brown, and an irresistible grin. Perhaps Basho, I thought, far from picking his way timorously down the mountain as I was doing, had skipped down as confidently as old Honda-san.

'I've been coming every year since I was eighteen,' he said. 'Used to be a lot tougher then, of course. There was no bus, you know, in those days. No bus till 1955, Showa 30 – I was thirty that year too. Before that we walked all the way from Haguro. Got up at one in the morning and walked all day. In white *tabi* and *waraji* – toed cotton socks and straw sandals. And had to fast all day before. Couldn't eat fish, couldn't eat meat. Good walkers', he added, poised like Pan on a boulder beside the path, 'used to make it from the top of Gassan to Yudono in twenty minutes.'

In fact we had been going steadily downhill for two hours and my legs were shaking so much I wondered if I could finish the course. By now the landscape was no longer alpine but tropical, bursting with green. As we scrambled across the rocks we had to push through bamboo and camellia thickets and thick ferns crowding across the path. The clouds had cleared now and the sun shone fiercely out of an oppressively blue sky.

Was it here, I wondered, that Basho saw the cherry tree, blossoming in July, three months out of season?

'Sitting down on a rock to rest for a while, I noticed a cherry tree, just three shaku (3 feet) high, still half in bud. Even when it was buried deep beneath the snow, I thought, in its heart this late blossoming cherry never forgot the spring. Its fragrance brought to mind the old Zen poem "plum blossoms in the scorching sun"; and remembering too the poignancy of high priest Gyoson's lines, I felt still more deeply moved.'

Gyoson, apparently, was a Tendai priest who lived in the Heian period, between 1055 and 1135. 'How pitiful', he wrote – 'the mountain cherry, blooming unseen by the eyes of men!'

We caught up with the rest of the group at a little stall selling 'yamabushi tea' at an exorbitant price per cup.

'Try some,' said Patrol-san. 'It's good for you.'

'Makes you clever,' sneered Endo-san – unfortunately I had failed to avoid him this time.

'If you're clever already it makes you stupid!' chuckled old Honda-san.

The last part of the descent was the worst of all. Around a corner the path came to an abrupt end. There was a cluster of pilgrims queuing to start down the first of what turned out to be a long series of rusty iron ladders, fixed precariously into the rocks.

As I hung above the void, feeling blindly for the next rung, gripping the sides of the ladder until my knuckles were white, there was a familiar voice beside me. 'Careful now, careful! Not much further now! Do your best.' Then a burst of impatience – 'Hurry up!' I stopped and laughed, causing chaos among the long line of pilgrims swarming down behind me. There was old Honda-san, bounding carelessly straight down the rocks, hardly bothering to balance with his staff.

As we scrambled down the last slopes, the nameless man was close behind me again. 'Come and see me,' he said urgently. 'I'll give you my address.' But the next group was pushing down behind us and it was impossible to stop.

In a way I preferred it that way. If I had ever met him again, somewhere other than this magic mountain, I'm sure I would have been disappointed. Whereas as it was – perhaps it was a rather sentimental thought – the whole beauty of the encounter lay in its frailty, its transience. Really nothing had happened at all. It had been as fleeting as the cherry blossoms.

Before going to worship at the inner shrine at Yudono, Basho and Sora performed thorough rituals of purification. They went down to the river Kiyomegawa, which flows through the valley, and poured water over themselves. Then they put on new *waraji*, straw sandals, swathed themselves in special sanctified white robes and headgear, and hung fresh ropes of white mulberry paper around their necks.

'Then', wrote Sora, 'we went humbly to worship.' He recorded some of the rules for worshippers: 'From here into the interior, all gold, silver and coins which you are carrying cannot be brought out again; they must be left behind. Nothing which is dropped may be picked up again.'

The path to the inner shrine was littered so thickly with coins and offerings left by all the faithful that the two travellers, as they entered, had to step on the precious coins. Sora, moved by this symbol of the devotion which the place inspired, wrote

Yudono yama	Mount Yudono
zeni fumu michi no	Treading the path of coins
namida kana	I weep . . .

Basho, who had written in detail of everything he had seen on Mount Gassan, now wrote simply, 'According to the rules for pilgrims, it is forbidden to reveal to others what is in Mount Yudono. Therefore I stop my brush and do not record it.'

But he was allowed to describe how deeply he was moved by the mysteries which he saw on the sacred mountain:

katararenu   Yudono
Yudono ni nurasu   Of which I may not speak
tamoto kana   Wets my sleeve with
                                tears . . .

As we tramped the last few yards down to Yudono shrine, threading our way between the thick ferns and briars overhanging the Kiyomegawa, everyone was walking faster and faster. Some of the pilgrims began to run. Everyone was full of excitement. We had reached our destination. We were going to see the holy shrine: *goshintai*, the divine body, the god himself in physical form; *Jodo no sekai*, Amida's western paradise manifested on this earth.

For me it was a different kind of excitement. I didn't know what it was that I would see. And I was not a devotee in the same way that everyone else was. It was not my religion. It was not my god. But still I wanted very much to see this mysterious and holy place, so holy that Basho couldn't write about it; and so holy that we too were forbidden to speak of or photograph it.

The rest of the group was waiting for us at the entrance to the shrine. 'Well done! You made it!' they bawled as we limped up. I had been expecting an awe-filled hush; but they were all shouting noisily.

There was more shouting: 'A snake! A snake!'

'Over there, on that wall,' said Takeda-san kindly, pointing. 'In Shinto, snakes are good. It's a good omen.'

'Shoes off!' said Suzuki-san anxiously, consulting his watch again. We took our shoes off and washed our feet, then joined the queue at the gate of the shrine.

Suddenly everyone was silent. In silence we shuffled through, into the inner shrine.

And here I too stop my brush.

Along the Coast

15

Octopus Dreams

Everyone was chattering and laughing again as we threaded our way down the hillside. They had done their job. They had achieved what they had set out to do. The silkworms would be healthy for another year. The rice harvest would be good.

Together we tramped the last half mile. We were down in the valley now, walking more and more slowly through groves of bamboo and maples into the dank heavy heat. The mountains soared all around us, covered thickly in forest. Here and there along the path were plump black snakes, nestled into the cool shadows of the rocks. The air was quivering with the shriek of semis. Flies hovered languidly.

We stopped on the red bridge from where you can look back along the gorge and catch a glimpse of the secret shrine behind an overhanging curtain of trees. In the old days, said Honda-san, zealous pilgrims used to wade up the river to the sacred waterfall, then stand under it so that the water plunged straight on to their heads, to purify themselves before going to worship. The yamabushi, grinned Patrol-san, still did.

Then there were photographs to be taken. And then our ways separated. The others rushed down to their bus to go to Yunohama, the hot-spring on the coast where they were to spend the night; after which they would all go back together to their silkworms in Fukushima. It was probably the only holiday they would have in the whole year. 'Come with us,' they pleaded. 'Come with us to Yunohama. It'll be fun!'

But I had a different path to take. There was still a large part of Basho's journey ahead of me, that gruelling two and a half months when he had trekked down the Japan Sea coast through the heat of summer. I was about to leave the mountain

247

country. In a day the land of Dewa, the country of the Ezo, with its lovely hidden valleys and sacred mountains, would be behind me.

The most immediate sadness was leaving my group. In that one day, struggling across Gassan, I had made friends, I had made enemies, and I had experienced the cosiness, the warmth and security of being an insider. For a day the door had opened. I had been gathered into Japanese society. From now on I would be on my own again.

I was both excited and frightened at the thought. It was a month since I had turned inland, and the mountains had become a home, a base. Their people – whose accents were no longer barbarous and incomprehensible – were my friends. The prospect of being on the road again, heading for unknown places with my pack on my back, was exhilarating. But as well as the knot of fear which I always felt at the insecurity of it, I was desolate at leaving the mountains. I wondered if I would ever see them again.

It was still early when I got back to Togei. At Hayashi's, nothing had changed. There was another bus in the car-park and another group in blue and white dressing-gowns crowding noisily into the shrine room. Everyone was busy. Hayashi in his immaculate white robes, his great shaven head towering over the rest, was making speeches and handing out paper necklaces and prayer books, while the women rushed around laying out trays of food. Only Obaasan sat quietly in the kitchen, playing with the little boy, who was, as always, bawling lustily and struggling to escape. I sat with her. Sadly, I realised it was time for me to go. There was nothing more for me to do here. It was time to move on.

As I trudged past the houses which marked the edge of the village, I stopped to look back. It was here, I remembered, that I had searched unsuccessfully for Benkei's stone. For a moment I wondered idly whether it really did exist or not. I made out Gassan, crouched far away on the rim of the plain, a rope of cloud coiled around the summit.

In front of me were rice fields. Once again I was looking at the great plain of Shonai, 'rice bowl of Japan', which I had skirted on my way up to Haguro from Karikawa. The rice was higher now, the rice shoots more closely packed, stretching away endlessly like a plump green quilt until the greenness paled and vanished over the horizon. Running straight across it like a causeway, the road I was to take dwindled away into the distance until it too finally disappeared.

The only relief from all this flatness, the only vertical object in the entire plain, was a giant red torii gate which straddled the road, silhouetted dramatically against the sky. It was one of those magical gateways that marks the place where two worlds meet. I stepped through it, out of the sacred world of the three mountains, back to the profane world of everyday life.

For Basho too, I suspect, the sacred mountains were the climax of the journey. While Sora, in his lovable plodding way, continued to note the weather each day, the places that they passed, the people that travelled with them and how much their lodgings cost, Basho, after devoting pages to the few days they spent on the mountains, suddenly became much more perfunctory. Nine days of their journey he compressed into a single sentence and once again began to complain about his illness.

The two travellers left their lodgings in South Valley on the tenth of the sixth month, July 26th. They paid a last visit to Bishop Egaku at the main temple on the mountain-top and had a farewell meal with him: the famous Haguro noodles, chopped small, with tea and saké. At the hour of the sheep, early in the afternoon, they went with Zushi Sakichi, the yamabushi who was Basho's student, down to Togei, where Zushi had arranged a horse for the old poet.

From here their destination was the venerable castle town of Tsurugaoka. At that time it was the seat of the Sakai lords, one of the most powerful families in the country. The first Sakai, a wily fellow by all accounts, had been shogun Tokugawa Ieyasu's *éminence grise*, his closest adviser, and for this he was rewarded with not one fief but two. As well as his castle in Tsurugaoka he had a second at Kamegasaki in Sakata, a few miles away on the Japan Sea coast; and when he died he was declared a god and enshrined in Tsurugaoka. His great grandson, the fourth Sakai, was ruling when Basho came.

In those days the road to Tsuruoka (as Tsurugaoka became) was not long and straight but narrow and winding and led through a dark tangled forest of cedars and pines. Tsurugaoka was an important castle town and it would not do for the enemy to be able to find it too easily. Zushi went along with Basho and Sora to guide them through the maze of muddy lanes. At the hour of the monkey, in mid-afternoon, they arrived 'at the house of a samurai called Nagayama Ujishige', tired and hungry. 'We asked for okayu, rice gruel,' wrote Sora, 'finished it, had a sleep, and in the evening finished with a round of haiku.'

They stayed three days at Nagayama's. Throughout the heady days tramping through the mountains, Basho had not been troubled once by his illness; but now that they were back on the plains, it began again and he was unwell for an entire day. Still they all sat together to write haiku and on the twelfth composed a round of linked verse. Basho, as the master poet, began the sequence

mezurashiya	Something rare:
yama o ide hane	In the Dewa mountains
no hatsu nasu	The first aubergine

'The following day', wrote Basho, 'we boarded the riverboat and went down to the port of Sakata.' It was July 29th, a month since they had first turned inland. It must have been very hot: the last three days of July are proverbially the hottest of the year, when you eat eel (for energy) and lay your pickled plums out to dry.

As they drifted down river to the broad mouth of the Mogami, the incoming tide was breaking on the grey mud flats and in front of them the sun, blazing like a fireball, seemed to plunge straight into the sea. Basho wrote one of his most famous haiku

atsuki hi o	Driving the hot sun
umi ni iretari	Into the sea –
Mogami gawa	Mogami river

After the silence and solitude of the mountains, Tsuruoka was a vast modern metropolis; though at another time it might have seemed old and quaint. It was a long time since I had been in a city. Bemused, I wandered the narrow streets, gaping around at the wooden shop fronts with their flickering neon signs, the lampposts festooned with bright plastic flowers and wires crisscrossing overhead like a giant cat's cradle.

I was not the only one down from the mountains. Between the lines of cars which pushed noisily to and fro, I caught a glimpse of an old woman waiting patiently at a crossroads, dwarfed by a coffee machine twice her height. She was so tiny and stunted – surely not more than four foot tall – and so badly bent that I couldn't see much more of her than an enormous straw hat and a pair of baggy blue trousers. The lights changed and she hobbled off very slowly and painfully, shoving along a gigantic heavy cart.

I was looking for Nagayama Ujishige's house, the house where Basho had stayed. It was clearly marked on my map of Tsuruoka; but no one I asked had heard of it. Finally I tried a chemist's shop near where I thought it should be.

I edged cautiously through the narrow shop, sliding between boxes piled high with papers and books and shelves loaded with huge glass jars. Some held pickled lizards and frogs suspended in brine, others neatly coiled snakes, dried antlers, pale ginseng with two spindly forked legs like a little shrivelled man, and other twisted nameless roots, row upon row of them.

'Nagayama Ujishige's house?' quavered the chemist. He was hidden at the back of the shop, bent over a desk behind a heap of papers. He scribbled a sentence then peered up at me over his glasses.

'Well now,' he murmured. 'Fancy you knowing that. Fancy you knowing about Ujishige's house. It was so recently it was found, too. There it was – it had been there all along, you know. And no one ever noticed!'

He beckoned me outside – he was stooped and balding and reminded me a little of the old *matsuhijiri* – and pointed to an alley on the other side of the road.

'Just down there,' he said confidently. 'Can't miss it.'

An hour later I was still tramping the maze of lanes, tired and hot. I had asked in the candle shop, the pickles shop, the writing brush shop and in a shop where straw snow shoes and long bamboo traps for catching eels hung from the ceiling. Everyone was kind and helpful and each set of directions was completely different.

Finally I found a plump young estate agent.

'I know,' he said ruefully, 'you'd expect an estate agent to know a thing like that, wouldn't you?'

But he didn't, and took me to see the woman over the street. 'She's lived here for a long time,' he said. 'She'll know.'

And there it was, down an alley in a decaying section of town, squeezed between the back wall of a long ramshackle wooden building from which came the thrumming and clattering of looms, and a grim rusting corrugated iron shack: not the dignified old samurai mansion I had been expecting but a rock in a small patch of wasteland, overgrown with grass and weeds. On it, smudged with moss, were the characters 'Basho' and 'Nagayama'.

There was a stale smell of sewage in the air. It grew stronger and stronger until I rounded a corner and found myself at the river, at the spot where Basho had boarded the boat to go down to Sakata. It was a sad sight, rolling listlessly between concrete banks lined with rusting little houses. But at least through the clutter of wires I could still make out the mountains, blue on the horizon.

I sat down gloomily at the side of the road and untied the bamboo box which Obaasan had given me. Inside, lovingly arranged on a large bamboo leaf, was my dinner: rice balls, mountain vegetables, a few sautéed grasshoppers, a simmered fig.

An old man was shuffling slowly along, using a huge umbrella as a stick. As he reached me, he came to a halt and bowed gravely, then folded one knotted hand over the other on top of his umbrella and peered at me ruminatively, his eyes pale and huge behind thick glasses. He must have been eighty or ninety, I thought, smiling at him, and quite a dandy in his day. He was all in beige – wide trousers, well pressed, linen jacket, trilby – with a wispy white beard and hearing-aid on a string around his neck.

Finally he opened his mouth. I thought he was going to ask my country. Instead he said in a quavering voice, 'Not on your own, are you?'

I nodded, feeling for once not at all like an adventurer but rather sad and lonely.

Basho, I think, felt the same. From Sakata he turned north and trekked twenty-five miles up the coast to Kisagata, a lagoon as celebrated for its beauty as Matsushima, the 'pine-clad isles' on the opposite coast. Nöin Hoshi, who wrote the famous lines on the Shirakawa barrier, spent three years living here in retreat; Saigyo wrote a poem on the cherry tree 'buried beneath the waves' –

Scudding over its blossoms,
The fishermen in their boats

But to Basho there was something dark about its beauty.

'Matsushima', he wrote, 'seems to be smiling, but Kisagata seems full of regret. There is a sadness added to its loneliness, as if the spirit of the place were in torment.'

The words are like a premonition – although Kisagata's destiny was much more dramatic than anything that Basho imagined. A hundred years after his visit, the wonderful lagoon was torn apart by one of those shattering convulsive earthquakes that make life in Japan so insecure. The whole sea bed was tossed into the air and where the lagoon had been – so lovely that the Empress Jingu chose it as her burial place – there was nothing left but the occasional rocky outcrop thatched with trees, jutting out of the rice fields.

I knew Kisagata's history; but still I felt duty bound to see it. I found a lorry to whisk me up the coast road, past patches of wasteland and rows of bleached wooden houses under a sweltering pale sky. Sometimes between the houses I caught glimpses of the sea, blue and still.

There was even less at Kisagata than I had expected. I was back in a Japan I recognised: wide streets swirling with dust, long factories with smoking chimneys, sad tin buildings and telegraph wires. The paddy fields surrounding the town were flat and anonymous, without even a rocky outcrop that I could see that might once have been an island.

Basho's mood remained gloomy. He headed back down the coast to Sakata and stayed there a few days.

'After piling up the days at Sakata, the clouds above the Hokurikudo – the Great North Road – summoned us. The thought of the great distance ahead burdened my heart, when I heard that it was 130 ri (320 miles) to the capital of Kaga.

'We crossed the barrier at Nezu, then walked with increased vigour through the land of Echigo, and arrived at Ichiburi barrier in the country of Etchu. I will not write of these nine days – my spirit was oppressed by the heat and humidity and my illness broke out again.'

The Hokurikudo is full of memories of Yoshitsune. It runs along the northern spine of Japan, through the desolate regions on the wrong side of the central mountain ranges, the Snow Country. It is the back way to the land of the Ezo. And when Yoshitsune escaped north disguised as a porter, in his cloak embroidered with plovers and worn black cap pulled down over his eyes, this was the route he took.

Like Basho, I was travelling in the opposite direction, towards Kyoto and the land of Yamato. I was through Nezu barrier before I had even realised; there was nothing on the road to mark it. Squashed sweatily in the back of an ancient Nissan Cedric, with hot dusty air swirling through the open windows, I left the land of Dewa and the country of the Ezo.

A couple of hours later I was trundling through the outskirts of the vast industrial city of Niigata. It was a landscape of nightmarish bleakness: a wasteland of roads and salt flats bristling with pylons and telegraph poles like a painting of the First World War trenches. There were no people about, only cars and lorries and huge garish hoardings for milk powder and wedding halls. The sky was a tangle of wires; and on the horizon was Niigata itself, a ghostly jumble of chimneys and concrete blocks looming out of a smog of pollution.

I stared around in glum disbelief. Up in the mountains I had forgotten that this other Japan existed. There was no going back now. I had left the middle ages. I was back in the modern world.

I was to spend the night in Sanjo, a distant suburb of Niigata. Miyabe-san, a friend of one of my Gifu acquaintances, collected me from the coffee shop where I was waiting.

'I hope you will not think it presumptuous,' he said as we drove off. 'I have taken the liberty of informing the Sanjo Shimbun, the local paper, of your visit and have arranged an interview for you at three o'clock.' It was a long time since I had heard such polished Japanese. I thought sadly of the mountain people and their rough northern accents.

We drove through Sanjo's gracious tree-lined streets to the library where the local paper was housed. We were greeted with great ceremony then ushered into a narrow room lined with ancient faded books, where we sat stiffly on squeaky leather sofas while a young reporter quizzed me about my journey. Then I had to pose for photographs, holding up a copy of the *Narrow Road*, with Miyabe-san standing proudly by. I was beginning to feel a bit like a dancing bear in a circus. This sudden rise to celebrity, as far as I could see, was based entirely on my foreignness. It made me both an honoured guest and an oddity.

Later we joined the editor for tea. He was one of those grizzled old men who have reached an age where one is allowed to say what one thinks.

'Of course . . .' He leaned forward confidentially as if to say, *this is off the record – you can tell us the truth now.* 'Matsuo Basho's haiku. You don't actually understand them, do you. After all, you're not Japanese. Only Japanese can understand Matsuo Basho.'

I sighed. Suddenly I felt tired. This was not a battle I wanted to engage in.

'Let's take "*furuike ya*", the "old pond",' I began patiently.

He nodded and murmured very fast, '*Furuike ya kawazu tobikomu mizu no oto*' (old pond/frog jumps in/sound of water) like a challenge, then glared at me fiercely.

I stumbled on, wishing my Japanese were better. 'There's no

set interpretation, is there? It has many different meanings. It depends on the person. There's no one meaning that Japanese understand and foreigners don't. You can appreciate it whether you're Japanese or not. After all, the Japanese appreciate Shakespeare.'

He grunted. He was not convinced. Shakespeare was different. Not so complex. Not so difficult to understand. Not so special. Foreign.

Later I told them about the farmers I had stayed with up north. He butted in again.

'How do they compare to farmers in England?' he asked.

I had no idea, I said. I didn't know anything about English farmers, only Japanese.

'Well,' he snapped, turning away in disgust. 'In that case you'd better become Japanese.'

I wondered what it was that had angered him. It was as if he was disgusted at my lack of national identity; as if he never forgot for a moment that he was Japanese. Did Japanese only ever see the world through the spectacles of their Japaneseness? Did books, films, articles about other countries always relate back to Japan? Was there no reason to study foreign ways, foreign customs – even foreign farmers – except to compare them with Japanese ones, to learn from them or criticise them? The answer to all these, I suspected, was yes.

I spent a luxurious night in Sanjo's only Western-style hotel. It was the first time I had been in a bed for ages. I woke early next morning and hung out of the window, looking at the pearly sky and the endless mosaic of grey tiled roofs, trees, and modern white geometrical blocks reflecting the dawn sun.

Later Miyabe-san arrived to show me around some of the sights and set me on my way.

'I am retired', he said, 'and it will be my great pleasure to be your host for half a day.'

He was a gentleman: courtly, silver-haired, with a sharp eye and sharp mind, overflowing with ideas and opinions. He belonged to a world immeasurably wider than that of the mountain people. His nephew, he told me, was studying in

Brazil, his daughter taught the piano, and he himself had been in Siberia after the war.

'I passed two years there', he said, 'in a prisoner-of-war camp. Towards the end our supplies became low and we had to ration our bread and water. Many men became ill and died. And here at home as well, we had such hardship to endure. Yet now we can have anything we want. Looking back at those days, it's like a dream.'

We were well south of Niigata by now, driving through a succession of tired little villages, each one a single line of weather-beaten wooden houses strung for miles along the coast – *fundoshi mura*, 'loincloth villages' as long and narrow as the loincloths, practically gee-strings, which labourers and ferrymen used to wear. Behind the houses were glimpses of the sea and faded fishing boats bobbing at anchor.

'This', he said, gesturing as we puttered through one small village, 'is the birthplace of Tanaka Kakuei. A great man. As great as your Churchill. In these parts we say he is a *kami-sama*, a god. There will be a shrine to him when he passes away.'

Of course. I had forgotten that Tanaka-san, the ex-prime minister who had been toppled by the Lockheed revelations, was a Niigata man. That explained many things. Tanaka-san took good care of his constituency. The only Bullet Train line to this neglected Japan Sea coast runs from Tokyo to Niigata; and all the industry which scars the landscape around the city is evidence of its wealth.

'Whenever we Niigata people need something – new roads, hospitals, factories – we have only to ask Tanaka-san and it is done,' beamed Miyabe-san. The roads around here were indeed noticeably better than those in the mountains.

'Everyone in these parts thinks of Tanaka Kakuei as a great man. In this village, for example', waving his hand towards the bleached wooden houses outside, 'nine out of ten houses vote for Tanaka-san.'

It was hard to reconcile this benevolent philanthropist, so well loved that he was like a god, with the ex-prime minister I had read about. Tanaka Kakuei had, apparently, intimate links with the *yakusa* underworld and had accepted a vast amount of money from Lockheed for his party faction and himself.

I listened with growing impatience to Miyabe-san's paeons of praise. Finally, as innocently as possible (I was, after all, his guest), I asked, 'But what about Lockheed?'

He chuckled at such naïvety.

'In the world of politics,' he explained kindly, 'money is a necessity. All politicians accept money; that is part of politics. When we Japanese heard about the Lockheed business, we all said "Bad luck!" It was too bad he was caught. That's all. It's like exceeding the speed limit. Everyone does it. There's nothing wrong with it. The only mistake is to be caught.'

We stopped at the fish market at Teradomari, that same 'Teradomari in Echigo' where, eight hundred years before, Yoshitsune landed after sailing up the coast through a fearful storm. The party had prayed in vain to the dragon gods; and it was only when Yoshitsune threw a silver dagger into the waves as an offering and his wife added 'a crimson skirt and a Chinese mirror' that the storm abated.

All along the road were great open warehouses, extending for half a mile or so. Inside it was as cool as a larder. Spread on trays of ice were basketfuls of fish – red, yellow, blue, grey – all glossy and dripping, some still alive, writhing and thrashing. I bought a grilled eel brushed with thick sweet soy sauce and coiled on to a bamboo skewer and walked back to the car gnawing at it, the warm juice dripping down my chin.

'I wonder if Matsuo Basho ate fish like these,' mused Miyabe-san. 'In his day, I think, people didn't know that one could eat all these different kinds of fish. Even when I was young, such great variety of fish was not available. We had squid, of course, octopus, little else.'

I smiled. The haiku Basho wrote about an octopus dreaming on a summer night floated through my mind

takotsubo ya	Octopus pot:
hakanaki yume o	Fleeting dreams
natsu no tsuki	Beneath the summer moon

Octopus Dreams

I strolled over the road and gazed across the water, still and pale in the heat. On the horizon was the hazy outline of an island: Sado-ga-shima, the island of Sado.

On that dreadful nine-day walk down the coast, Basho too stopped here. It was night time, a clear summer night, and the Milky Way – Ama no Gawa, the River of Heaven – glimmered across the sky

ara umi ya	Rough seas:
Sado ni yokotau	Stretching out to Sado
ama no gawa	The River of Heaven

Miyabe-san took me as far as a town called Kashiwazaki, where we said goodbye. I watched, waving and bowing, as he disappeared back towards Sanjo, then turned wearily and began to hitchhike again.

A huge lorry stopped almost immediately. I had to stand on tiptoe to shout to the driver, then lobbed my pack up into the cab and scrambled in after and we rumbled off along the coast road. By now the villages had a dusty tropical look to them: old wooden houses whitened, sun-bleached, casting long dark shadows across the street; women, almost as old, in baggy blue trousers and enormous straw bonnets, hobbling along wheeling barrows loaded with melons.

'Good skiing up there,' bellowed the driver, waving towards the distant mountain peaks pale on the horizon, on the far side of the coastal plain. He was a swarthy, thickset man with a prosperous rice belly swelling beneath his white vest.

'Like skiing, do you?' I yelled back.

He snorted with laughter.

'Me? Ski? I'm a working man. No time for that.' He worked a six-day week, he bawled, and had a week's holiday a year – three days for the summer festival, four days at New Year.

'We're not rich like you people, we Japanese. We have to work.'

He turned down the baseball a fraction and set about grumbling – about the lowness of his wages, the cost of his mortgage and life insurance, the heat, the traffic, the baseball scores . . .

I was well ahead of Basho by now.

It was nearly the end of August by the time he and Sora reached Ichiburi, the barrier between the provinces of Echigo and Etchu. That day – the last of the nine – they had had to cross 'the most dangerous places of the north country', where the cliffs plunged sheer into the sea and the only way to get through was along the edge of the water, clambering from boulder to boulder through the crashing waves.

Nowadays there is a spectacular road bored into the cliffs, high up along the very edge, lined with great concrete pillars to stop the traffic rolling into the sea. Here and there it suddenly shoots out into space across a shadowy ravine. The passes still bear the same fearful names: *oya-shirazu* – 'abandon your parents'; *ko-shirazu* – 'abandon your children'; *inu-modori* – 'dogs turn back'; *koma-gaeshi* – 'send back your horses'.

The two travellers reached the checkpoint late in the evening. They showed their papers to the guards, then stumbled into a nearby inn 'overcome by exhaustion' and lay down to sleep. But they were disturbed by voices from the next room, floating clearly through the flimsy paper walls. They were 'the voices of young women, two of them. The voice of an old man was mixed in with theirs and, listening to their story, it seemed that they were "play women", prostitutes, from a place called Niigata in the country of Echigo.

'They were on pilgrimage to the great shrine at Ise; the old man had come with them as far as this barrier, and they were writing letters and little messages for him to take home the next day. "Roaming the white wave beaten shores, daughters of fisherfolk fallen to this life of shame, how we grieve for our false vows, for the karma we pile up day by day . . ." – hearing these words I drifted off to sleep.'

The next day, as Basho and Sora were setting off, the women approached them tearfully. They were afraid, they said. The road they had to travel was completely unknown to them. Would the reverent fathers be kind enough to let them follow behind, so that they might feel safer? They would, of course, keep a discreet distance; and it might help them too to turn to the way of the Buddha.

Despite their pleas and tears, Basho refused them. 'We are stopping in many places along the way,' he said, and advised them to find a more reliable traveller to accompany them.

'"The gods are watching over you; you will undoubtedly travel in safety," I said as we left; but still for some time my heart was full with the piteousness of them.'

With a little wry amusement at the incongruity – two grizzled old poets in priestly robes sleeping alongside prostitutes – he wrote

hitotsu ya ni	In the same house
yujo mo netari	We slept with play
hagi to tsuki	women –
	Bush clover and
	the moon

A few days later, Sora was suddenly taken ill. They had been on the road now for four and a half months; and the long trek down the Japan Sea coast had exhausted them both. Ironically enough, they had just reached Yamanaka, a particularly famous spa deep in the mountains outside the city of Fukui, famous for the healing powers of its waters, which are supposed to guarantee longevity. Here Sora had some sort of stomach attack. He was in such pain that he was unable to continue the journey and set off immediately for Nagashima, in the province of Ise, where he had relatives.

Suddenly Basho was on his own.

'The sadness of one who leaves, the bitterness of one left behind: we were like a pair of wild ducks separated and lost in the clouds.'

When they left Edo together, they had painted the words 'Pilgrimage of Two' on their bamboo hats. Now, wrote Basho despondently

keu yori ya	From today:
kaki tsuke kesan	Let the dew on my hat
kasa no tsuyu	Wash away those words

He still had many places to visit before the end of his journey. But the next day, trudging the dusty lanes alone through the heavy heat, he didn't manage more than a few miles. In the evening he reached Zenshoji temple. Sora had stayed there the previous night and had left a poem for him. Lonely and in pain, unable to sleep, he had written

yomosugara	All through the night
aki kaze kiku ya	Listening to the autumn wind
ura no yama	In the lonely hills behind

'We were only a night apart,' wrote Basho. 'But it might as well have been a thousand ri.'

Zenshoji temple was at the end of a maze of little lanes, in the suburbs of Daishoji, not far from Fukui. I was nearing the end of my journey now. The land of Dewa, the country of the Ezo, was nearly four hundred miles away; the old capital, Kyoto, and the prosperous heart of Japan, the pleasant land of Yamato, little more than fifty. The faces around me were softer, more rounded, paler, and the voices spoke a Japanese that I could understand. There were still plenty of bent backs and stumpy bowed legs and wrinkled old monkey faces; but most people were in western clothes, skirts and dresses, not smocks and baggy blue trousers.

I had dawdled a little along the way. I stayed with friends in the grand old castle town of Kanazawa, cycling around the modern city centre and down the alleys of old samurai mansions and admiring the vast endless fish markets. Then I went to Ataka and wandered the windswept sand dunes, through the groves of spindly pines where the old barrier used to be, where Benkei and Yoshitsune had their celebrated confrontation with Togashi, the border guard. And, like Basho and Sora, I stopped to take the waters at Yamanaka spa.

There was no 'autumn wind' when I visited Zenshoji. It was still early August. The sky was pale with heat and the air was still. Slowly, heavily, I plodded the bleached concrete streets. Once I passed a couple of plump women, each with a pink lacy parasol, walking along even more slowly than I was. Somewhere an invisible crow cawed again and again.

The temple was right at the foot of the hills. Around it bamboos swayed and nodded in the dead air. I was hoping to wander around on my own. But when I slipped off my sandals and slid open the doors into the dark cool interior, a woman rushed up to usher me in. She had a sharp pinched face and hair a suspiciously uniform shade of black.

'Watch your feet,' she said, handing me a pair of slippers. The temple was astonishingly dilapidated. Where there should have been tatami, there were only dusty floorboards, with wide gaps between them through which I could see the ground a good few feet below, dappled with sunlight. The tatami mats were stacked against a side wall, covered in a thick lace of cobwebs.

She shepherded me into a tiny room right at the back, closed her eyes and began to recite, swaying gently.

'In this room they stayed, one night Kawai Sora, Matsuo Basho the next.' It was a shabby little room, covered, like the rest of the temple, in a thin layer of dust. 'Here Kawai Sora wrote "The lonely hills behind".' She flung back a paper window and there was the hill right outside. I could almost have reached out and touched the moss and bamboo. 'Here he heard "the autumn wind".'

I would have liked to have stayed and savoured the atmosphere. But the woman opened her eyes – they were startlingly black – and swept me out again, closing the door briskly behind her.

Did they still take in guests, I asked, toying with the idea of a night in the little room.

'No one stays in temples any more,' she said as we picked our way back across the gaps between the floorboards. 'They all go round in big groups and stay in inns, not temples.' Apart from the two of us, the place was deserted.

Basho would have liked it as desolate and lonely as this. It would have suited his mood. When he came, there was a lively community of Zen monks here. But he didn't stay in a small, secluded room at the back of the temple, as the woman had claimed; he was put up in a dormitory full of noisy novices. As dawn broke, the air was full of 'the clear tones of sutra-chanting, and the thud of the wooden gong' announcing breakfast, and he had to roll up his bedding and join the queue of monks filing into the refectory.

He was impatient to get going. 'I wanted to get to Echizen that day,' he wrote. He had not been expecting to travel on his own; and now he was eager to finish the journey. He was on the point of hurrying off when some young monks came running down the steps after him, holding out sheaves of paper and an ink stone, begging the great master not to leave without penning some lines for them.

He looked around hastily for inspiration. There was a willow tree in the garden and its leaves were already beginning to flutter to the ground. Remembering that guests in a Zen temple usually offer a little work in exchange for a night's lodging, he wrote

niwa hakite	I sweep your garden
ideba ya tera ni	Then leave:
chiru yanagi	Your scattered willow
	leaves

'Without taking any trouble over it, I scribbled it down, tying on my straw sandals at the same time.'

The woman seemed glad of company. She showed me a small wooden image of Basho, cross-legged like a Buddha, in a shrine in a corner of the temple. I held it for a moment. It was surprisingly light and warm, with a wise old face. Framed over the shrine was the haiku.

'In his own hand,' she said proudly. I doubted it. The temple folk had long since forgotten his impatience – perhaps they never noticed – and remembered only that the famous poet stayed here with them in their temple and wrote a haiku for them.

I too was becoming impatient to leave. I wandered out into the grounds with the woman still scurrying behind me. There was a tall willow there among the pines and rhododendrons. It pleased me to think that it must be a descendent of Basho's willow tree. As I walked through the gate, the woman was wailing, 'But don't you want to see our five hundred images of the Buddha's apostles?'

I didn't. But I did want to see the Pines of Shiogoshi, which had been admired for centuries.

Every poet since long before Yoshitsune's time journeyed up here from the capital to see the marvellous sight of the great gaunt pines and the full moon cradled in their branches, stark against the iron sea behind. The Shiogoshi pines had inspired thousands of poems – so many, Basho wrote, that 'there is no more to be said. To add one more word would be like adding a sixth finger to the hand.'

Instead he quoted the most famous of all, which Saigyo, Yoshitsune's contemporary, wrote

All through the night
Battered by
Waves and storm –
Dripping with moonlight
Shiogoshi pines

It took me an hour and a half to walk from Zenshoji to Yoshizaki inlet on the coast, where Basho took a boat across to the pines. There I asked directions of the old women in the dark little shops along the road. Strangely, no one seemed to have heard of Shiogoshi or its famous pines. Finally I tried the local temple.

'The Shiogoshi pines . . .' grunted the priest. He was standing outside, sunning himself. He looked faded, as faded as the wood of his temple and the houses along the road. His black robes were nylon, thin, almost transparent, like net curtains.

'Not here any more,' he said gruffly, looking at his watch as if I were wasting his time. 'Cut down twenty years ago. To make a golf course.'

Twenty years ago, after being treasured for centuries . . . for a golf course.

I walked away sadly, scuffing my feet in the dust. Well, I reasoned, golf courses were important to the Japanese. They were a sign of prosperity. A status symbol. A sign that the place was doing well. But still I was astonished at the mindless vandalism of it. It seemed for a moment – perhaps unjustly – to epitomise this Japan I had found on the other side of the north country. Was it no more than a fluke that the north was still unspoilt? Was it just a matter of time before the hidden valleys and sacred mountains would be destroyed just as blithely, just as carelessly, to make way for the modern world?

But there was still one discovery to be made.

16

The Temple by the Sea

I left Fukui early next morning and took a train out past little corrugated iron houses, through shadowy fields where the rice was already fading and yellowing, to Tsuruga, at the southernmost tip of the Echizen coast. There was a hint of autumn in the air. The old couple next to me pulled down the blind to keep out the shafts of sunlight, took off their shoes and propped their feet on the seat in front. She had on stockings, he black transparent nylon socks and a rusty grey suit. They sat in silence, studiously poring over a pile of leaflets – one, I noticed, from Zenshoji – studying the characters one by one through a magnifying glass while outside tiny stations rolled by, ranks of bicycles lined up in front.

I was on the last lap of my journey. From here I would be turning inland, rattling across the last of Basho's eight hundred miles to the town of Ogaki in the heart of Yamato, where the old poet ended his journey among friends. Ogaki was also, purely by chance, only one stop up the line from Gifu, the town where I had first lived in Japan. So I too would end my journey among friends.

But first I had a detour to make.

Strangely few people got out at Tsuruga. I put my bag in a coin locker and enquired about buses out to the lonely tip of Tsuruga peninsula. One had just gone. The next was in five hours' time. I was rather pleased that I had no choice. It seemed right to make this last small journey on foot.

I ambled along Tsuruga's windswept streets, disfigured like every Japanese town with wires, plastic flowers, plaster façades like mock-Tudor Disneyland castles, covered arcades echoing with the Beatles or the 'Four Seasons'. Still, it had the spacious feel of a seaside town. The streets were broad and empty and the air smelled of the sea.

I passed Kehi shrine where Yoshitsune and Benkei prayed all night for safe passage before setting off on their journey north. They had hoped to hire a boatman to take them up to Dewa from Tsuruga Harbour, but there were none that were willing to risk the 'fierce gales of the early second month'. So, after another night in Tsuruga, they started on foot the long and perilous journey that was to end at the Castle on the Heights in Hiraizumi.

Basho was here too, hoping to see the full autumn moon on the fifteenth of the eighth month, September 29th. The previous night, the sky was particularly clear.

'"Will it be fine tomorrow night too?" I asked.

'"Here on this side of the mountains we always say 'Fine harvest moon eve don't vouchsafe fine weather on the morrow'", replied the innkeeper.' Sure enough, the following night it rained.

meigetsu ya	Harvest moon:
hoku koku bi yori	The fickleness
sadame naki	Of northern weather!

The road led out of town around the edge of the bay, past a few last factories, through groves of ancient pine trees up on to the cliffs. Gradually the traffic and noise of the mainland faded away and for a while the only sound was the lapping of the sea on the pebbles way below. Then, behind me, there were voices. A woman and a child were ambling along together hand in hand, singing a haunting little song.

It was beautiful weather for walking. The sky and the sea were intensely blue and the air was crisp. In the distance were the rugged hills of Echizen, pale on the far side of the bay.

It would have been several hours' walk if a car had not stopped. The driver was a young man with a dark, high-cheekboned face above a dapper pin-striped suit. Improbably, he was an estate agent, he told me, on his way to price some plots of land which were up for sale in this remote peninsula. As we zigzagged along the cliffs, with the luminous sea far below us, we discussed our occupations, the weather, the area, my country. Then he slowed down a little, turned to look at me and said with disarming innocence, as if he were simply continuing the conversation, '*Asobini ikimasho* – Let's go and play.' At first I didn't understand. Then I remembered Basho's 'play women' and laughed. I made my excuses and we continued as if nothing had been said.

He dropped me off at a tiny windswept village. It was hardly a village at all, just a single row of houses, some wooden, some tin, sheltering in the lee of the cliff. Outside each house signboards creaked, painted with huge vertical characters: *minshuku*, 'bed and breakfast'; 'fishing boats for hire'; 'fresh fish cuisine'. But the street was empty. There was only the wind, full of the salty smell of the sea, no people. The beach was the colour of coral, covered in tiny shells, and tied up all along it were rusty fishing boats.

The temple I was looking for was right at the edge of the sea. It was satisfyingly old and weather-worn, with a huge cast-iron bell hanging outside. I stood in the doorway shouting '*Gomen kudasai!*' until a woman hurried out, drying her hands on her apron.

'A student of Basho, aren't you,' she smiled and settled me in the shrine room with a book of haiku while she disappeared again.

Basho came here with Tosai, an old friend from Fukui, on the sixteenth, September 30th, the day after failing to see the harvest moon. In those days there was no road out, winding along the cliffs. The weather had cleared and the two hired a boat to scull the seven ri, seventeen miles, across the bay to Iro-no-hama, Beach of Colours. They took a picnic and made a day of it. 'A man called Tenya kindly provided boxes of food, bamboo flasks of saké and the like, for our use, and sent several servants in the boat along with us; and blown along by the wind we arrived in no time.'

The place was even more desolate than it is now. 'On the beach were a few fishermen's huts and a dilapidated Hokké temple. Here we drank tea and heated up saké and savoured the loneliness of the darkening night.' Thinking of Suma, the place of Prince Genji's exile and the epitome of the melancholy beauty of loneliness, Basho wrote a haiku

sabishisa ya	The loneliness:
Suma ni kachitaru	Surpassing even Suma,
hama no aki	Autumn on these shores

The woman had slipped back with a plate of peaches, peeled and cut into slices, which she put on the floor. Above us, a pair of swallows darted around the room. It was large and airy, open along the front, overlooking the sea.

'Of course you want to see Tosai's account, don't you,' she said. She brought out a yellowing, faded scroll, untied it and spread it out reverently. At Basho's request, Tosai had made a record of the day's events and left it in the temple. I looked at the spidery calligraphy, dark, fading away, then dark again where he had redipped his brush in the ink.

Basho really was here, I thought. Here he sat, where I am now – not in the same building (the temple must have been pulled down and rebuilt many times since then) but on the same spot and in a room which must have looked very similar – and drank his tea and saké as dusk fell.

Holding the parchment at arm's length, the woman read it out in a gentle rhythmical singsong: 'After admiring the scenery of the coast at Kehi, we came to the coloured beach at Iro-no-hama, where Priest Saigyo wrote of the small *masuho* shells . . .'

So that was why Basho came to this remote, out of the way place: because Saigyo had come. He came to look for the little pink shells of which Saigyo had written

Gathering
Small *masuho* shells
Salt-water dyed . . .

– as well as to enjoy the lonely beauty of the place.
Basho's haiku was

nami no ma ya	Between the waves:
kogai ni majiru	Mixed with the little shells
hagi no chiri	Scraps of bush clover

The Temple by the Sea

'I knew you were a student of Basho,' confided the woman. Ageless, she seemed, in her shapeless blue dress and blue apron, with her soft round unwrinkled face and curly hair. There was something warm and comfortable about her. 'They all are, you know, everyone that comes here.

'I didn't know anything about Basho', she went on, putting a cocktail stick into a pale crescent of peach and offering it to me, 'when I came here as a bride. But we have so many visitors – students, teachers, poets . . . In the old days, they used to come by boat, like Basho.'

It was only a few years ago that the road was completed. 'Time and time again they tried to build a road here,' she said, 'but the waves always washed away the stones. I had to go to Tsuruga sometimes, to sell fish and buy vegetables and rice. Sometimes I went on the boat. Six thirty in the morning, it left. Or I walked – *shikata ga nai* – what else could you do. I used to walk along the edge of the water. When my *zori*, my straw sandals got wet, I put on new ones. It's like a dream, those days, looking back.'

The swallows still swooped round and round above us and the waves lapped on the beach outside. Kneeling on the pale tatami with its smell of fresh straw, the woman chattered away, beaming, as if it was months since she had had the chance to talk.

'It's inconvenient out here, mind you. I wouldn't mind if I had been born here. But I'm an outsider, I grew up in the city, so I notice the inconvenience. I remember when I was sent here as a bride. That was Showa 21, when I was twenty-three.' More than forty years ago: yet she still spoke of herself as an outsider. 'I missed my friends so much. I used to cry. In the evening, all you could see was the sea and the mountains, nothing else. I used to cry, I was so lonely.'

She went to get more tea and I sat, idly turning the pages of the book, thinking of the young girl sent all alone to this remote place, to marry someone she did not know. On each page was a single haiku, each brushed in a different hand, signed and dated.

'The people we've had here!' she chattered as she filled my

271

cup. 'Famous people, too. And they all wrote a haiku for us. Everyone that comes here writes a haiku.'

She took the book and began to read them out, stopping every now and then to explain: 'the Crown Prince it was who wrote this', 'the Princess, his wife', 'Professor Ueda', 'his daughter – eight years ago they came, together . . .' Beside her on the tatami was an ink stone, some ink ready ground in it, and a writing brush.

I knew it was discourteous to wait to be asked.

'I'd love to write something for you,' I said, 'but I'm not a poet, and my Japanese isn't very good.'

But she looked so surprised and disappointed, as if no one had ever refused before, that I decided to try. Listening to the swallows flitting overhead, I painted into the book, in large, clumsy characters

tabi owari	Journey's end
umi no otera ni	In the temple by the sea
tsubame kana	Swallows . . .

Epilogue

From the Beach of Colours I went back to Tsuruga, then took the train to Ogaki, where I met up with friends. Together we went to look at the shrine which marks the site of Bokuin's house, where Basho stayed. From there I was to go with them to Gifu, to stay for a few days, then on to Tokyo and finally back to London.

Basho knew the dignified old town of Ogaki well. He came here many times; and it must have been like a homecoming after his long journey around the remote places of the north. His friends and followers flocked to greet him, 'arriving by day and night, rejoicing and fussing over me, as if I had just returned from the dead', and Sora, who had recovered his strength, came up from Ise.

Old and worn out though he was, he was too much of a wanderer to stay in one place for long. After a couple of weeks the road gods summoned him again. The shrine buildings down at the great shrine of Ise had been rebuilt and he wanted to be present at the opening ceremony. On the sixth of the ninth month, October 18th, 'once again I boarded a boat . . .'

Thinking of Futami, a little town near Ise, famous for its clams, and playfully punning on *futa*, lid, and *mi*, flesh of the clam, he wrote a farewell haiku

hamaguri no	Parting for Futami
futa-mi ni wakare	Like clam from shell
yuku aki zo	I go – and autumn too!

It was another two years before he was back in Edo, in a new cottage in Fukagawa with a banana tree outside. And it was here that he completed and published his greatest work, *The Narrow Road to the Deep North*, in 1693.

The following summer he set out on another journey. He was fifty years old. He visited his family in Iga Ueno, then went on to the great city of Osaka. Here he was taken ill. His friends and disciples gathered at his bedside and he dictated his last haiku

tabi ni yande	Ill on a journey,
yume wa kareno o	My dreams wander on
kakemeguru.	Across withered fields.

Select Bibliography

English
On haiku and Japanese literature

Aitken, Robert, *A Zen Wave. Basho's haiku and Zen*, Weatherhill, New York and Tokyo, 1978.

Britton, Dorothy, *A Haiku Journey. Basho's 'Narrow Road to a Far Province'*. Kodansha International, Tokyo, 1974.

Henderson, Harold G., *An Introduction to Haiku*, Doubleday Anchor Books, New York, 1958.

Keene, Donald, *Anthology of Japanese Literature*, Grove Press, New York, 1955 and Penguin Books, London, 1968.

—— *World Within Walls: Japanese literature of the pre-modern era 1600–1867*. Charles E. Tuttle Co., Tokyo, 1976.

—— *Landscapes and Portraits. Appreciations of Japanese Culture*, Kodansha International, Tokyo, 1971.

Lafleur, William R., (translator) *Mirror for the Moon. A selection of poems by Saigyo (1118–1190)*, New Directions Books, New York, 1978.

Mayhew, Lenore, *Monkey's Raincoat. Linked poetry of the Basho school with haiku selections*, Charles E. Tuttle Co., Tokyo, 1985.

Miner, Earl, *Japanese Linked Poetry. An account with translations of renga and haikai sequences*, Princeton University Press, New Jersey, 1980.

—— *Japanese Poetic Diaries*, University of California Press, Berkeley, Los Angeles, California, 1969.

Ueda, Makoto, *Matsuo Basho. The master haiku poet*. Twayne Publishers Inc., New York, 1970 and Kodansha International, Tokyo, 1982.

Yuasa, Nobuyuki (translator), *Basho. The Narrow Road to the Deep North and other travel sketches*, Penguin Books, London, 1966.

Select Bibliography

On Japanese history and culture

Aston, W. G., (translator). *Nihongi. Chronicles of Japan from the earliest times to AD 697*, Kegan Paul, Trench, London, 1896.

Blacker, Carmen, *The Catalpa Bow. A study of shamanistic practices in Japan*, George Allen & Unwin, London, 1975.

Brown, Jan, *Exploring Tohoku. A guide to Japan's back country*. Weatherhill, New York and Tokyo, 1982.

Dunn, Charles J., *Everyday Life in Traditional Japan*. Charles E. Tuttle Co., Tokyo, 1969.

Frédéric, Louis, *Daily Life in Japan at the time of the Samurai, 1185–1603*, (translated by Eileen M. Lowe), Charles E. Tuttle Co., Tokyo, 1972.

Latham, Ronald (translator), *The Travels of Marco Polo*, Penguin Books, London, 1958.

McCullough, Helen Craig (translator), *Yoshitsune*, Stanford University Press, 1966.

Morris, Ivan, *The Nobility of Failure: Tragic heroes in the history of Japan*, Charles E. Tuttle Co., Tokyo, 1975.

Piggott, Juliet, *Japanese mythology*, Library of the world's myths and legends, Newnes Books, London, 1984.

Sansom, G. B., *Japan. A short cultural history*, Charles E. Tuttle Co., Tokyo, 1931.

Varley, H. Paul, *Japanese Culture*, Charles E. Tuttle Co., Tokyo, 1984.

Japanese

Basho zenshu, Prose and poetical works of Basho, Nihon koten zenshu kanko-kai, Tokyo, 1926.

Hagiwara Yasuo (editor), *Oku no hoso michi*, Iwanami, Tokyo, 1979.

Ogawa Hiromi, *Dewa sanzan no shiki*, Shinjinbutsu oraishi, Tokyo, 1984.

Togawa Ansho, *Haguro-san ni hyaku wa*, Chuo shoin, Tokyo, 1972.

Ebaga Taizo, Ogata Tsutomu (editors), *Shintei oku no hosomichi*, Kakugawa shoten, Tokyo, 1967.

Index

Note Major mentions of haiku have been indexed, but not individual pieces of verse

Index

Index